APPLICATIONS IN CRIMINAL ANALYSIS

APPLICATIONS IN CRIMINAL ANALYSIS

A SOURCEBOOK

Marilyn B. Peterson

Westport, Connecticut
London

The Library of Congress has cataloged the hardcover edition as follows:

Peterson, Marilyn B.

    Applications in criminal analysis : a sourcebook / Marilyn B. Peterson.
      p.   cm.
    Includes bibliographical references and index.
    ISBN 0–313–28577–2 (acid-free paper)
    1. Criminal investigation—United States—Handbooks, manuals, etc.
    2. Law enforcement—United States—Handbooks, manuals, etc.
    I. Title.
    HV8078.P47   1994
    363.2′5—dc20   94–11219

British Library Cataloguing in Publication Data is available.

A hardcover edition of *Applications in Criminal Analysis* is available from
Greenwood Press, an imprint of Greenwood Publishing Group, Inc.
(ISBN 0–313–28577–2)

Library of Congress Catalog Card Number: 94–11219
ISBN: 0–275–96468–X (pbk.)

First published in 1994

Praeger Publishers, 88 Post Road West, Westport, CT 06881
An imprint of Greenwood Publishing Group, Inc.

Printed in the United States of America

The paper used in this book complies with the
Permanent Paper Standard issued by the National
Information Standards Organization (Z39.48–1984).

P

Copyright Acknowledgments

The author and publisher gratefully acknowledge permission to reproduce the
following copyrighted material:

Figure 4.4, "Sexual Homicide—Motivational Model," from R. K. Ressler, A. W. Burgess,
and J. E. Douglas, "Sexual Homicide Patterns and Motives," *Journal of Interpersonal
Violence* (September 1986): p. 50. Copyright © 1986 Sage Publications, Inc. Reprinted
by permission of Sage Publications, Inc.

Figure 4.5, "Criminal Profile Generating Process," from John E. Douglas, Robert K.
Ressler, Ann W. Burgess, and Carol R. Hartman, "Criminal Profiling from Crime Scene
Analysis," *Behavioral Sciences and the Law*, Vol. 4, No. 4 (1986): p. 407. Copyright ©
1986 John Wiley & Sons, Ltd. Reprinted by permission of John Wiley and Sons, Ltd.

Extracts from Marilyn B. Sommers (Peterson), "Law Enforcement Intelligence: A New
Look," *International Journal of Intelligence and Counterintelligence*, Vol. 1, No. 3
(1986): pp. 34–36.

This book is dedicated to the former employees of the Pennsylvania Crime Commission who took on the challenge of keeping the public aware of the dangers that organized crime and public corruption posed to the Commonwealth. Because of the latter, the agency was de-authorized on June 30, 1994. Its absence will leave a gaping hole not only in law enforcement in the Commonwealth, but in America.

Contents

Chapter 3   Report Applications   **61**

Chapter 4   Violent Crime Applications   **89**

Figures

Acknowledgments

Explorers use stars to guide them. Some of the stars that lighted the way during my analytical explorations have been (in chronological order) William B. Anderson, Charles H. Rogovin, R. Glen Ridgeway, Paul P. Andrews, Jr., Malcolm K. Sparrow, Robert J. Kelly, and Steven Gottlieb.

Special mention goes to the most constant star—Charles H. Rogovin—who has offered insightful comments throughout my career. Also, special thanks are due to Paula A. Carter, a solid analyst who took the time and care to review this manuscript and give me many constructive suggestions.

Finally, deep thanks must go to all those who cheered me on through the writing of this book: my husband, Lind Aitken; my son, Jon; my stepdaughter, Michelle Aitken; my parents; my brothers; and my friends Doreen Tancredi and Kathy O'Steen. I also thank my Greenwood editor, Mim Vasan, for her patience.

Acknowledgments must also go to all the agencies and individuals who submitted information or had information in the public domain on analytical techniques and analytical experts. Their information greatly enriches these pages. They include the following:

Arizona Department of Public Safety

California Department of Justice, Bureau of Investigations

Drug Enforcement Administration

Federal Bureau of Investigation

Middle Atlantic–Great Lakes Organized Crime Law Enforcement Network (MAGLO-CLEN)

National Institute of Justice

New Jersey State Commission of Investigation

New Mexico Department of Public Safety
New York State Organized Crime Task Force
Pennsylvania Crime Commission
Rocky Mountain Information Network (RMIN)
Royal Canadian Mounted Police
Western States Information Network (WSIN)

A–Z Line Art, of Lawrenceville, New Jersey, was responsible for interpreting the graphic figures for this text.

APPLICATIONS
IN CRIMINAL
ANALYSIS

Chapter I

Introduction

INTRODUCTION AND DEFINITIONS

Criminal analysis is the application of particular analytical methods to data collected for the purpose of criminal investigation or criminal research. It is practiced in law enforcement, in the criminal defense field, in the military, and in private security organizations around the world. In some organizations, it is used informally as part of an investigator's or prosecutor's work. In others, it is applied by uniquely trained personnel who are commonly called "intelligence analysts," "crime analysts," or "criminal information analysts." These terms are often used interchangeably.

A sourcebook on the applications of criminal analysis is tasked with several purposes. First, it must explain the context of criminal analysis: what it is, from where does it come, what training supports it, and what standards for it are now in place. Second, the sourcebook must detail analytical methods in a manner which nonanalysts can understand. Third, the practical applications of analytical skills and methods within the investigative process and within criminal justice management must be shown.

This volume may serve as an overview of analytical techniques for those in the field and as an introduction to the world of analysis for those who are not. The need for analysis in the investigative/prosecutorial world is seldom questioned; the purpose of this sourcebook is to serve as a guide to the concepts and practices of analysis which can benefit the student, the teacher, the practitioner, and the manager.

Definitions

The word "analysis" is defined as the "separation of a substantial whole into its constituent parts" to allow an examination and interpretation of the thing (American Heritage, 1992). Equally important is the "synthesis" of the data, that is, the reassembly of those constituent parts into a restructured whole which gives us new information (Andrews and Peterson, 1990).

"Criminal analysis" is a broad overview term which has been chosen to depict the body of analytical work which occurs within criminal justice. It includes "crime analysis," "intelligence analysis," and "strategic analysis." Criminal analysis is the application of analytical methods and products to data within the criminal justice field. It should be pointed out, however, that some of these same methods can be applied to criminal violations or potentially criminal situations which arise outside traditional criminal justice—in the private security firm arena, in the military arena, or even in the corporate arena. Moreover, they can be applied to civil investigations and prosecutions as well.

The term "applications" as it is used in this text means the types of cases and specific ways in which criminal analysis has been used or could be used.

The term "criminal analysis" has not been broadly used to cover this area of endeavor in the past. The most common reference to this type of work has used the term *intelligence* analysis. This was coined in the days when the raw data collected in the field by investigators were considered "intelligence," and the collection/analysis/conclusion data cycle was termed "the intelligence cycle." Most of what is taught as "intelligence analysis," however, is analysis to be used in aid of an investigation; hence it has also been termed "investigative analysis" (Sommers, 1986) or "tactical analysis" (Harris, 1976).

Intelligence or investigative analysis has generally been held separate from "crime analysis," which, in its simplest form, is done within police departments to determine patterns of burglaries, auto thefts, and so on. Crime analysis has been a patrol oriented form of analysis: that is, its conclusions are often used to support decision making on the deployment of patrol officers. That deployment is often done as a measure to attempt to prevent further crimes of the type that was the subject of the crime analysis. Investigative analysis, on the other hand, has been used to support the major crimes or organized crime functions within law enforcement, to help solve a particular case.

HISTORICAL BACKGROUND

In order to understand the role of an analyst in the law enforcement community, one must first be familiar with the information-gathering function of a paramilitary organization such as the police. Intelligence traces its roots back to ancient Chinese strategy and to Biblical times. Books on war and on intelligence show a crucial step between gathering information, analyzing the data, and using them. On the international scene, analysis has been an integral part of the work of intelligence agencies like the Central Intelligence Agency, Israel's Mossad, the Soviet KGB, and the British Secret Service for some time.

Intelligence found its way into law enforcement in the United States in the 1920s and 1930s when police began collecting information on anarchists and mobsters. When the 1950 Kefauver hearings brought the term "Mafia" to everyone's lips, new efforts were made in large departments to collect information on this threat to public safety.

The use of analysis within law enforcement intelligence units began, in a limited sense, during the late 1960s. The 1967 President's Commission on Organized Crime supported law enforcement use of intelligence, and soon after, *Basic Elements of Intelligence* became the guidebook to the intelligence field (Godfrey and Harris, 1971). The California Department of Justice, followed by the New Jersey State Police, began developing and using some analytical techniques. Soon association analysis, telephone toll analysis, event flow charting, and visual investigative analysis (VIA) were used in a handful of organizations. VIA, for example, was employed to coordinate the investigation into the murder of presidential candidate Robert F. Kennedy.

Initially, computerized applications were limited, since the software available was in the complex and mathematical Fortran programming language and if changes were called for, a rigorous process of reprogramming, testing, debugging, and verification was necessary. Consequently a program was seldom modified and mainframe installation and maintenance required skilled programmers. Few law enforcement agencies had computers in the 1970s.

In 1976, a revised edition of *Basic Intelligence* was released; it showed that federal agencies such as the Bureau of Alcohol, Tobacco and Firearms; the Federal Bureau of Investigation; and the Drug Enforcement Administration were using some analytical methods (Harris, 1976). At the same time, private corporations and public agencies began offering analytical training. Law enforcement, defense, and private industry analysts were taught the basics of association, telephone, event, financial, visual investigative, and other variations of analysis. Not all were destined to become analysts, however. Most were investigators, interested in weaving the techniques into their personal store of investigative aids. Law enforcement managers also saw the value of analytical training for themselves and used the methods to help organize cases and to analyze management-related data.

As a result, by 1980 analysis was more widely known and state and local agencies began applying it to their cases. The early 1980s brought the simplified computerization of analytical techniques (e.g., telephone record analysis, association analysis, event flow analysis) using shelf software packages. As analysts became more conversant with data bases and user-friendly subprogramming, they were able to develop more tailored and specific analytical computer routines to deal with large quantities of records and varied data.

Analysis came into broader use during the decade, partly because of the federally funded Regional Information Sharing Systems (RISS), which included analysis as a major service—ranging from telephone record analysis and association analysis to strategic assessments. Using flexible data base and reporting software, the RISS projects were able to computerize all types of investigative records and to analyze those records once the computer reorganized them.

The RISS projects made sophisticated analytical products available to over four thousand law enforcement agencies across the country. They also educated tens of thousands of law enforcement officers and managers about the uses of analysis through training classes, conferences, and briefings. Soon officers and managers were developing analytical units within their agencies or creating analytical subprograms on their personal computers to aid their investigations. Some agencies, for example, had RISS personnel train their newly developed analytical units on site.

A professional organization, the International Association of Law Enforcement Intelligence Analysts (IALEIA), was created in 1980 by a cadre of U.S. and Canadian analysts. It grew to over eight hundred members in the United States, Canada, Australia, Hong Kong, England, and other countries by 1994. IALEIA's overall goal has been to professionalize the field of analysis within law enforcement. It sponsors regional and national training on analysis and related intelligence/organized crime topics; publishes a quarterly professional journal, formerly the *Law Enforcement Intelligence Analysis Digest* and now the IALEIA *JOURNAL;* distributes a quarterly newsletter; and has various expert committees dealing with training, career development, private security, standards and accreditation, technology awareness, international affairs, and other matters. It holds yearly meetings and issues awards.

In 1994, there were active IALEIA regional chapters in Florida, New York, Arizona, Texas, California, Washington, D.C., Canada, the Midwest (U.S.), the Mid-Atlantic (U.S.), Oregon, the Czech Republic and New England. Regular membership in IALEIA is open to intelligence officers and analysts. Criminal justice students and researchers can become associate members.

Another group of criminal analysts is the International Association of Crime Analysts (IACA). This group was formed in 1990 to provide assistance to agencies starting crime analysis units and to make crime analysis training available. By 1994, it had nearly two hundred members and worked in conjunction with state-level crime analyst associations, particularly in the western United States. It has yearly training conferences.

Other groups have exhibited support for the use of analysis in law enforcement. The International Association of Chiefs of Police has given space to IALEIA at its annual conferences. Its organized crime committee developed a management manual, *Criminal Intelligence,* which included data on intelligence standards and the analytical function (IACP, 1985). The Law Enforcement Intelligence Unit (LEIU), a private organization of law enforcement agencies, has held training sessions in analysis.

The International Association for the Study of Organized Crime was established in 1984; it includes criminal justice academic researchers as well as practitioners. It prints research papers in its publication, *Criminal Organizations*.

As in any growth field, however, progress has occurred in fits and starts. In some agencies, managers who had been exposed to analytical concepts and products were frustrated by subordinates who did not know how to produce them at the desired level. In other agencies, investigators and analysts who wanted to do analysis were stymied by managers who did not understand or appreciate the value of the techniques.

The year 1990 saw the beginning of the Society of the Certified Criminal Analysts (SCCA). This group, which is loosely associated with IALEIA, has created standards and tests to certify and recertify analysts (see also Training, Education, and Standards, this chapter). Minimum experience, education, and training standards have been established for regular certification, recertification, and lifetime certification. After a lengthy development phase, the first certified analysts were inducted after completing the application process in August 1991. One goal of this organization is to encourage writing and teaching in the field.

During this time the Australian Institute of Professional Intelligence Officers was begun in Australia. It grew out of an IALEIA chapter there and now has over two hundred members. It holds an annual training conference, and publishes a journal and a newsletter.

Also in 1990, the first hard-bound text on law enforcement analytical techniques was published—*Criminal Intelligence Analysis* (Andrews and Peterson). This book details seven analytical methods: association analysis, case analysis, telephone record analysis, inference development, collection plans, conversation analysis, and report writing. The text, which combines the work of academicians and practitioners in the field of analysis, can be used in a college-level course. It received the 1989–90 IALEIA award for the most significant contribution to the literature of intelligence analysis for that year.

The availability of basic analytical training expanded in 1991 to include a two-week curriculum at the Federal Law Enforcement Training Center in Glynco, Georgia. This course relied on federal and state experts to teach a variety of subjects from the basics (e.g., Law Enforcement Sources of Information and Introduction to Charting) to the more complex (e.g., Accounting for Non-Accountants and Profiling and Indicators).

In 1993, the Federal Bureau of Investigation Academy in Quantico, Virginia, instituted Crime Analyst Training. The first session of the Academy, held in 1994, provided free training to those involved in both crime and intelligence analysis.

The 1990s promise to be a third breakthrough decade for the field of analysis. More people are applying new techniques, talents, and technologies. Analyst certification and recertification should lead to more advanced training and written reports on analytical techniques. The continued use of computerized techniques for organizing data to be analyzed should become common by the year

2000, so that analysis will then be a standard operating procedure for every police department and private security unit in America and around the world.

To gain the recognition it deserves in law enforcement, analysis must be responsive to the needs and concerns of investigators, prosecutors, and police managers.

INVESTIGATIVE USES

Most techniques explained in this volume can be used within the investigative realm, although some derive from a broader, more proactive context.

To say that analysis is used in every investigation every day of an investigation is hyperbolic in the strict sense, but true in a general sense. Police investigators use analytical techniques every day. They must analyze something to draw a conclusion from it. They must organize investigative data to write a weekly report on a case. To know how to proceed in an investigation, they must know what is there and what is missing. These require analytical skills, analytical techniques.

Analysis is an investigative technique, just as surveillance or interviewing or electronic monitoring is an investigative technique. Knowing analytical concepts and methods makes good investigators better. This is why the vast majority of people who take analytical training are investigators. They are not interested in changing their career paths; they want to apply the proven techniques of analysis to their cases. Some of the best analytical minds combine law enforcement investigative experience with analytical methods.

Any case which needs serious investigating needs analysis. It is the most effective way of dealing with incomplete information—to tell you what you still need to get or to tell you what can be concluded from the information you have. The entire range of investigative work can benefit from the application of analytical techniques: from homicides to missing persons to burglaries to auto theft to major conspiracies. However, most agencies have only limited numbers of analysts to assist with limited types of investigations. This is why analytical training for investigators is so crucial.

Analysts in Cases

The optimum use of analysts in an investigation is to bring them into the case at the onset. This allows the investigators to rely upon the analysts to undertake various types of products which can support the investigator's work as well as the investigation as a whole. Products are the charts, graphs, tables, summaries, and other analytical compilations which are produced in the course of an analytical review of materials. Analysts can perform public document searches, one of their most common uses, and establish files and computerized data bases tailored to the investigation. The document management function, critical in large cases with volumes of subpoenaed records, is another analytical function.

Analysts can provide weekly summaries of the cases's progress for the investigator to pass on to his or her supervisor. When toll billings are needed, the analysts can keep track of the notification requirement and generate a request to the telephone company that they delay advising the subscriber of the agency's review of their records. Indeed, analysts can be an integral part of the investigative team. The analyst's writing, computer, and organizing skills can save countless investigative hours while assuring the potential success of the investigation. The use of analyst hours can save many investigator or attorney hours.

Why, then, doesn't every agency use analysts? One reason is that most analysts are civilians and many police agencies are limited in the number and the salary level of civilians they can employ. This, combined with a general belief that police do not make the best analysts because they are trained to look at an incident as an independent event, rather than being taught to hypothesize from an incident to a possible pattern, causes some agencies not to use analysts. To circumvent this problem, some agencies use sworn officers as analysts or a combination of civilian and police officer analysts.

Most analysts are civilians working in a sworn environment; that is, they work for and with people who have the sworn power to arrest lawbreakers. Thus they are a suspicious minority because they did not attend the police academy or work "out on the street."

Police agencies are generally unionized, with rules which limit the number of nonunion (i.e., nonsworn) employees who can be hired. The types of civilian positions found within a police agency have traditionally been low-paying clerical or dispatch jobs. In some agencies, an analyst must be willing to work for little more than a clerk's wages or wait for the agency to get approval for a new type of personnel to be hired and compensated at a higher level. Within the bureaucracies of most cities or states, this is a lengthy and arduous task.

Some unions, on the other hand, take the attitude that these jobs could and should be done by uniformed officers, such as those who have been injured in the line of duty and thus cannot be assigned to the street. It is difficult, then, for some agencies to "break into" employing analysts.

There is a potential for friction between analysts and investigators stemming from differences relating to background, education, and job concerns. Analysts have not gone through the rigors of a basic police training class. While many sworn officers served in the military, many analysts attended college instead. Many analysts are women; most officers are men.

The analysts' lack of "street time" may make them appear naive about how investigations work or how crime operates. If an analyst makes recommendations about a case based on the data that have collected, the investigator may be hesitant to accept those recommendations because of a lack of faith in the analyst's judgment. Conversely, the analyst may view the investigator as someone who is trying to fabricate a case because the investigator keeps all the facts in his or her head, rather than putting down a lot of quantifiable, factual data on paper. An investigator may be working off a "hunch"; the analyst wants more empirical data on which to base a hypothesis.

Job concerns play a large role in police/analyst friction. Investigators have concerns that the analyst will take credit for the case or that the analytical product, rather than the months of investigation, will be highlighted. Investigators may worry that analysts will see that the case has not been done thoroughly and will point this out to management. The fact that analysts bring out what is missing in an investigation may make them appear critical of investigators.

Many investigators view cases as their private territories and do not want anyone else intruding, analysts, other investigators, or police managers. To protect this territory, investigators may withhold information needed to make an analysis, causing the resultant analytical product to be incomplete and therefore inaccurate.

Analysts, on the other hand, think of investigators as having more status in the police environment. Investigators have a wide range of promotional steps through which they can climb. Civilian analysts can only go so far within a police agency, regardless of time on the job, education, or knowledge. Often, they cannot rise to the top of the analytical unit since this post is reserved for a sworn police officer.

This lack of status often drives analysts from the field. Some become investigators or lawyers. Others leave law enforcement to work in computer positions or to teach. Only in a few federal agencies have analysts been able to use their analytical experience and skills to gain management positions within law enforcement.

PROSECUTIVE USES

The goal of every investigation is a successful prosecution. Accordingly, the use of analysis in the investigative arena also supports the prosecution of the case. The function of analysis is of equal importance at the prosecutive level as at the investigative level.

Just as investigators use analytical skills or techniques in their cases, attorneys perform varied types of analysis on the material brought to them for presentation in court. Most often, that analysis falls within the realm of "legal analysis," that is, reviewing the case materials for evidence which matches the elements of the crime(s) charged and determining legal sufficiency.

There are numerous times, however, when legal analysis falls into the realm of criminal analysis. Many tasks necessary to the course of a prosecution can be done by analysts, such as the preparation of visual exhibits for use before the judge and jury, the synopsizing of previous testimony or statements, the reviewing of electronic intercept tapes, the organizing of case material into the form needed to prove the elements of the crime.

Analysts can work best on the prosecution if brought into the case early. They may also form a bridge between the investigation and the prosecution of a case.

If used during the investigatory stage of the case, they become experts on the data. If that is not possible, or if the investigating agency did not use any analysts on the case, then a prosecutive agency analyst should be assigned immediately to pull the materials together so the prosecutor can see how strong the case is and/or assign his or her own investigators to get the information to fill in gaps. The analyst is an integral part of the case through the trial phase.

Yet even fewer prosecutive agencies have analysts than do police agencies. Prosecutive agencies are attorney-based (as opposed to investigator-based) organizations. Although the union problems seen in police agencies generally do not exist, there is a hierarchy within the agency. Attorneys are the highest paid; investigators are the second highest paid. All others (analysts, clerical workers, administrators) are considered less important. So while pay scales in prosecutive agencies may be higher or may afford more opportunity for hiring nonunionized, nonsworn personnel, the status of analysts is viewed as distinctly below that of the attorneys and investigators.

But in many cases, analysts are not even hired by prosecutive agencies. Attorneys, like policemen, have been through arduous training and feel most comfortable with the judgment and work of those with similar training. They would rather have the attorneys working on the cases do the necessary analysis than have analysts assist the attorneys.

Although this is not cost-effective and does not use the most capable people, it is the norm. Few prosecutive agencies have a complement of analysts of any significant size. Training of paralegals in analysis as well as legal research might make analysts more acceptable to the prosecutive community.

Some prosecutors see analysis solely as an investigative tool, rather than a prosecutorial one. Some also do not realize that analytical products can be effectively used in pretrial conferences and in court. In a pretrial conference, for example, or under discovery, the defense may counsel a client to plead guilty if confronted by analytical depictions of the crime which the defense knows will sway a jury. This can save thousands of dollars in court costs and dozens of hours of attorney time.

Within a grand jury or trial setting analytical products can be and have been entered as evidence when investigators or analysts have testified about the methodology used to complete the analysis. Analysts can be used as expert witnesses with good results.

The use of analysis within the prosecutorial setting is generally an untapped field which may result in development of new techniques and more beneficial uses. Cross-training between paralegal techniques and analytical techniques would benefit paralegals as well as analysts.

PLANNING AND REPORTING USES

Analysis assists law enforcement in police planning and reporting. These are more integrated uses of analytical skills in law enforcement that may open other career paths to analysts.

Traditionally, intelligence personnel have reported directly to top management in police agencies, as have planners. Their jobs often require similar skills.

Police planning is an extension of the criminal analysis function in its broadest and most strategic sense. To determine appropriate budgeting and the future use of resources requires an analysis of current resources and current crime problems. Crime analysis, inference development, and strategic assessments are needed to set policy.

There are two barriers to applying criminal analysis skills in police planning. Shortages of funds first cut "nonessential" programs such as training and planning. Enforcement is traditionally a reactive, rather than a proactive, concern. Long-range planning is looked upon by even enlightened police as unnecessary when its predictions are erased by an unforeseen event or technological advance. The status of civilians in a sworn environment is again critical. If police executives do not trust civilian analysts to make recommendations about current cases, they will not ask for their advice on future planning. Instead, sworn police personnel are used in planning positions.

Analysts should work as police planners because they can take the knowledge and concerns of management as a framework for their analysis and planning, combining experiential knowledge and logical method.

Analysts commonly write reports and speeches and serve as public information officers. Good writing skills are essential; these skills include more than good spelling, or grammar, or even knowledge of what to say. Good writing is a function of good organization. Knowing how to organize the facts in a logical manner is necessary in an intelligence report, in an agency's annual report, or in a speech for the police chief or the governor. Analysts are able to organize facts and ideas in words as well as in graphics. The marriage of text and graphics is a necessary part of any public report, and analysts can best shepherd such projects. Analysts are trained to work with graphic professionals to assure a good product.

Almost all areas within a police agency benefit from the application of analytical skills. How, then, are those skills developed? How can police managers choose analysts who will be most flexible and useful?

EDUCATION AND TRAINING

Analysts form possibly the most diversified group of individuals in law enforcement. Some are police officers, while others are researchers. Still others are persons who have been promoted through the clerical ranks to become analysts. Their educational backgrounds vary as well as their experience levels. Some police officers are not college graduates, and some people who have worked their way up to becoming analysts have had little to no college courses; others have advanced degrees.

Training has been fairly standard since only a few vendors or agencies have offered analytical training; thus it has been similar around the country and even in other parts of the world. What differs is the availability of training, particularly of advanced training.

Education and training provide the basis for a competent and successful professional. The analytical skills learned are then applied to the investigative, prosecutorial, planning, or reporting uses detailed in this volume. A closer look at standards and offerings in these areas follows.

Education

Minimum educational requirements for law enforcement professionals have become common. High school degrees have long been a requirement for police officers, and some police organizations now mandate college degrees for advancement within the ranks. Certain police agencies are now requiring college degrees for admittance to their police academies, although this is not the norm.

Analysts are expected to have college degrees more often than law enforcement officers. Many analysts are recruited directly out of undergraduate (or graduate) schools through intern programs or open (public) recruiting. Criminal justice programs in colleges and universities have many students who are eager to gain entry to a law enforcement agency, whether it be as an investigator or as an analyst. Some view the analyst role as easier to qualify for and offering the opportunity to advance to investigator.

The college graduates who become analysts are from varied subject fields since, until recently, there have been no schools which offer degree specialization in criminal justice research and analysis. Some graduates have backgrounds in mathematics; others majored in criminal justice, political science, sociology, history, English, prelaw, journalism, social work, business, or education. No one major has been found to produce more able analysts than others. Certain majors, such as business or mathematics, may produce specialists in financial analysis or in complex computer analysis. Other majors, such as journalism or English, may produce analysts with writing skills who may be good generalists.

Is a college degree really necessary for analysts? It is not necessary, but it is preferred. Analysts need four basic skills: writing ability, verbal ability, organizational ability, and cognitive ability. Analysts must be able to write, to talk, to organize materials, and to think. While these do not require a college degree, the college experience provides an opportunity to hone these skills. Courses which require the completion of research papers and focus on analyzing what one is researching produce analytical skills. College enables students to experience a broad range of concepts, people, and information.

The question of a degree requirement was faced by the Society of Certified Criminal Analysts in determining its standards for analysts. Its criteria for regular (three-year) certification include a minimum of an associate's degree (two year degree) or five years of documented experience in a related criminal justice position. Although the Society originally intended to require a four-year degree of all analysts, it was felt that this would place certification outside the grasp of most American analysts and analyst/investigators. The Society hopes to raise the standard for all certification to require a bachelor's degree by the year 1997. Those who apply for Lifetime Certification through the Society should have a bachelor's degree.

There has been no indication that postgraduate study produces better criminal analysts than an undergraduate degree, although some analysts do have advanced degrees. Moreover, there is again no differentiation between the analytical viability of persons with advanced study in particular fields, such as law or business, over those with more general degrees. The key to success in analysis is to write and communicate ideas at the level of the police or prosecutorial audience. Many persons in that audience are not holders of advanced degrees, nor are they familiar with the style of writing mandated in some master's or doctoral programs. As a consequence, those who have spent long periods in an academic environment may find it hard to adapt their writing style to everyday police work.

The ideal educational background of a candidate would be a bachelor's degree including courses in economics, accounting, history, sociology, political science, writing, logic, foreign language, criminal law, criminal justice advanced courses, statistics, computer science, and research. With the benefit of this broad range of courses, applicants have knowledge of many concepts which support law enforcement analysis. Also, they have probably completed research papers or analysis treatises which prospective employers can review to judge their writing and research skills.

Undergraduate education, if at all possible, should include an internship in a criminal justice agency. An internship is one way to identify potential employees and provide them with a trial work period. It may also aid prospective employees in determining whether they are interested in work with that particular agency. Neither of these will be achieved if the employees are relegated to photocopying and other tasks with a similar skill level. There are many nonconfidential functions within any agency which could serve as a testing ground for analytical skills such as collecting and reporting agency statistics or compiling crime rate information.

A prospective candidate's skills can also be tested during the applicant screening process. Some agencies use a test which requires applicants to summarize a two- to three-page report. This demonstrates their ability to retrieve the salient facts and to state them in a logical manner. Some agencies administer written tests to determine general analytical knowledge. These can include twenty-five to fifty questions, often of the multiple-choice or true/false variety. Other agencies give practical exercises which require one or more products to be compiled from several pages of investigative material.

Some colleges and universities have begun to develop programs which they believe will prepare students for careers in law enforcement, international, or corporate analysis. Mercyhurst College in Erie, Pennsylvania, has initiated a

Research Intelligence Analyst Program (RIAP). The program includes liberal arts courses, a foreign language requirement, computer systems courses, and specialized intelligence and analysis lectures. The college also arranges internship programs for its students with selected federal, state, and local agencies.

In Australia, the Queensland University of Technology has a Security and Intelligence Certificate program within its criminal justice department. This one-year program includes four units on intelligence theory and application, automated systems, investigations, analysis and report writing, and interdepartmental liaison. It also offers a three-year degree program in justice studies which includes courses in criminology, intelligence, ethics, national security, intelligence organizations, intelligence research, protected automated systems, and protective security.

Other schools in the United States including Michigan State University and Northeast Missouri University offer courses on intelligence and analysis but do not offer a degree specialization program in the field. Contact people for these programs are listed at the end of this chapter.

The educational backgrounds of analysts should be general enough to give them an understanding of the multifaceted criminal environment, yet specific enough to develop their writing and organizational skills. It is to be hoped that in the near future, other colleges and universities with programs in criminal justice will begin developing and offering analytical concentrations within those fields so that entry-level analysts are better prepared for their careers. These programs could use practitioners as adjunct professors or could be developed by teams of professors and practitioners, with the former presenting occasional guest lectures.

Training

Because practical law enforcement research skills are not taught in many colleges, the responsibility for training analysts has fallen upon their agencies or upon consultants who provide the service to law enforcement organizations. As a result, even reputable agencies may employ undertrained analysts. And, while several basic analytical courses have been developed, few advanced courses are available to those wishing to expand their skills.

Some agencies offer only on-the-job training, where analytical techniques or methods are sometimes haphazardly passed down from the more experienced employees to the new ones or, worse yet, the new employees are left to their own devices and must reinvent the methodological wheel. One on-the-job training method involves reading the literature in the agency's library and past analytical products of experienced colleagues. After several weeks (or months), they are moved on to assist journeymen analysts on cases until gradually they are ready to provide analytical products on their own. While on-the-job training is valuable in imparting to new employees the agency's protocols and accepted formats, it is not a preferred method of training unless the job to be done by analysts is so limited to those protocols and formats that there is no creative or discretionary work required of them.

Other agencies rely on the training program offered by ANACAPA Sciences of Santa Barbara, California. ANACAPA offers several courses. The basic course is a one-week session which covers association (link) analysis, net worth analysis, inference development, probability assessment, and charting methods. This one-week course is geared toward investigators but can provide effective entry-level training for analysts. At a minimum, it familiarizes students with analytical terminology, teaches rudimentary charting, and gives them a taste of what analytical products might be able to be produced. The course has both a pretest and a posttest and is given at locations around the United States and in other countries.

ANACAPA also provides a two-week course, which includes the following segments:

- the analytical process,
- telephone toll analysis,
- logic,
- inference development,
- network pattern recognition,
- analysis of money flow,
- charting techniques,
- white collar crime indicators,
- concealed income analysis,
- frequency distribution,
- data correlation,
- computer analysis, and
- case charting.

This two-week course is also given in various locations. ANACAPA courses are usually open to private security personnel and the military, in addition to law enforcement workers.

Training seminars presented by other agencies have generally been based upon these ANACAPA models. The topics are usually the same and the techniques and exercises may bear a resemblance. Moreover, many analytical courses run by agencies at the state and local levels have only been offered to internal employees or were discontinued after some period. In 1990, however, the Federal Law Enforcement Training Center in Glynco, Georgia, developed a nine-day Criminal Intelligence Analysis Training Program which is open to federal, state and local law enforcement personnel. This course covers the following topics:

- sources of public information,
- sources of law enforcement information,
- indexing data,
- introduction to accounting,
- report writing,
- introduction to charting,
- telephone record analysis,
- association analysis,
- profiling/indicators,
- computerized applications,
- visual investigative analysis,
- event and commodity flow charting, and
- legal issues.

The FLETC class is a comprehensive analytical class. It draws on instructors from federal agencies assigned to the Training Center, from specialty instructors in federal field offices, and from state and multistate agencies. A lengthy practex, which requires several products over the course of the second week, is included. Computerized analysis is provided through the use of laptop computers lent to the students for the duration of the course. "Shareware" computer programs are provided for the students to take back to their agencies.

During 1993, the Federal Bureau of Investigation Academy in Quantico, Virginia, developed a three-week training course for analysts sponsored by its National Center for the Analysis of Violent Crime. This program, called Crime Analyst Training, is designed to provide training in crime analysis, intelligence analysis, and criminal investigative analysis (profiling) to analysts from around the country. The topics included in the pilot course of this training were as follows:

Establishing a Crime Analysis Unit
Research Methods
Law Enforcement Statistics
Crime Analysis
Forecasting
Association Analysis
Pattern Recognition
Event Flow Charting
Financial Analysis
Visual Investigative Analysis
Criminal Investigative Analysis

Computer Skills
Writing Skills
Communication/Speaking Skills

Other common ways to obtain analytical training are through organizations which have a training mandate. The Regional Information Sharing System (RISS) projects, for example, are conduits for regionally held analytical and intelligence seminars. The analysts' organization, the International Association of Law Enforcement Intelligence Analysts (IALEIA), has regional chapters which offer seminars from several hours to several days in length. Consultants to the Bureau of Justice Assistance and the National Institute of Justice develop training with analytical components in support of priority programs.

On a regional basis, individuals who are now in or are retired from law enforcement offer basic analytical classes, some of which are quite comparable to the ANACAPA course.

Within the field of crime analysis, no large-scale national contractor has emerged to provide crime analysis training, yet it is available throughout the United States. One vendor, The Alpha Group in California, offers a one-week course on a limited basis. This course includes time series analysis, statistics, mapping, forecasting, pattern recognition, and other topics. Concurrent with that training, one principal of Alpha, Steven Gottlieb, published a text, *Crime Analysis*, in 1994. (Training vendor contact information is given at the end of this chapter.)

Advanced analytical training is significantly less obtainable than basic training. In many cases, training on specific types of criminal investigation (e.g., money laundering and nontraditional organized crime) is the topic of ''advanced'' analytical training. In others, the advanced training provides further examples of techniques taught in basic training and serves as a refresher.

Over the past decade, ANACAPA developed three additional courses:

- Financial Manipulation Analysis, which focuses on money flow, manipulation, and analysis of business records; particularly suited to those who specialize in asset investigation or business analysis
- Advanced (Computer Aided) Intelligence Analysis, which provides a specific computer software package developed by ANACAPA to produce network diagrams in IBM or Macintosh computer environments
- Management Utilization of Criminal Intelligence, which focuses on analysis as an aid to managerial problem solving and strategic and tactical decision making; suitable for police executives or managers.

A number of agencies and organizations have offered analytical training beyond the basic level on a onetime basis. These courses usually bring together several experts on specific topics in a half- to several-day curriculum. Often, these courses are crime-related; that is, the experts provide information or techniques on specific crime groups or activities. Variety is the key to this type of training; the subjects are changed frequently to appeal to a limited repeat audience.

Other advanced courses have included one in which a set of complex practical exercises formed the week's training along with in-depth looks at financial analysis, collection plans, event flow charting, and inference development (Andrews and Peterson, 1985). Another, developed in 1993, provided advanced exercises in event flow analysis, financial analysis, oral briefings, strategic analysis, and indicator analysis/profiling, along with a half-day practical exercise related to homicide (Peterson, 1993). Teacher interaction with students, including individualized advice, feedback, and critiques of products, was essential to both courses.

A training program on strategic analysis within law enforcement has been developing for over five years. The first class, given in 1989, included instruction and practical exercises on several topics:

- strategic thinking,
- choosing topics for strategic analysis,
- collection plans,
- trend analysis,
- forecasting,
- premonitories,
- vulnerability assessments,
- threat assessments,
- strategic planning, and
- evaluating strategies (Peterson).

This course also includes numerous practical exercises and interaction on products between teacher and students.

A second strategic analysis course, presented in 1993, included law enforcement statistics, trend analysis, forecasting, collection plans, report writing and organization, oral briefings, threat assessments, developing strategies from analysis, and strategic planning and evaluating strategies (Peterson).

Also in 1993, a two-day seminar on interpretive analysis was developed and given by the California Department of Justice, Bureau of Investigations. This included strategic thinking, brainstorming, inference development, descriptive trend analysis, descriptive forecasting, indicator analysis/profiling, and numerous exercises which applied the techniques to work in progress at the Department (Peterson, 1993).

One drawback to producing analytical training, particularly of an advanced nature, has been its level of use relative to its comparative cost. There are fewer than two thousand law enforcement analysts in the United States. Most of them are concentrated in areas like Washington, D.C., New York City, Florida, Arizona, and California, with no more than one hundred in any one metropolitan area (with the exception of Washington, D.C.). And, as earlier noted, these working analysts come from varied educational backgrounds and perform a variety of duties.

Thus, to appeal to a moderate sized audience, training must be general in nature, rather than specific as advanced training should be. Much of the basic training that is developed, in fact, is designed to appeal to investigators as well as analysts so that it may attract a larger audience.

The comparative development cost of advanced analytical training may be high. Lesson plans, handouts, practical exercises, and visual aids to support a course of several days can take months to develop. If the course is given a second time, modifications or updates are usually made. They can also be time consuming, but less so than the initial course development. Three to four schedulings of a particular course may be necessary to complete the fine-tuning of its presentation. It is not, therefore, efficient to develop a course which will be given only once or twice.

What results is one of several things: first, few new courses are developed, leaving trainers to use exercises from courses developed by others with which they may not be particularly familiar or comfortable (Peterson and Ridgeway, 1990). Second, courses that are offered as "advanced analytical" courses are often remakes of investigative courses which provide valid data on crime groups or criminal activity, but do little to hone analytical skills. Finally, in the void of available courses, analysts become stagnant in their jobs, wishing for training or interaction or affirmation of their work products but not getting it. Those analysts are often the ones who leave the field after a few years.

There is a potential solution to the dearth of advanced analytical training. If a national, international, regional, or multistate initiative, such as IALEIA, the RISS projects, a consultant group, or a federal agency, would support the creation and presentation of advanced training, then courses could be developed which would be applicable to a wide audience and would thus be cost-effective.

Education and training are the building blocks of analytical skills and judgment. If we are to have professional analysts who make a significant contribution to the business of law enforcement, then these factors become critical.

STANDARDS AND ACCREDITATION

Data require analysis by managers, investigators, or analysts. The advent of more sophisticated methods of data collection (electronic surveillance, for example) and of computerized methods of collating data for analysis has created a significant need for trained and experienced analysts within the law enforcement environment as well as in the private sector.

That need is expected to grow in the future, as more agencies become technologically aware and as more complex investigations become commonplace.

To meet that need, a cadre of qualified analysts who will serve both investigative and prosecutive agencies must be developed. In addition, career paths for analysts which include police planning, police information, and police management specialists are expected to develop further as the application of analytical skills increasingly comes to the attention of police management.

The diverse backgrounds of analysts have worked against the creation of standards in the field. The International Association of Law Enforcement Intelligence Analysts (IALEIA) has had a goal to "develop qualification standards and indices of competence for the profession" in its bylaws since 1980. One of its ongoing committees is the Standards and Accreditation Committee. That committee surveyed members' agencies within Florida during 1984 and within the nation in 1993 to compile data on analyst job descriptions, training requirements, salaries, experience, and educational backgrounds. The 1984 survey found that 53 percent of the agencies responding required a bachelor's degree while 12 percent required a two-year associate's degree, 24 percent required high school diplomas, and 11 percent did not have an educational requirement for entry as an analyst. In the 1993 survey, the percentage of agencies requiring bachelor's degrees for analysts rose to 67 percent. Thus, the studies concluded that the minimum standard should be a bachelor's degree or four years of law enforcement experience which required the ability to collate, assemble, and analyze pertinent facts and present them in clear and concise written reports (International Association of Law Enforcement Intelligence Analysts, 1984, and Peterson, Summer 1993).

It should be noted, however, that the general standard for analysts in other countries is not at this level. Few agencies in Canada and Australia, for example, require university degrees of their analysts.

Another barrier to the standardization of analyst qualifications is that titles and pay ranges for analysts vary within law enforcement. In federal, state, and local agencies some analysts are designated and paid as clerical support (at one extreme) while others are used and paid as management professionals (at the other). The difference in classification and pay may reflect the analyst's experience to a degree, but may equally reflect the value placed on analysis by the management of the organization. In other words, analysts with similar experience and education could be holding widely disparate titles and making widely disparate salaries in agencies, even within the same geographic region. The types of jobs titles analysts have include intelligence clerk, intelligence specialist, intelligence analyst, criminal analyst, criminal information analyst, information research specialist, management analyst, administrative analyst, research analyst, research assistant, and management specialist. Law enforcement officers, including investigators, detectives, troopers, and police officers (including line supervisors), may also be involved in analytical work though their job title and description do not indicate that they are.

The 1984 Florida survey cited previously found a range of entry-level Florida salaries between $10,080 and $23,120. Nationwide salaries offered to beginning state level law enforcement analysts were also surveyed; they showed a range of $12,456 to $30,014. The 1993 survey reported a range of analytical salaries from $12,000 to $70,000.

While the "typical" analyst might exist on paper and in a few agencies, there is a diversity in the duties analysts are called upon to perform. The role of the analyst must be defined within the jurisdiction the analyst serves, but with some overlap with analysts employed elsewhere. The political considerations of analysts' jobs, paychecks, and duties must be taken into consideration because any standards must be applicable and workable. Generic job descriptions for criminal intelligence analysts and crime analysts appear at the end of this chapter.

A third barrier to standardization is the politics of standard setting. Drawing the line for any standard implies that there will be people left on the "wrong" side of the line. Where, in such a diverse community, can the line be drawn?

Several programs to accredit and certify analysts have begun to attempt to meet the need for standards. The Society for Certified Criminal Analysts was begun in 1990 by nine practitioners with combined experience of more than a century in analytical methods, teaching, and supervision who formed its Board of Governors. All were members of the IALEIA group; most were past or present board members of that organization. All were familiar with IALEIA's efforts to create standards; several had served on the IALEIA Standards and Accreditation Committee. The standards put forth by SCCA were arrived at by the consensus of that group, which worked for over a year on that issue alone.

SCCA developed minimum educational, training, and experiential standards for certification, recertification, and lifetime certification. In 1991, it certified the first group of analysts from a pool of international applicants.

SCCA attempted to have its standards reflect the diverse backgrounds of analysts by instituting guidelines which use those backgrounds to create a common core of "standard experience." For example, the SCCA requires applicants to be "working, or having worked for at least three years, as an analyst, analyst supervisor, or analyst manager for law enforcement, private security, or the military." In this way, certification is open only to those who work or have worked in the field. At the same time, less experienced analysts who have just entered the field can be welcomed into the analytical community and certified. Further, the applicability of certification is broadened to include analysts working in private security and the military.

A broad standard is also found in the educational area. A minimum of an associate's degree or equivalent (sixty hours of study) or five years of documented experience in a related criminal justice position is required. This allows investigator/analysts without the desired college credits to qualify for initial certification.

Previous analytical training is a requirement for certification. The basic training required is the equivalent of an ANACAPA course, that is, a course which covers the basic methods used in analysis: specifically, training on network analysis, flow analysis, telephone record analysis, and financial analysis are required, along with at least two of the following modules: statistics, inference development, crime analysis, or introduction to analysis, all within at least a twenty-four-hour course. Training must be given by a recognized provider or agency or administered through an on-the-job training program. Applicants are required to be members of the International Association of Law Enforcement Intelligence Analysts.

The analyst's experience, training, and education are detailed on a lengthy application form. If the analyst is applying for regular (three-year) certification, the form and a fee are submitted and the analyst is scheduled for the certification test. The test includes a written component of over two hundred questions as well as a practex component which requires the analysts to complete analytical charts based on data provided. A study guide is provided to applicants before the test is scheduled. Once the test is completed, the test grades and applications are reviewed by the Board of Governors and a vote is taken to certify or not to certify the individual.

Benefits of SCCA certification include certificates, notification of training classes, circulation of monographs developed by certified analysts, and inclusion in a registry of certified analysts. Those certified may also use "Certified Criminal Analyst" after their names. Information from the registry may be made available to law enforcement managers who are seeking qualified analysts or analyst supervisors.

Lifetime Certification is also available, with somewhat more stringent requirements. Lifetime certificants must have at least ten years of "active duty as an analyst and/or an analyst supervisor, manager or teacher of intelligence/analysis in law enforcement and/or the military." They must have completed their bachelor's degree and a basic analytical course. Testing is not required for Lifetime Certification applicants. The submission of the application form and fee is standard.

Regular certificants must apply for recertification every three years. Again, criteria are more stringent for recertification than for certification. Recertification requires that the applicant

- have been involved in developing, giving, or taking advanced training;
- have written an article or document on an analytical method;
- have participated in a complex case or assessment;
- or have completed a special project, such as being an active contributor to an intelligence publication or organization.

All applicants must agree to abide by the Analysts' Code of Ethics, which appears at the end of this chapter. Failure to abide by these dicta is one cause for expulsion from the Society.

Since the beginning of the SCCA, discussion has been heightened regarding standards. The chairman of IALEIA's Standards and Accreditation Committee sits, ex officio, on the SCCA Board of Governors, and, as mentioned, several SCCA Board of Governors members also serve on the IALEIA Board of Directors. By requiring membership in IALEIA, SCCA encourages support for that organization. Not all IALEIA members agree with the standards set by SCCA; not all those members can meet those standards. The SCCA organization has, however, met the goal of IALEIA, to ''develop qualification standards and indices for competence.''

A California certification program was begun in 1992 at the California State College campus at Fullerton. It was initiated by Steven Gottlieb, who is a practicing crime analyst and teaches at Fullerton. A certificate program was developed: individuals can take a series of classes at California State (in Fullerton or other locations) and, when they are completed, receive a certificate from the California Department of Justice. The classes required for certification are as follows:

• Crime Analysis Data Analysis (12 hours)

• Crime Analysis Applications (24 hours)

• Basic Elements of Criminal Intelligence (18 hours)

• Criminal Intelligence Analysis (18 hours)

• Criminal Investigative Analysis I (12 hours)

• Criminal Investigative Analysis II (24 hours)

• Law Enforcement Research and Statistical Methods (36 hours)

• Practicum in Crime and Intelligence Analysis (400 hours)

Continuing education credits are also given for the courses. The California Department of Justice will acknowledge each person who completes the program as a ''Certified Crime and Intelligence Analyst.'' Some of the courses toward the certification are also available through Gottlieb and the Alpha Group outside California.

The proposed FBI crime analyst training program may also have a certification component. Concurrently, the International Association of Crime Analysts is also working toward developing standards for criminal analysts.

While standards which are universally acceptable are difficult to compose, basic job descriptions for analysts are available. Descriptions of both criminal intelligence analyst and crime analyst positions are given at the end of the chapter.

CONCLUSIONS

The use of analysis within law enforcement and private security continues to evolve. Some analysis is done so automatically by investigators that they do not realize they are doing it. Other techniques are complex and warrant the use of experienced analysts.

As analysis becomes an integral part of the investigative process, the need for training, for advanced training, and for standards grows. Analytical applications are limited only by the minds of developers and the users of those applications and products. Training on evolving methods should be documented and developed. And as the body of analysts grows and their training and experience levels grow, so too will standards governing those levels evolve to a higher plane.

APPENDIX A: ANALYTICAL ORGANIZATIONS, EDUCATION, AND TRAINING

Organizations

International Association of Law Enforcement Intelligence Analysts, Emma E. Fern, President, P.O. Box 52-2924, Miami, FL 33152-02924. TEL: 305/653-3010.

International Association for the Study of Organized Crime, Patrick Ryan, Executive Director, Department of Criminal Justice, Long Island University, Brookville, NY 11548. TEL: 516/299-2594.

International Association of Crime Analysts, Sergeant Mark Stallo, President, Dallas Police Dept., Crime Analysis Unit, 2014 Main Street # 300 A, Dallas, TX 75201. TEL: 214/670-4539.

Society of Certified Criminal Analysts, R. Glen Ridgeway, Chancellor, Main P.O. Box 583, Purchase, NY 10577.

Australian Institute of Professional Intelligence Officers, Don McDowell, President, Post Office Box 1007, Civic Square, Australian Capital Territory (A.C.T.), 2601 Australia.

Books

Criminal Intelligence Analysis. Paul P. Andrews, Jr., and Marilyn B. Peterson, eds., Palmer Enterprises, P.O. Box 1714, Loomis, CA 95650. TEL: 916/652-3225.

Crime Analysis: From First Report to Final Arrest. Steven Gottlieb. Alpha Publishing, P.O. Box 8, Montclair, CA 91763.

University Programs

Mercyhurst College, Robert Heibel, Coordinator Research Intelligence Analyst Program, Department of History, Erie, PA 16546 TEL: 814/824-2117.

Queensland University of Technology, School of Justice Studies, Bevin Wigan, Coordinator, Security and Intelligence Certificate, Locked Bag No 2, Red Hill, Queensland, 4059 Australia.

Michigan State University, Dr. David L. Carter, School of Criminal Justice, 560 Baker Hall, East Lansing, MI 48824-1118. TEL: 517/355-2197.

Northeast Missouri State University, Dr. Charles Frost, Justice System Programs, Kirksville, MO 63501. TEL: 816/785–4667.

California State at Fullerton Crime and Intelligence Analysis Certification Program—Steven Gottlieb, Coordinator, P.O. Box 34080, Fullerton, CA 92634-9480. TEL: 714/773–2411.

Training Vendors

Federal Law Enforcement Training Center, Criminal Intelligence Analysis Training Program, George Jackson, Coordinator, SSD, Building 67, Glynco, GA 31524. TEL: 912/267–3215.

ANACAPA Sciences, Douglas H. Harris, Chairman, 2000 North Pantops Drive, Charlottesville, VA 22901-8646. TEL: 804/295–1929.

Federal Bureau of Investigation, National Center for the Analysis of Violent Crime, Gregory Cooper, Program Director, or Jane Whitmore, Coordinator, Crime Analysis Training, FBI Academy, Quantico, VA 22135. TEL: 703/640–1467.

The Alpha Group, Steven Gottlieb, P.O. Box 8, Montclair, CA 91763.

APPENDIX B: CRIMINAL INTELLIGENCE ANALYST GENERIC JOB DESCRIPTION

Definition

Technical work in the (agency name) is receiving, analyzing and assessing criminal information of a confidential nature and disseminating the information in keeping with agency procedures and regulations.

An employee in this position requests and receives information of a confidential nature and other data and analyzes, correlates, reviews and disseminates information pertaining to analytical products and assessments. Work is performed under the general supervision of the (position which supervises this function).

Examples of Work

Receives and analyzes information of a confidential nature, placing pertinent facts in proper relationships; evaluates the information; and prepares comprehensive analytical products and reports based on available data.

Reviews all incoming newspaper and other publication articles relative to developing trends and patterns of criminal activity and culls any information of importance.

Accesses data from a variety of law enforcement and other sources and prepares reports on same to assist in criminal investigations or intelligence assessments.

Uses link analysis, event flow analysis, and activity charting to develop inferences about the intentions and vulnerabilities of criminal groups, their key individuals, their methods of operation, and the extent of their criminal influence and scope; makes recommendations for investigative strategies.

Performs telephone record analysis; identifies significant contacts, frequency distributions and patterns of calls; completes written reports and link charts when appropriate.

Uses crime analysis techniques, statistical analysis and time series analysis to view, evaluate and draw conclusions regarding patterns of crime.

Uses other analytical methodologies including, but not limited to, financial analysis, case analysis, visual investigative analysis and strategic analysis on an as-needed basis.

Researches and reviews, prior to the initiation of a major investigation, all data on file on the subjects and prepares a preliminary report on the data.

Supports and assists investigators directly in the compilation and analysis of confidential information regarding complex criminal investigations and recommends specific investigative directions based upon conclusions drawn from the analysis.

Establishes and maintains professional contacts with experts, analytical counterparts, educators and researchers.

Creates and uses appropriate manual and automated files for performing analytical and research functions.

Makes sound decisions regarding which analytical techniques, methodologies and technologies should be employed to meet the objectives and goals of the analytical task.

Participates in formal or on-the-job training courses in electronic data processing operations and analytical methodologies.

Provides oral briefings, court testimony or other presentations on analytic products or techniques.

Required Knowledge, Skills and Abilities

Experience and proven ability in the area of research techniques and written communications.

Experience in working with computers and data and word processing applications software.

The ability to organize facts, reports and work assignments.

The ability to learn and apply methods and techniques appropriate for analyzing, evaluating, and presenting criminal information and preparing reports of assessments and conclusions.

The ability to prepare graphs, charts, tables, maps and other illustrative devices for visual presentation of data and information.

The ability to communicate effectively both orally and in writing and to prepare clear and comprehensive reports.

The ability to apply logic and sound judgment in assessing and predicting characteristics of criminal groups or criminal operations using data obtained from a variety of sources.

Minimum Experience and Training

A bachelor's degree from an accredited college or university OR

An associate's degree from an accredited college or university and two years of progressively responsible technical or professional experience in the field of law enforcement OR

Five years of progressive responsible technical or professional experience in a law enforcement agency.

Source: Standards and Accreditation Committee, International Association of Law Enforcement Intelligence Analysts, 1992.

APPENDIX C: CRIME ANALYST GENERIC JOB DESCRIPTION

Definition

Responsible administrative work in the collection, storage, retrieval and assimilation of specific crime data. Work is performed under general supervision.

Duties

Collects and organizes pertinent crime data for analysis through review of police reports and computer files. Attempts to identify evolving or existing crime problems and patterns, geographically and for similar offense patterns.

Prepares tables of suspect descriptions and persons arrested for similarities. Reads reports and prepares tables of modus operandi of persons committing selected offenses for correlations and patterns.

Maintains several pin maps or computer-generated maps to show clusters, concentrations and patterns of similar offenses, calls for service and other data. Furnishes geographic crime data reports for patrol and detectives.

Issues crime analysis bulletins that address specific crime problems, listing all possible information, including details on time, day, month, etc.

Issues monthly crime bulletins showing grids of the city with crime occurrences by selected offenses and overall. Makes conclusionary statements regarding patterns and trends which are evolving or have developed.

Performs comparative analysis on the incidence of crime and rates per population in other cities of the state, or cities of comparable size, versus this city.

Knowledge, Abilities and Skills

Knowledge of the functions, principles, practices, procedures and techniques of information and data collection, analysis and utilization with particular emphasis on statistics and computer system interface. Knowledge of municipal law enforcement and criminal justice system.

Ability to establish and maintain effective public and employee relations. Ability to plan and conduct research projects. Ability to write clear, concise reports, memoranda and letters. Ability to work independently and exercise good judgment.

Minimum Qualifications

Graduation from high school or possession of an acceptable equivalency diploma, supplemented by college course work in statistics and law enforcement. Five years experience in statistical collection and analysis. A comparable amount of training or experience may be substituted for the minimum qualifications.

Source: Extrapolation by author based on description submitted by the Ft. Pierce, Florida, Police Department.

APPENDIX D: ANALYSTS' CODE OF ETHICS, SOCIETY OF CERTIFIED CRIMINAL ANALYSTS

The intelligence function must maintain a standard of excellence in its personnel and in their performance. Analysts must exemplify high standards of integrity and professionalism. Accordingly, an analyst must:

1. Maintain a professional responsibility to his/her agency and maintain professional relationships with other analysts, enforcement officers and superiors in the field.
2. Refrain from discriminating against others on the basis of gender, sexual preference, race, creed, or religion.
3. Refrain from accepting or soliciting gifts, favors or bribes in connection with official duties.
4. Refrain from knowingly making false or misleading statements, or concealing material facts, in the course of his/her official duties.
5. Refrain from willfully disclosing to any person, whether or not for pecuniary gain, any information not generally available to the public pertaining to any criminal investigation, agency matter, or other official business which he acquires in the course of and by reason of his official duties.
6. Avoid personal or business association with persons known to be connected to or engaged in criminal activities.
7. Avoid engaging in criminal, dishonest, disreputable, or disgraceful personal conduct.

CHAPTER II

Techniques in Criminal Analysis

The steps taken to employ particular techniques of criminal analysis have been described by Morris (1982) and Andrews and Peterson (1990), but no text has provided a clear and complete survey of a majority of the techniques and their components as they are used in law enforcement. This chapter provides an alphabetical listing of twenty-six methods and thirty-seven products. An asterisk (*) denotes that the preceding method or product is discussed in detail elsewhere in this chapter. While it does not give readers enough information so that they can employ the analytical methods without further study, it provides a basis for understanding the concepts, methods, and products used. The Glossary in Appendix 1 provides definitions of terms used in this book.

ACTIVITY FLOW CHART

An activity flow chart shows the general steps needed to complete a particular process. An activity flow chart differs from an event flow chart in that the latter is more specific and uses exact occurrences and dates, while an activity flow chart provides an overview of occurrences and generally does not use dates.

Activity charts are made by gathering information on the events which occurred in a process or series of similar processes and generalizing them to depict a hypothetical, rather than a specific, process. For example, an event flow chart might include the statement "Mr. A. sells a kilo of cocaine to Mr. B. for $25,000." That same action, depicted in an activity chart, would be expressed "A drug distributor sells kilo quantities of cocaine to other distributors."

Activity flow charts include boxes or other symbols with information statements inside the symbols. The final sentence of the last paragraph would be considered an information statement. These boxes are connected by lines (solid for known connections, dotted for suspected connection) with arrowheads show-ing the direction of the flow of activity.

Activity flow charts can be used to explain complex processes such as money laundering or securities manipulation. They can also be used in place of event flow charts to provide general information rather than specific, confidential in-vestigative information.

Examples of activity flow charts can be found in Chapters 3, 4, and 7.

ASSESSMENTS

Assessments are a product of the strategic analysis* process. They are written reports which can include the results of surveys,* independent research, infor-mation gathered from investigative files, and data received from other law en-forcement sources.

Assessments can include a number of analytical products, including charts, tables, graphs, and maps. The determination of what products to include depends on the information gathered and the purpose of the assessment.

General assessments can be done to provide an overview of criminal activity or a criminal group. Specific assessments include threat assessments and vul-nerability assessments. An example of a conclusion from an assessment is given in Chapter 3.

ASSOCIATION ANALYSIS

Association analysis depicts the relationships among people, groups, busi-nesses, or other entities in a way which provides the investigator, prosecutor, or jury with information on the nature of the group and the manner in which the group interacts. For the purposes of this volume, persons banding together in some criminal enterprise are referenced; a general association analysis can be done to show noncriminal group activity as well.

To complete an association analysis, materials are gathered; they can include police reports, surveillance reports, field interviews, corporate records, testi-mony, informant data, public record data, and other information. They are re-viewed for references to people, groups, or businesses that are associated with one another. The association data extracted from these records are entered into a manual or computerized data base* which includes the names of the persons or things related, the nature of the relationship (association), and, where appro-priate, the time frame of the relationship. It is also important to include reference information in the data base so that the accuracy of these relationships can be verified.

After organizing the information in this manner, an association matrix* (if desired) and/or an association chart* is developed. The association matrix is generally considered to be an interim working product; a chart is drawn from it.

The completed association analysis package could include an association chart, a summary* of the chart, conclusions that can be drawn from the chart, brief biographical sketches* on each of the people or entities on the chart, overall conclusions* of the analysis, and recommendations* for further investigation or action. The summary, conclusions, and recommendations may include information on the organization—its hierarchy, its strong and weak points, the strength of the relationships among the people or entities, and possible members who could be used to infiltrate the group—and requests for data on additional suspected relationships.

ASSOCIATION CHART

An association chart is used within an association analysis* to depict the relationships among people or entities graphically. An association chart is usually drawn from the materials collected in an association matrix* but can be drawn directly from data in reports and other documents, or from an association data base. It is organized by the number of connections people or entities have. Larger numbers of connections by an individual or business cause that individual or business to be placed toward the center of the chart, while fewer connections place a person or entity on the periphery. This "rule" of placement is necessitated by the practical requirement of the need to connect the people or entities to more or fewer other symbols.

The symbols used on association charts have been standardized, with people shown as circles and business shown as boxes (squares or rectangles). They are connected by solid or dotted lines. The solid lines between the symbols denote strong or known relationships; dotted lines denote weak or suspected relationships.

Different symbols or lines can be used in a chart as necessary, so long as a legend is placed on the chart to explain the meaning or purpose of the symbols or lines.

The way in which the chart is organized may provide new information to the analyst or investigator on the hierarchy of a network or the operational mode of a conspiracy. Once a chart is completed, the analyst must summarize what it says, interpret it, and draw inferences* about its meaning.

There are a few cautionary comments about interpreting an association chart accurately. First, someone who appears in the center of the chart is often not the leader of the surrounding group. Those in the center are usually those most in communication and, therefore, are the most vulnerable. Leaders often appear in peripheral chart positions, insulated from everyday communication. Second, association charts are freeze-frame pictures of relationships which, by their very nature, are constantly changing. The conclusions drawn from them are only as timely as the information available to be analyzed.

The summary* of the chart should include what we know about the nature of the conspiracy and the roles assigned to people in it. The inference, or conclusion, drawn about the subjects as a result of the analysis is based on what we know and what we might presume. The chart, along with a written report, forms the basis of association analysis. Examples of association charts are found in Chapters 5, 6, and 7.

ASSOCIATION MATRIX

An association matrix is a row and column arrangement of information on relationships among people and/or groups or businesses. It is a working analytical product, an interim step in the production of an association chart* that can also be used separately. Matrices* in general are covered later in this chapter.

The data included in an association matrix is taken from available sources including investigative reports, public records, and testimony. Some association matrices are triangular, similar to mileage charts on maps. Others are square, allowing names to be placed on two sides of the matrix rather than one, as in the triangular version.

In an association matrix, a mark is placed in an intersecting cell to depict the relationship between the people or things corresponding to the row or column. In association matrix practices, solid circles are generally used to show strong or known relationships and open circles to show suspected or weak relationships. If someone is the owner, manager, director, or president of a company or group, the strength of that relationship can be shown by a plus sign or asterisk.

The placement of names along the association matrix can be done in alphabetical order or by listing businesses separately from individuals. The key to reading a triangular association matrix is to remember that each person or entity has both a column and a row which must be reviewed to comprehend the full extent of the associations depicted. The numbers of those associations shown on the matrix are counted, and the association chart that is drawn from it is based on the number of connections needed and where those connections appear. Examples of association matrices are seen in Chapters 3 and 5.

BANK RECORD ANALYSIS

Bank record analysis is the review of bank account deposits, withdrawals, and monetary instruments to determine the amounts of monies received and disbursed by a suspect. It can be used to estimate the suspect's living expenses or to determine the potential presence or use of illegal income, skimming, business fraud, or money laundering.

First, bank records are legally obtained (generally by subpoena) from a banking institution. In some cases, suspects have multiple bank accounts at different banks which must be discovered. A significant part of a money laundering investigation is the careful uncovering of links to other bank accounts and entities through checks written to them or received from them, endorsements on checks, and money transfer instruments including wire transfers, official checks, and money orders.

Once received, the records are computerized or placed into a manual accounting format which allows for their summarization by time frame, usually by month or quarter. Multiple accounts are compared, particularly to the extent that the movement of funds into or out of one account coincides with activity in another account.

Products of bank record analysis are generally determined by the type of investigation under way and the purpose of the analysis. If a net worth analysis* is needed, living expenses are estimated and the total disbursements for the period in question are determined. A source and application of funds,* similar to a net worth analysis, also requires the review of bank records to determine expenditures for the periods being compared. If potential illegal income is under investigation, then deposits which are not accounted for by paychecks or other explainable sources of income and large cash transactions should be highlighted. Financial summaries* are the most common products of bank record analyses. These provide summaries of deposits, withdrawals, checks written, debit and credit memos, starting and ending balances, primary payees, and unusual payments on a monthly, quarterly, or yearly basis as needed. These are presented within a written report that draws conclusions* based on the materials and provides investigative recommendations* when warranted. In some cases, commodity flow charts* are used to show the movement of funds between accounts. In others, event flow charts* may be used to show the chronology of deposits or payments.

Business fraud and tax evasion may be uncovered by an examination of the uses of funds disbursed for non business purposes which have been withdrawn from a business account. Skimming, or the removal of business profits for the purpose of avoiding paying taxes on them, may be reflected in large cash deposits to personal accounts. Money laundering can be shown by the movement of funds into accounts held by fronts or "paper" corporations.

An example of a bank record analysis is found in Chapter 7.

BAR CHARTS

A bar chart is a graphic depiction of a certain activity in relation to or in comparison with another factor such as time, cost, or another occurrence, both of which can generally be measured in numbers. It can be used in conjunction with a number of other analytical techniques.

To complete a bar chart, the activity and the units of measurement to be compared (numbers, percentages, dates, etc.) are placed along the two dimensions of the chart. The data to be measured are placed in the grid of the bar chart as appropriate. The bar chart is then interpreted to ascertain its meaning. Sometimes patterns can be seen which have occurred over time or in connection with the particular activity. For example, the number of telephone calls per day placed into a bar chart could show large numbers of calls leading up to a date on which a major criminal violation occurred in which the subscriber was believed to be involved.

Bar charts are used in statistical analysis* and can depict frequency distributions.* An example of a bar chart is found in Chapter 7.

BIOGRAPHICAL SKETCHES

Biographical sketches are products which compile all known data on individuals or entities to provide investigators or prosecutors with these data to augment other types of analytical products or methods being used, or to be used alone.

To complete a biographical sketch, an analyst culls the agency's files to determine what is known about the individual. Other sources may also be tapped, including criminal history data bases such as NCIC (National Crime Information Center); financial data bases, such as Dun and Bradstreet; or regional information systems such as FinCEN or the RISS projects. The information gathered is put into a succinct format and included in the analytical package.

At a minimum, a biographical sketch on an individual would include a name, any aliases, an address, identifying numbers (social security, arrest numbers, etc.), vehicle identification, names of associates, place of business, former or current criminal activity, and nature of involvement in the current investigation or crime group activity.

A biographical sketch on a business or entity would include its name; an address; the names of any officers, directors, or major stockholders; the nature of its business; and its relation to the current investigation or criminal activity being studied. An example of a biographical sketch is found in Chapter 5.

BRIEFINGS

Analytical briefings are the oral presentation of findings or products based on the data analyzed. They are most often given to law enforcement managers and prosecutors.

Briefings usually have three components. First, the analyst provides a fact pattern* of the case, that is, a summary of what occurred in the investigation or an overview of an assessment. Second, the analyst shows and interprets analytical charts,* tables,* or other graphics and gives summary statements including conclusions or hypotheses. Third, the analyst responds to questions from those persons being briefed. The analyst may also have to explain the analytical methodologies used to arrive at the products and hypotheses.

Preparing for a briefing includes refining the graphic products for presentation, preparing the fact pattern, envisioning what questions might arise, and preparing answers for those questions. In the course of thinking what questions might arise, the analyst may need to do further research or get more information from investigators to be able to answer those questions.

A briefing may be used as an intermediate step in the investigation, to pull together all available material in support of management decision making related to further investigation, potential changes in investigative technique, or potential expansion of investigative targets.

An extension of the briefing process is providing testimony before a grand jury or in a trial. Experienced analysts can not only present analytical products in court, but be used as expert witnesses.

CASE ANALYSIS

Case analysis is an overall treatment of investigative materials to provide a comprehensive look at the investigation and provide recommendations for its completion. It can be done on cases in progress or on cases which have been dormant and now require a fresh look. Case analysis is generally complex and self-directed and requires the abilities of an experienced analyst.

To complete a case analysis, all the materials relating to the investigation must be reviewed to determine what is needed to assist the investigation and what data are available to be analyzed. Information which raises questions not answered by the files should be given to the field investigator, as he or she may have information not included in reports.

Data are extracted from the files and organized either manually or in a computer. Certain types of data—for example, telephone records or financial records—can be analyzed by using the specific methodology required. Other information may be placed into a multipurpose computer data base* that includes relational information (names, manner in which linked) and chronological information (dates, times). This allows the computer to generate reports to support a time-based analytical product (event or commodity flow analysis*) as well as relation-based association analysis.* It is important to incorporate data from telephone or financial analyses* into this multipurpose format as this allows the integration of such data with surveillance reports, corporate documents, and other materials, thus providing a comprehensive report.

Once the appropriate analytical products are done, their meaning should be ascertained, and they should be compared to one another. The charts which more clearly depict the particulars of a case than others should be chosen for the final report. Some products, when compared, provide new data which should be reflected in the conclusions. A written report should be made to summarize all of the final products used and to include conclusions and recommendations.

A case analysis applies analytical techniques and methods to all the information available on a case. It breaks that information down into pieces to analyze it, then puts it back together (synthesis) to provide a new look at the information. The analyst, as someone outside the investigation, may see gaps or leads which investigators who are working close to the case may miss. This can result in a case's successful conclusion.

CHARTS

Charts are the graphic depiction of data which may include numerical data, name data, event data, or other synopsized information. They include association charts,* telephone record charts,* bar charts,* pie charts,* VIA charts,* and event and commodity flow charts.*

Charts are used within most types of analytical methodologies. They show an activity or relationship in a simple manner and augment the presentation of data. Key to chart making are certain guidelines relating to scale, symmetry, symbols, and clarity. The accuracy of scale, for example, is crucial to the objectivity of the chart. Symmetry in charting is not as mandatory for working charts, but should be present in those used for public purposes. Symbols should be consistent in their application within a particular chart. Clarity is also important, with a minimum of crossed lines or confusing placement of symbols necessary. A legend should be used in most charts to explain the use of symbols, lines, or other markings. There are examples of charts in Chapters 3, 4, 5, 6, 7, and 8.

CHRONOLOGICAL TABLE

A chronological table, also known as a timeline, depicts the events that have occurred or are planned to occur within their specific time frame. The events are generally listed down the left side of the table, with the times (dates) shown across the top of the chart. (This can be reversed if there are more times than events.) The time at which something is to occur can be denoted by an X or similar mark or, if the event is to occur over time, an arrow can be placed over the multiple times to reflect that fact.

A chronological table is not as simple to read as an event flow chart* since it is tabular, rather than graphic, but it is a way of depicting numerous events which would not fit well into a chart format without being accompanied by a lengthy descriptive treatment. The chronological table shows the temporal (time-based) relationship of the events which have occurred or will occur. It can be a planning aid for mapping out major projects or investigations.

COLLECTION PLAN

A collection plan is a preliminary step toward completing a strategic assessment* which shows what needs to be collected, how it is going to be collected, and by what date. It can include a survey instrument, a chronological table,* and possible hypotheses which you intend to prove or disprove. A collection plan is generally approved by analytical unit management or agency management.

When assessing a criminal group, there are standard questions which can be asked as part of a collection plan. These include the hierarchy of the group, its criminal activities, its legitimate and illegitimate business activities, its financial health, its connections to other groups, its political connections, the membership of the group, and the geographic territory of the group (Sommers, 1986). There are also standard questions to be asked if the assessment is being done on a criminal activity, rather than a group.

In addition to the standard questions, a collection plan should include group- or activity-specific questions. If a sports betting network is being assessed, for example, who the bankers or layoff people of the organization are needs to be determined.

If a narcotics organization is being investigated, the person or location that is the source of the narcotics should be sought. If there is a potential terrorist threat, one of the first questions to be asked is what political affiliation the group has and what specific calendar dates are important to that political affiliation. Group- or activity-specific questions can best be determined through interaction with investigators with expertise in this branch of criminal activity.

Just as important as knowing what to ask is knowing whom to ask. Identifying potential sources of information is crucial to a collection plan. Some of the data may be found in the agency's intelligence files or in the local library. Other data may have to come from a survey of a group of people or agencies, or from the files of other agencies. Other information may come from public record sources, including the census, labor statistics, or newspaper/magazine reports.

Once what is to be asked and where it can be found has been determined, decisions must be made about what to do with the data which have been collected. General data manipulation steps which can be detailed within the collection plan include review, compilation, analysis, and conclusion drawing.

The fourth component of the collection plan is the estimated date to complete the steps in the plan. This not only gives the analyst targets for completion, it gives management a sense that the project will be completed in a known time frame. Assessments often take two to six months (or longer) to complete. While ending dates can change during the progress of the assessment, changes should be done only with the understanding and approval of management. Interim reports can also be used to keep management aware and interested in the outcome of the assessment.

A collection plan is used more in strategic analysis than in tactical analysis and can also support project management and long-range planning.

COMMODITY FLOW ANALYSIS

Commodity flow analysis is the analysis of the flow of goods or currency among persons or businesses to determine the meaning of that activity. It may give insights into the nature of a conspiracy, a hierarchy of a group, or the workings of a distribution network.

Commodity flow information is extracted from the materials gathered in an investigation or assessment which may include surveillance reports, testimony, and confidential information. The information is placed into a data base or manual filing system; it includes the names of the persons or businesses between (or among) whom the commodity has traveled, the direction of the flow of goods or services, the type of goods or services flowing, and the dates or times of the flow (if known).

This information can be translated into a commodity flow chart* or can be described in writing. If a commodity flow chart is used, a written summary of the chart should also be done. Biographical sketches* on each of the persons or groups involved may also be drawn up. Using the data shown on the chart (or written description) and the biographical sketches, conclusions* about the activity or organization involved can be made. On the basis of the facts and conclusions, recommendations* for investigative action, further information collection needs, and/or prosecution can be made.

COMMODITY FLOW CHART

A commodity flow chart is a graphic depiction of the flow of goods or services among persons or entities. It can give an insight into distribution patterns, hierarchies, the nature and extent of a conspiracy, or the procedures of a criminal organization.

A commodity flow chart is made up of boxes (or other symbols) connected by lines with directional arrows on the lines. Inside the boxes are the names of the people, groups, or businesses among which the goods or services are flowing. Activity is generally shown outside the boxes of the chart, along the lines. That is where the "flow" is occurring, so the amount of dollars, amount of a drug, or other commodity is shown there. Dates are also shown, when possible, to record the time span of the activity.

Once a commodity flow chart is completed, the analyst studies it to determine what it means. Who ends up with the largest amount of the commodity in question? Are there places (or people) shown to which (whom) the commodity is siphoned? If a criminal hierarchy is involved, what does the flow of the commodity indicate to us about the relationships within that group?

Often, a commodity chart reflects a criminal organization. It can give insights into who are the apparent and more covert people who benefit from the criminal activity. It can cause us to hypothesize about the nature of the group and the extent of its activity. Obvious uses for commodity flow charts include applications to stolen property, bribery, drug flow, and money laundering. Examples of commodity charts are shown in Chapters 6 and 7.

COMMODITY FLOW MATRIX

A commodity flow matrix is made in a similar manner to a telephone record matrix.* It is square, and the data inserted into it reflect the goods or currency flowing among the people and/or businesses involved.

The names of those from whom the commodity flowed are arranged across the top of the matrix or down the left side. The names of those to whom the commodity flowed are arranged on the remainder of those two sides. The bottom and right side are left free for "from" and "to" totals.

This design of the matrix allows the analyst to keep track of the flow of the commodity from its origin to its destination. Using this compilation method, a commodity flow chart* can then be drawn.

COMPOSITE TABLE

A composite table is drawn from incident information or suspect information to determine the most common factors occurring within the incidents. It is made by identifying the various factors involved in an incident, or the various bits of data related to a suspect description. These pieces of data are placed in a tabular format to ascertain any commonalities or patterns. In a series of armed robberies, for example, the factors may include time of day, location, type of establishment robbed, number of perpetrators, use of weapons, language used, manner of dress of perpetrators, and type of financial instruments taken.

The information known about each of the armed robberies committed could then be placed into the table. The table would then be reviewed for possible patterns, commonalities, and differences. Conclusions about the persons responsible for the robberies might then be drawn.

Composite tables are used as part of several analytical methods including case analysis,* crime analysis,* indicator analysis,* and profiling.* An example of a composite table is given in Chapter 4.

CONCLUSION

A conclusion is the meaning or new material resulting from the analytical process. It can be in the form of a hypothesis,* a trend,* a forecast,* or a prediction.*

Conclusions are arrived at by reviewing the facts gathered and the analytical products derived from the facts. Conclusions can be reached deductively or inductively: that is, they can state only what has been gathered in the facts (deductive), or they can make a statement which goes beyond the facts (inductive). A trend, forecast, or prediction is an example of an inductive conclusion because it goes beyond what is already known.

CONTENT ANALYSIS

Content analysis is the classification of material into types of data and the analysis of those types of data to derive the meaning of the piece of communication. The information derived from the content analysis may give the analyst greater knowledge about the sender of the message, the receiver, and the message itself (Weber, 1990).

Content analysis can be used to determine the psychological state of a person or group, to detect the presence of propaganda; to reflect cultural patterns of the sender(s), and to identify the intentions of the communication. By breaking down the words used into groupings of general intent, the content analyst determines the overall meaning of the message. A word-frequency listing can be created to show the number of times particular words are used in a document.

Content analysis is generally done on written documents but can also be done on recorded documents. A related form of analysis, called conversation analysis,* is done on spoken communication.

Content analysis is done infrequently in a law enforcement setting. It is has been known to be effective in analyzing documents sent by terroristic groups or other criminals who communicate in writing.

CONVERSATION ANALYSIS

Conversation analysis is the review and compilation of data gleaned from a conversation to determine the meaning of the exchange. It is used on tapes that result from some form of electronic surveillance.

To do a conversation analysis, the legally obtained conversation is reviewed and summarized as to its participants and its overall conclusion or meaning. For the purpose of prosecution, these summarizations are then presented in such a way as to prove the guilt or complicity of those involved in criminal actions or conspiracies.

Key to such proof are the roles of the participants in the conversation. Those roles are examined to determine who was the instigator of talk about illegal activity. The responses given to talk of illegal activity are also analyzed to determine whether there was implied consent of the receiver, or if the person was only indicating a willingness to talk further. Certain key phrases are noted as "markers" in a conversation as opposed to agreement (Shuy, 1990).

Once the conversation, or group of conversations, is reviewed with these criteria in mind, the roles of the participants in the conversation can better be determined. The strength of those roles shown through the conversation analysis can result in a win or loss in court.

CORPORATE RECORD ANALYSIS

Corporate record analysis is the acquiring, review, and comparison of a company's records to determine potential business-related fraud or other illegal activity.

Corporate records are seen in varied documents—from bank records, to sales tax records, to company ledgers, to quarterly wage reports, to corporate filings. All of these have components which can be analyzed. These records are obtained from the corporation as part of the investigation, usually in response to a sub-poena.

Data from these records relating to names, or events, or financial activity can be extracted and placed into manual or computerized files. Bank records can be analyzed in a manner similar to bank account analysis to determine the use of the funds; summaries of payments by month, quarter, and year; unusual payments; and so forth. The bank records can be compared to information shown on income, sales, or wage tax statements to see whether the amounts shown for income, and so on, are consistent.

Amounts spent on particular items or services can be compared to those spent by similar companies to determine whether the activities of the company are within the industry standard or are potentially illegal.

To perform this analytical technique most accurately, it is helpful to have some understanding or knowledge of the industry or the general commercial environment being analyzed. This can be obtained through research, through contact with experts in that industrial or commercial environment, or through analysis of a number of similar businesses so that a model of activity is developed.

CRIME ANALYSIS

Traditional crime analysis includes both the breaking down of criminal incidents into their composite parts (factors) to determine patterns and similarities which may lead to the apprehension of the perpetrator(s), and the statistical analysis of crime to forecast future crime.

Information on a series of crimes which have been committed is used to complete a crime analysis. This information may include victim data; suspect data; dates, times, and locations of crimes; physical evidence; weapons used; and fruits of the crimes.

These data are entered into a manual or computerized data base which can generate composite tables* or frequency distributions* that allow identification of the patterns in the occurrences. As a result, conclusions* may be drawn about the identity of the suspect, when a similar crime will be committed again, who (or where) a likely victim is, or how a crime was committed. The information can be geographically mapped to provide locational indicators.

To do statistical analysis, crime analysts review data on the incidence of crime—numbers of particular crimes, crimes per gradients of population, seasonal crime fluctuations—and arrive at summaries, conclusions, and predictions regarding those crimes.

The overall field of crime analysis includes the use of time series analysis,* statistical analysis,* forecasting,* composite building, criminal investigative analysis (profiling),* indicator development,* and frequency distribution analysis.* Crime analysis is discussed in more detail in Chapter 8.

CRIME BULLETIN

A crime bulletin is a short report developed by analysts and disseminated to patrol officers, investigators, and/or the public to make them aware of a criminal pattern that is occurring.

It can include a composite drawing or photograph of a suspect, a physical description of a suspect, the modus operandi of a suspect (including preferred victims), the known geographic range of the suspect, and a warning relating to the subject's potential for violence. Another term used for a crime bulletin is "BOLO" (Be On the Look Out).

Crime bulletins can be used to alert people to a series of crimes or to give them information on how to prevent crime from occurring. A sample of a crime bulletin is given in Chapter 4.

CRIMINAL INVESTIGATIVE ANALYSIS

Criminal investigative analysis is the use of components of a crime and/or the physical and psychological attributes of a criminal to ascertain the identity of the criminal. This technique has been refined by the FBI in the area of homicides and sexually motivated crime. Some analysts refer to it as profiling.* In actuality, a profile of a criminal is a product developed as a result of the criminal investigative analysis process.

To complete a criminal investigative analysis, the analyst or investigator must have all known information on the crime available—crime scene data, witness testimony, and so on—to create a picture of the crime and thus of the criminal.

The products used within criminal investigative analysis can include data bases,* composite tables,* geographic maps,* and association charts.* Certain records of the suspect or victim can be obtained and analyzed such as telephone records or travel records. Criminal investigative analysis is detailed more thoroughly in Chapter 4.

DATA BASES

A data base is a format for structuring information which is to be analyzed. Data bases are the most frequently used analytical working product as they allow the analyst to compile the information to be analyzed into a format which supports that analysis.

Data bases may be manual or computerized, depending upon the number of records to be analyzed. A data base can be a simple table* or a several-thousand-record computerized file. The types of data bases used can be standard or can be tailored to the particular analysis. A data base is an intermediate analytical product from which other analytical products may be made.

The creation of a data base requires the analyst to consider the factors present to be analyzed. If one were analyzing checking account records, for example, some of those factors would be the type of transaction (deposit, withdrawal, check), the date of the transaction, the amount of the transaction, the person the check was payable to, who signed the check, who endorsed the check on back, the presence of a notation on the "memo" line, any secondary endorser, the location of the bank where the check was cashed or deposited, and the number of the account in which it was deposited (if any). If one were analyzing associations, some of the fields in the data base would be name of first individual or business, name of second individual or business (that first individual/business is associated with), date of association, type of association (business, personal, criminal), specifics of association, document reference number, and other comments.

Computerized data bases are created by using data base software (such as Dbase IV, FoxPro, Paradox, or Q & A), or by programming specific data base commands and parameters into a computer. The key to a successful data base is being able to retrieve data in any grouping or format needed to perform the analysis and produce summary reports which become part of the analytical product. Examples of data bases are seen in Chapter 5 and Chapter 8.

DEMOGRAPHIC ANALYSIS

Demographic analysis is a basic social science tool which has been adapted for use in a law enforcement setting. It analyzes the demographic characteristics of a particular community (place or group) and can include such factors as age, race, gender, level of education, ethnic origin, and income.

Demographics play an important role in law enforcement analysis, particularly in relation to forecasting of crime rates and criminal markets. Crime incident reports, for example, might show us that the majority of violent crime is committed by males between the ages of eighteen and twenty-five. Thus, any fluctuation in the composition of the populace of an area which increases or decreases the number of males between eighteen and twenty-five could have a significant impact on the violent crime rate.

A high incidence of a particular population can indicate the potential market for a particular criminal product and, therefore, for a particular criminal group. In ethnic communities where the population's culture embraces gambling, for example, illegal casinos or other forms of gambling may be found.

Demographic analysis is used most often in strategic assessments and law enforcement planning. It is critical to analysis of community settings done in support of community policing or problem oriented policing.

DESCRIPTIVE ANALYSIS

Descriptive analysis is the written summarization of an event, activity, group, or person which imparts data of an evaluative nature and from which conclusions and recommendations may be drawn.

Many analyses are not easily depicted in chart form, but information can be gathered, compiled, and presented in written, or descriptive form. The technique used in descriptive analysis is an extension of basic research and inference development skills. All materials available are read and factual information is extracted. The materials are organized in a logical manner and summarized. Certain portions may be highlighted for end-user interest. Conclusions* are based on the materials collected.

Descriptive analysis is found in analytical reports of all kinds, particularly in those which deal with organized criminal groups. The changes in the group (leadership, territory, membership, criminal activities, business interests, etc.) are reported through descriptive analysis.

EVENT FLOW ANALYSIS

Event flow analysis is the compilation and analysis of data relating to events as they have occurred over time to allow the analyst to draw conclusions and/ or make recommendations based on the analysis. They are used most frequently in relation to specific criminal violations, where the events leading up to (and away from) the violation are important to be noted.

Event flow analysis is a chronology of what occurred within the framework of the criminal activity. That is, only the events which impacted on, or were part of, the criminal activity should be noted. Otherwise, the events included become so numerous that the facts of the criminal violation are obscured.

To complete an event flow analysis, one must review all case documents for events which occurred. These events are placed in a manual or computerized data base which allows for their retrieval by date and, if necessary, also by time of day. Once put in proper order, the events are reviewed to determine their value for inclusion in the chronology.

An event flow chart* which graphically depicts those occurrences in an easy-to-read format can then be drawn. Another way to depict events is through a chronological table,* that is, a table which shows the date or time of the event in one column and a short description of the event in another. Using either of these products, a summary of what occurred is then written and conclusions are based on the totality of occurrences.

Event flow analysis can result in the creation of a modus operandi if the events which occurred in a series of crimes are compared for similar attributes.

EVENT FLOW CHART

An event flow chart is the visual depiction of a series of occurrences. It is used as part of an event flow analysis.

An event flow chart uses boxes or rectangles (or other symbols used consistently in a given chart) which are connected by lines with arrowheads denoting the direction of the flow. A summation of the event occurring is put in the box along with a date (or time) as available. The flow of the chart is usually left to right, top to bottom.

Event flow charts are most often used in cases that involve specific criminal violations. The events leading up to the violation can then be depicted in an easy to understand manner. The chart can be used to explain the occurrences to management, to a prosecutor, or to a jury.

Once an event flow chart has been created, the analyst must study it to determine what it says about the activities in question and what conclusions can be drawn from it. These become the basis of the conclusions of the event flow analysis.* Examples of event flow charts are seen in Chapters 4 and 8.

FACT PATTERN

A fact pattern is a descriptive paragraph which summarizes the facts which have occurred. It is commonly used by prosecutors as part of a legal analysis but may also be used in case analysis and other individual analytical methods. It differs from a descriptive analysis in that the latter is a process, while a fact pattern is a product.

The fact pattern includes salient information on occurrences which are significant to the investigation or prosecution. It is an analytical product which can be used in virtually all types of analysis. It supports other types of analytical products including briefings* and written reports.*

FINANCIAL SUMMARY

A financial summary is an analytical product which depicts the activity in a financial account such as a bank account or a corporate account. It summarizes financial activity during a given period, usually monthly, quarterly, or yearly. Financial summaries can be expressed in a table format, in a bank statement format, or in an accounting format.

The most common information found in a bank account financial summary, for example, would be the number, date span, and total of deposits; the number, date span, and total of checks; the number, date span, and total of cash withdrawals; the number, date span, and total of other debits or credits to the account; and the opening and closing balances. An example of a financial summary of a bank account is seen in Chapter 7.

FORECAST

A forecast is the end product of the forecasting process. It is a prediction, a conclusion about what will happen in the future. When disseminating a forecast, it is important to indicate the basis used for the forecast. Some analysts show several predictions based on different bases and then choose one and provide the reasoning behind the choice.

FORECASTING

Forecasting is a process which predicts the future on the basis of past trends, current trends, and/or future speculation. Within the field of analysis, both numeric and descriptive forecasting are done. Numeric forecasting is statistically based and generally rests on past and current numbers of occurrences.

Descriptive forecasting takes both quantitative and descriptive trend data to predict the future. The projected strength of an organized crime group in five or ten years could be based on numerical indicators (changes in the number of members, in the businesses owned, and in other assets) as well as on less quantifiable data such as the ascendancy of an ambitious leader or the popularity of a new criminal product the group offers.

Forecasting is used in both crime analysis* and strategic analysis.*

FREQUENCY DISTRIBUTION

A frequency distribution is a data analysis product which is used in a number of analytical methods. It counts the number of times something occurs and in some cases helps to identify behavior patterns in a criminal activity or enterprise.

Within a telephone record analysis,* for example, the numbers of calls made during particular hours, or dates, or to particular persons, or to states, are counted. From them listings are made of the primary persons contacted, the common calling hours, the dates of heaviest calls, or the commonly contacted states. Frequency distributions are often a significant part of statistical analysis,* crime analysis,* and content analysis.*

A frequency distribution is a preliminary step in making a bar chart.* Frequency distribution tables are also used to display frequency data. A frequency distribution is shown in Chapter 5.

GEOGRAPHIC DISTRIBUTION ANALYSIS

Geographic distribution analysis looks at the occurrence of something over a particular geographic area to determine what can be concluded about the activity or group as a result. This distribution is usually represented on a map, but its results can also be expressed in a descriptive manner.

In one instance, it could look at the locations of businesses or residences of members of a criminal syndicate to show the geographic range of the group. In another, it could show the locations of narcotic-growing areas or processing labs to determine the most likely smuggling routes for the drugs. With a different set of facts, it could show the locations of burglaries within a neighborhood, beat, or district.

To complete a geographic distribution analysis, data on the locations of criminal activities or crime groups should be collected. A map which covers the jurisdiction in question can then be computer-generated or drawn and the locations accurately indicated on it.

Next, the map is reviewed to create a summary of what it depicts and from which to draw conclusions about what it might mean. Examples of geographic distribution maps can be seen in Chapters 3, 6, and 8.

GEOGRAPHIC FLOW CHART (MAP)

A geographic flow chart (map) shows the flow of particular illegal activities or services from one location to another. In meaning, a geographic flow chart is no different from a commodity flow chart based on the same material. A map is usually more eye-catching, however, than a commodity flow chart because people relate to maps, which illustrate the distance and location of the flow of goods and services.

To complete a geographic flow chart, the analyst must gather all available data and extract any information related to geographic locations of activities and movement of goods or services over time and location. This information is placed on a computer-generated or hand-drawn map with appropriate notations as to what goods or services is moving from place to place.

When the information is all in place, a summary of the activity can be made and conclusions can be drawn about the activity.

INDICATOR ANALYSIS

Indicator analysis involves the compilation, review, and analysis of the activities which occur around a particular activity to develop a model of what occurrences may be used to predict the presence of that activity in other locations. Criminal investigative analysis, or profiling, can be viewed as a part of indicator analysis, as it comprises determining a criminal's potential behavior based on past behavior or incidents.

Indicator analysis has been used, for example, to develop models of the presence of organized crime, the infiltration of business by organized crime, and the presence of white collar crime. For example, some indicators of business infiltration by organized crime could be that the business has no-show employees on the payroll, is primarily a cash business, and has its profits being ''skimmed'' (taken out of business accounts for other use without being declared for tax purposes). Large international corporations and banks often use this type of analysis in evaluating countries for possible business locations, assessing the likelihood of terrorism or other negative acts against its property or employees.

Indicator analysis is generally a strategic analytic product which can then be used to support tactical investigative work. However, it does have strong ties to crime analysis in that it uses the bases of crime analysis (factors and frequency distributions) to measure the strength of the indicators.

Examples of indicator analysis can be seen in Chapters 4, 5, 6, 7, and 8.

INFERENCE DEVELOPMENT

Inference development is the drawing of conclusions based on facts. Within law enforcement, these facts are generally the data collected in the course of an investigation or analytical study.

Inferences can be in different forms. Conclusions, hypotheses, predictions, and forecasts are all inferences. Some inferences are deductive (reflect only what is already known), and some are inductive (arise out of what is known to speculate on what may be). It is in the latter category of inferences that new material may be derived from the reconfiguration of facts gathered.

All analytical products should include inferences. These conclusions are based on the facts as they occur in the investigative data and on the reworking of those facts (analysis) through analytical charts, tables, or other products.

An inference contained in a threat assessment is shown in Chapter 3.

MAPS

Maps are used as a geographic flow chart* or as part of a geographic distribution analysis.* They are a simple graphic depiction of a specific region used to show some activity or occurrence related to criminal activity.

The decision to include a map as an analytical product is usually based on an incidence of locational information present in the material to be analyzed. Information gleaned from a map can relate to territories covered by a crime group or to sources and routes of goods or services being transported by crime groups. Examples of maps are seen in Chapters 3, 6, and 8.

MARKET ANALYSIS

A market analysis is the review of information to determine the likelihood of the existence of a market for an illegal good or service. It is a form of strategic analysis,* proactive in nature, and gives a different perspective from which to look at a particular criminal activity.

A market analysis could look, for example, at the demographic aspects of a community or jurisdiction such as the age range and the ethnicity of the population. The types of illegal activities now supported are also a key factor. The presence of known or suspected criminal groups needs to be determined, along with the illegal goods or services these groups currently provide.

By looking at the data, the analyst might predict the interest that the populace will have in a particular illegal activity and thus the success that the criminal group providing it will have. This is done in cases where there are new emerging illicit goods (such as narcotic derivatives like "ice"—crystallized methamphetamine—or "crack" cocaine) or an emerging group which specializes in a particular good or service. By being aware of the level of interest in the community in the good or service, law enforcement can prepare itself to deal with this activity or group.

MATRICES

Matrices are used in analysis to organize data in such a manner that it can be compared to similar data. A matrix can be in either triangular or square form. The triangular matrix is most commonly used as an association analysis matrix.*

The arrangement of columns and rows in a triangular matrix is similar to a mileage grid on a map. You read a map matrix by going down one column which is marked "Philadelphia" and across a row which is marked "New York" and in the intersecting box (or "cell") of that row and column you read "90," which is the number of miles between the two cities. Mileage matrices are in a triangular shape so that each name only has to be inserted once, as that covers both a column and a row.

Another form of matrix is a square, which can show connections between, for example, people on the left side of the square and businesses on the top side, but cannot show relationships among those along one side; thus it is limiting. A square matrix form can be used to depict telephone connections between individuals, with the persons calling shown on one side of the matrix and the persons being called on the other side. This allows for both incoming and outgoing calls to be noted in the case of a multiple-subscriber analysis or when there are collect or third party calls in the telephone record analysis.

The square matrix can also be used in a commodity flow analysis where payments both to and from individuals or corporations need to be organized prior to their depiction in chart form. The matrix also allows the analyst to easily determine the net position of each person or entity—that is, the total of the funds flowing in minus the total of the funds flowing out. Examples of matrices are seen in Chapters 3 and 5.

NET WORTH ANALYSIS

Net worth analysis is the review of a person's financial records to determine whether that person has been living within the confines of a legally reported income.

Net worth analysis requires the ability to access significant amounts of financial data on an individual. The technique was developed by the U.S. Internal Revenue Service as the primary organization with access to tax data. Information complied in net worth analysis can also be helpful in determining assets for possible forfeiture in RICO cases. If it can be proven that these assets have been bought with ill-gotten gains, that property may be forfeited to the government.

The general formula governing net worth analysis is that assets minus liabilities (what one has minus what one owes) equals net worth. Increases in net worth over a period of years either can be traced to legal, taxed income or cannot. In the latter case, this may indicate that the individual has been involved in illegal activity.

The standard form used in net worth analysis lists assets (houses, cars, jewelry, cash on hand, etc.) and liabilities (mortgages, car loans, etc.). Also shown are reported (taxed) income and living expenses. The former can be verified through employers or other income sources. The latter can be estimated on the basis of an analysis of the individual's bank accounts (see Bank Record Analysis*).

Living expenses are subtracted from the reported income and the change in net worth from one year to another is factored in, resulting in a final figure which may indicate illegal income. If this figure is relatively small (under $50,000), the illegal income aspect may not be pursued further as there is a substantial margin of error in these calculations and the amount in question would not generate a significant return in taxes. If it is over $100,000, there is a good possibility that it indicates substantial illegal income and that the case should be pursued.

Another technique similar to net worth analysis is called the source and application of funds.*

PIE CHART

A pie chart is a graphic depiction of the parts of a whole: the pie equals the whole of something and the slices equal smaller parts.

Pie charts are often used to depict percentages adding up to 100 percent, or monetary amounts adding up to a dollar. They are used in statistical analysis. They can be applied to law enforcement to show the occurrences of particular crimes in relation to the overall crime rate or the relative amounts/percentages of income from illegal sources.

An example of a pie chart is seen in Chapter 3.

PREMONITORY

A premonitory is a short-range strategic analysis product which assesses the viability of successful investigation and prosecution of a target or set of targets.

To do a premonitory, one has a target of a person, group of persons, or entity or group of entities. There may be some indication of illegal activities going on among the targets, or such activity may be suspected because of the group affiliation or other known activities in which the targets are involved.

Data to be reflected in a premonitory can include surveillance information, background record checks on the targets, information on similar groups or activities, and informant data. The four areas key to completing the premonitory would be what illegal activities the targets may be involved in, what the strengths and weaknesses of the group are, what recommendations for investigative techniques can be stated, and what the probability of success in the case is.

Premonitories are generally written products but may also be presented in the form of an intelligence briefing. Association and/or event flow charts* are some of the products that can be the premonitory. Biographical sketches* of all major targets are also generated.

The key difference between a premonitory and other strategic analyses is that the premonitory is intended as a short-range assessment of an identifiable criminal concern which is being considered for further investigative action. General strategic assessments are more long-range in nature.

Premonitories are usually internal, highly confidential documents which include corroborated as well as uncorroborated information.

PROBABILITY FACTOR

The probability factor is the degree of likelihood that a particular inference or hypothesis is correct. Probability factors are generally shown in percentages. The hypothesis or inference (or forecast) can be either negative or positive (expressing that something will or will not occur, for example).

Probability factors of over 80 percent indicate that something is most likely to occur; from 60 to 80 percent it is somewhat likely to occur; from 40 to 60 percent there is a relatively even chance it may occur; from 20 to 40 percent it is somewhat unlikely to occur; and below 20 percent it is very unlikely to occur.

Probabilities are important to the conclusion drawing and predictive aspects of analysis. In some instances, an analyst might present two or three predictive alternatives, giving a probability for each. This allows management to know and choose the most viable alternative.

PROFILE

A criminal profile is the product of a criminal investigative analysis in which indicators of behavior or activity are used to create models.

Most notable examples of profiles have been done in narcotics and serial crime investigations. A profile is created by gathering all possible information on a type of behavior or occurrence and then analyzing and comparing that behavior to cases or incidents at hand. On the basis of such analysis, for example, one might find that the typical cocaine courier using public airlines is a female, aged eighteen to thirty-five, traveling alone, returning from a cocaine source country after staying only a few days, who has hidden the cocaine in her luggage and has brought in from five to ten kilos. That information, when passed on to the appropriate customs authorities, might result in significant seizures.

Within violent crime investigation, models of criminal behavior are developed against which suspects can be measured. This type of profiling incorporates psychological and sociological data on criminals. Some indicators used to build profiles are shown in Chapter 4.

RECOMMENDATIONS

The analytic process can be used not only to make the meaning of gathered data clear, but to make recommendations on the basis of that uncovered meaning. The types of recommendations made by analysts fall into two categories: investigative and deterrence.

When analysis is used in a tactical mode during an investigation, one of its functions is to discover what data are missing that could be necessary to the solution of the case. The analyst, as an information manager, has the overview perspective necessary to identify missing pieces such as further records to be subpoenaed, additional interviews or reinterviews to be conducted, and records checks needed. Bringing these to the attention of the investigator or prosecutor is one way in which the analyst furthers the case.

Other recommendations are aimed toward deterrence and may arise from a crime analysis, rather than an investigative analysis. After a series of armed bank robberies, for example, the analyst might identify the possible location, time, and day of the next robbery. From that, a recommendation would be made for increased police presence in that area during the time in question.

Some types of warnings can also be considered deterrence recommendations. A crime bulletin* informing senior citizens of a fraudulent driveway paving scheme in the area may prevent them from being defrauded, thus deterring crime.

REPORT

A report is a final product of an analysis in which all the data gathered are synthesized into an appropriate format. A report can range from a few pages to a few hundred, depending on the type of report and the requirements of management. The longer reports are generally strategic in nature and require months to complete. The format for a report may be prescribed by the department or it may evolve as a result of the material being analyzed.

A report is a key product within an analysis. Charts,* tables,* graphs,* and maps* provide pictorial representations of information, but summaries of those products, along with conclusions and recommendations, finish the analytic process.

SOURCE AND APPLICATION OF FUNDS

Source and application of funds is a financial analysis technique which looks at what a suspect has legally earned or received and what the suspect has spent a specific period to determine whether illegal funds were available to him. It is similar to net worth analysis,* with the difference that net worth analysis looks at changes in balances of loans or the amount of assets (and liabilities) a person has, rather than at what the person has spent. In spite of the differences in format or formula, the net result—the amount of potentially illegal income—remains the same.

An example of the source and application of funds format is seen in Chapter 5.

STATISTICAL ANALYSIS

Statistical analysis is the review of numerical data to summarize it and to draw conclusions about its meaning. It incorporates a number of different techniques including frequency distribution.*

Statistical analysis is commonly used in crime analysis* and police planning. Crime rates, forecasts, and probabilities are all forms of statistical analysis.

Crime rates, for example, indicate the occurrence of crime as compared to population. If a town of 10,000 had 3 homicides, then there would be 0.3 homicide per 1,000 residents. (The crime rate is determined by dividing the number of homicides by 10,000 and then multiplying the result by 1,000.) During the same period, a city of 50,000 having 65 homicides would have a crime rate of 1.3 homicides per 1,000. Using further statistical methods to compare the two rates, the city would have a rate 433 percent higher than that of the town.

As is true of all analytical techniques, it is important not just to show statistical data in a table, bar chart, or pie chart, but also to summarize it and interpret it.

STRATEGIC ANALYSIS

Strategic analysis includes several different types of analysis, including threat assessments,* vulnerability assessments,* warnings,* market analyses,* general assessments,* and premonitories.* The key to all forms of strategic analysis is that they are generally predictive and medium- to long-term in nature, and that they form some assessment of a situation along with recommendations on how to handle it.

Strategic analysis is done by looking at what has occurred and what is occurring and then predicting what may occur. This requires the assimilation of data from a variety of sources, among them police records, public records, demographic data, economic data, and other documents. Many of the techniques used in strategic analysis are borrowed from military, international, or business intelligence formats. A collection plan* is used to initiate a strategic analysis and an assessment* is usually the end product of a strategic analysis.

Strategic analysis is a lengthy process which may take weeks to months to complete (the generally accepted average length is six months). It can, and should, be used to form the basis for law enforcement policy-making and strategy development.

SUMMARY

A summary is a written representation of the information and the products resulting from an analysis. While analytical products are meant to be as simple as possible, they are often not self-explanatory and should be accompanied by a summary.

A summary also helps the analyst to generate a concise synopsis of the analysis which can then form the basis for the conclusions or inferences* that are drawn.

Summaries are also an integral part of the research process as they are needed to place often voluminous data into a readable form.

SURVEY

A survey is a set of questions designed to elicit information in support of a strategic analysis or a less-encompassing analytic study.

Survey design should follow traditional research methods: the number of questions should not be lengthy, there should be more yes/no or "closed" questions than open-ended questions, and the open-ended questions should be asked toward the end of the survey. Questions should be worded as simply as possible, leaving little room for misinterpretation. Broadly worded, open-ended questions can garner responses that are almost impossible to compare to others.

Prior to releasing a survey, thought should be given to what form the answers might take and how they will be tabulated and analyzed. Surveys are analytical tools and should be constructed with care. Where possible, responses should be estimated in terms of their ability to be computerized for ease in data manipulation.

Surveys are used to gather information from other law enforcement agencies or from the public (fear-reduction surveys, community/problem-solving surveys). To increase the number of responses to surveys, they can be administered in person (with an advance copy sent for preparation purposes) or over the telephone. The analysis of survey data often includes a series of frequency distributions and percentages of responses. Examples of surveys are found in Chapters 3 and 8.

TABLE

A table is a format in which to depict data that allows us to find the information quickly. The data included are often being compared in one or more areas to other data found in other columns of the table.

Once it has been determined that a type of data should be tabulated, then the variables (other data) which are to be shown with it need to be determined. Then, the sizes of the format and columns can be determined and the material inserted.

After the materials have been tabulated, they should be reviewed to determine their meaning or relationship. Examples of tables can be found in Chapters 3, 4, and 5.

TELEPHONE RECORD ANALYSIS

Telephone record analysis is the review of data garnered from telephone bills or nonaudio wire intercepts (e.g., dialed numbered recorders or pen registers) to provide information on potential conspirators and on the patterns of traffic on a given telephone line or set of lines.

Long-distance telephone bills are legally obtained from telephone or long-distance service providers. (Cellular phone service companies can also provide data which include all calls made, both local and long-distance.) Or, pen register/dialed number recorder (DNR) machines provide information on all calls made from a particular line. That information is placed in a manual or computerized data base* (many pen registers are now computerized to eliminate the data entry step).

The computer organizes the data as directed by the analyst (places the calls in order of date, time, number called, etc.). Various "runs" of the computer generate printouts of the data organized in the different ways. One print out showing calls by number called gives a listing of all other phone numbers contacted, along with the dates and times of those contacts as well as the number of calls made to each number.

Other listings provide information on date spans of calls, hours the phone is in use, patterns of calls, and unusual calls. Much of the information is listed in tables that show frequency distributions.

This information is incorporated in a written report which can provide additional leads to the investigator. The calls may uncover previously unknown coconspirators. In some cases (such as in a gambling investigation), the calls and their timing can help prove a criminal violation.

The analysis of calls from several phones (multiple subscriber analysis) is used in many conspiracy or criminal enterprise investigations. In these, calls from the various parties are compared to determine similarities among them—particularly calls which bring two or more of the conspirators into contact with another party who may be a previously unknown member of the enterprise.

The completed telephone record analysis should include a written report with conclusions and recommendations as well as a telephone record chart.* The most common use of telephone record analysis is to show probable cause for installing an electronic wire intercept on the telephone line.

An example of a frequency distribution table in a pen register record analysis is shown in Chapter 5.

TELEPHONE RECORD CHART

A telephone record chart is a visual depiction of the activity between or among certain telephone numbers which were included in a telephone record analysis.*

Symbols for the telephone chart are also similar to those of the association chart—circles for people, boxes for businesses or entities. Two major differences appear. First, there are arrows where the line meets the circle or square to show the direction of the call. Second, along the line drawn is a smaller circle in which the number of calls is shown. Sometimes, the direction of the call is also shown in these smaller circles—"C" usually means collect calls have been made, while "T" indicates the presence of third-party (generally credit card) calls.

Charts are most often drawn in multiple-subscriber analysis, where the records of several subscribers are obtained and compared. This comparison often yields numbers which were contacted by two or more of the subscriber/suspects and those numbers may help to uncover previously unknown members of the conspiracy.

The completed chart should be analyzed to determine its meaning, and the conclusions drawn should form the basis of the written report of the telephone record analysis. An example of a multiple subscriber telephone record chart is seen in Chapter 5.

TELEPHONE RECORD MATRIX

In telephone record analysis charts are often based on a telephone matrix, which is similar to the square association matrix* format. This can be completed with "calls from" numbers on one side of the chart and "calls to" numbers on another side. Reading and counting the numbers of calls made proceed in a manner similar to that used for the association matrix; the telephone chart is organized on the same basis.

THREAT ASSESSMENT

A threat assessment is a strategic document which looks at a group's propensity for violence or criminality, or the possible occurrence of a criminal activity in a certain time or place. It is generated out of the military/international intelligence community concept of "warning intelligence."

A strategic warning is a judgment issued early enough to permit decision makers to undertake countermeasures (Grabo, 1987). This judgment is based on certain indicators. Within a military setting, indicators include military action, political factors, and economic and social data. Within a law enforcement setting, they include criminal activity, economic and social data, and organizational strength. Political factors can intrude when the crime threatened has a political basis or connection such as terrorism or racism.

To construct a threat assessment, data on the possibility of the threat (the chance it will actually occur) are gathered. Then, an assessment is made of the potential degree of threat present in those predicted to do the criminal act(s). The projected time frame of the threat and the possible target(s) of the threat are also examined. At the target end, the threat assessment merges into a vulnerability assessment.*

Conclusions about the probability that the threat will materialize into action must be made, along with recommendations for countermeasures or (if prior action is impossible) response to the threatening action once it occurs. These recommendations presume some knowledge of the analyst of what actions are available to the agency and the feasibility of those actions. As this may not always be the case, the analytical data can be presented to a group of investigators or managers for consideration (brainstorming) of possible countermeasures or responses; the alternatives developed by that group can then be presented as part of the threat assessment.

TIME SERIES ANALYSIS

A time series analysis is a crime analysis* technique used to show the occurrence of similar criminal activities over time. Time is one of the critical factors used in crime analysis; it refers not only to time of day, but to day of the week and day of the month. A series of twelve muggings, for example, could occur in eight locations to victims in a range of ages. The only similarity to be found among them could be that eight of them took place between midnight and 2:00 A.M. The eight which were in a similar time frame would then be considered as potentially having the same perpetrator, and an attempt to gather other evidence to reinforce this hypothesis would be made. Time series analysis is often done in conjunction with geographic distribution analysis.*

TREND ANALYSIS

Trend analysis is the use of numeric or descriptive data to arrive at conclusions* about what occurred from the past to the present. It can also be used to support the construction of a forecast.*

A trend could be seen in the occurrence of vehicle thefts in the town of

Marysville. During 1990, there were 132 thefts of motor vehicles, followed by 148 thefts in 1991, 156 thefts in 1992, and 160 thefts in 1993. Using these figures, a trend could be extrapolated using traditional statistical methodologies.

TREND

A trend is the direction or tendency in which something is moving. It is the product of a trend analysis* and can form the basis of a forecast.* Both numeric and descriptive trends can be seen in law enforcement.

VISUAL INVESTIGATIVE ANALYSIS

Visual investigative analysis (VIA) is the analysis of the steps taken, or necessary to be taken, in the course of an investigation or in the course of a criminal act.

Its purpose is to determine what remains to be done before the conclusion of an activity. Used in an investigation, it is a method of visually managing a complex case or task force investigation. Used to view occurrences relating to a crime, it may help to reconstruct what occurred.

Using VIA, case managers can track the deployment of personnel and equipment, can see the status of leads, and can see what needs to be accomplished next in the case. After a certain point in an investigation, a retrospective VIA can be done to determine what may have been overlooked in the case.

VIA CHART

A VIA chart is the graphic depiction of the specific steps taken or needed to be taken within a criminal occurrence or criminal investigation.

VIA charts use a standardized charting format where symbols appear along a line and depict the actions taken. The symbols are numbered and dated and appear in chronological order. Radiating from symbols are lines on which the nature of the action and its results are recorded.

Because of its representation of every action taken in an investigation, VIA is a space-consuming product. It is generally done on paper spread out on the walls of an office to make room for all the data.

Some VIA charts have several lines of action when events occur simultaneously. By viewing a VIA chart, one may see what has been done and what still needs to be done in an investigation. An example of a VIA chart is given in Chapter 6.

VULNERABILITY ASSESSMENT

A vulnerability assessment is a type of strategic analytical product which can fall into the premonitory type of product or can be viewed as its own distinct form.

Vulnerability can be either immediate and practical or more conceptual in nature. A museum which has an exhibition of priceless jewelry will be interested in an assessment of the possibility of the jewelry's being stolen or damaged while in its care (its vulnerability to harm). A premonitory (short-range) assessment of that vulnerability can be prepared. On the basis of it, the museum and police can take action to lessen that vulnerability.

On the other hand, the emergence of a new synthetic drug which had similar psychoactive properties to cocaine could cause a police chief to request a vulnerability assessment on his community's potential use of such a drug. As the result of such a report, the chief could issue intelligence warnings to patrol officers, the laboratories which analyze narcotic samples, hospitals, and so on.

Vulnerability assessments are done with whatever data can be accumulated. This information may range from informant data to data from other departments to scientific data to public record data on the community.

The following are the keys to vulnerability assessments: What is the potential threat? In what ways is the community or event or situation vulnerable? What can be done to lessen that vulnerability?

A vulnerability assessment can include other analytical charts and products and is generally completed in a written format. Its results can also be communicated in an intelligence briefing.* An example of a vulnerability assessment is seen in Chapter 5.

WARNING

A warning is the product of a threat or vulnerability assessment* and provides specific facts about a potential future occurrence which may threaten the individual or group warned. It can contain a forecast* or prediction about future activity. Warnings can be used in both crime analysis* and strategic analysis. The form a warning would take in crime analysis would be a crime bulletin* or crime alert. In a strategic setting, a warning would be the conclusions drawn at the end of an assessment of threat or vulnerability.

CHAPTER III

Report Applications

Both published and internal reports are the mainstay of analytical work. No analysis is complete without a written summary of its findings, conclusions, and recommendations. Conversely, few reports are sufficiently informative or complete without the application of analytical methods. Good reports reflect strong analytical skills; they are well researched, well documented, well written, well organized, and well presented.

Reports range from internal documents—intelligence reports, premonitories, long-term assessments—to documents which are disseminated within the law enforcement community only, to those which become standard references for the media, researchers, and other law enforcement agencies. Report formats published by specialists including Frost (1990, Frost and Morris, 1983) have emphasized the exacting requirements of internal reporting by intelligence officers, rather than the broader use of reports as vehicles of intelligence dissemination or public awareness.

Early writing on law enforcement analysis considered objectivity. As Godfrey and Harris state:

The intelligence report must be objective in order that the decision maker, the one who determines which future courses of action will be followed, will know exactly what existing information and analysis can tell him. The report should be written in such a way that there is a clear delineation between positive information or facts, those pieces which have gone into developing a hypothesis, and the conclusions which are drawn from both facts and the hypotheses. (1971, p. 28)

Reports developed by crime analysts include crime bulletins, alerts, and memoranda to the patrol divisions about crime patterns and trends. Investigative analysts' reports include the analytical products they have completed along with a summary of the products, their conclusions, and their recommendations. Strategic analysts' reports reflect the depth of information available on the subject matter and a discussion of that material, as well as products, conclusions, and recommendations.

Frost gives examples of reports as intelligence dissemination vehicles, including periodic reports, "spot items," and "gist and comment" items. Periodic reports include the weekly, monthly, quarterly, or annual intelligence summaries produced by various agencies and referred to later in this chapter. Spot items and gist and comment items are short pieces traditionally found in intelligence bulletins. A spot item gives brief information about an emerging trend or activity. A gist and comment item takes the emerging trend or activity, appends other data on that trend (previous article information, historical data, etc.), and fleshes it out to give an encapsulated analysis of the occurrence (Frost and Morris, 1983). The everyday analytic report is not the focus of this chapter; rather, the more in-depth public and internal reports are.

Agencies which developed specialties in analysis, including the California Department of Justice, the Royal Canadian Mounted Police, the Pennsylvania Crime Commission, and the New Jersey State Commission of Investigation, have provided dozens of examples of analytic reports. These have ranged from limited dissemination reports to public annual reports. They have included information from organized crime family hierarchies to the way the agency's budget was spent in the past year. Their value to criminal justice practitioners and to the public has been great.

This chapter discusses how reports are prepared and some of the analytical techniques involved in producing these reports. It gives examples of publicly disseminated reports and publicly disseminated information on internal reports. It shows how analytic reports support planning and decision making. And it identifies and interprets some of the analytical hypotheses found in the reports to show the true goal of an analysis: deriving meaning from facts.

PREPARING REPORTS

Law enforcement reports can range from a few pages to several hundred. They can cover the basics of the agency's work over the year, the numbers of cases investigated or prosecuted, referrals made, how its budget was spent, and so on; they may include in-depth investigative materials which encompass several cases or years; or they can reflect an exhaustive study of an organized crime group or criminal activity.

Law enforcement agencies with a mandate to produce reports would find it hard to fulfill that mandate without access to analysts, or to people with analytical training or skills. The purpose of most reports in criminal justice is to take the work of the agency and summarize it into something the audience will understand and support. These documents must synthesize the data uncovered and report them in a logical, accurate, and interesting manner.

Reports are painstaking to produce and require varied resources. Some issues involved in producing them include content direction, research, data collection, data collation, writing and editing, graphic direction, legal review, management approval, publication logistics, indexing, dissemination requirements, and follow-up.

Content Direction

The content of the report is generally guided by the management of the agency which is producing the report. If it is an ongoing periodical report—annual or quarterly, for example—the content is probably preestablished. A change in management of the organization or in the person responsible for producing the report can result in changes in the content or format of the organization's reports. Brainstorming among management, analysts, investigators, and attorneys can result in a tailored and informative report. Content should be a reflection of the targeted audience, the purpose of the report, and the desired outcome of the report. The purpose of an annual report, for example, could be to inform the legislature and the public about the work the agency has done the previous year; the desired outcome would be continued legislative support and possible increases in funding or personnel slots.

The report's format is guided by its content and the relative importance of the different topics covered. In general, overview sections or historical sections are placed near the beginning, while case results or research findings are placed in the middle and conclusions or future issues at the end. Sections with extensive use of statistics are often presented as a summary in the text, with the statistical tables forming appendices.

Many reports now begin with an executive summary which takes the most salient points and conclusions and places them where they will be most noticed. This section usually must be written last as it ties together what is written in the report and needs to flow from a relatively finished version of the report.

Research

Research is the second step toward producing a report; it includes reviewing not only information on the subjects to be covered, but previous reports by the agency and similar reports by other agencies. An understanding of the "standard" for producing these documents is necessary to meet, or improve upon, that standard.

Researching previous reports can be particularly helpful when the agency to produce the report has not previously established a standard for a report of this type. The analyst can then show management different examples of similar reports from other agencies, giving them the opportunity to choose what format will be best.

Research also provides the management with information on what types of data are available to be used in their report and what impact the data will have on the content and format.

Data Collection

Once the general content is determined, the collection effort must begin. Data collection can range from a review of the agency's management information system (for basic statistics), to the summarization of hundreds of investigative reports, to the compilation of data from dozens of outside sources. Surveys are sometimes used to collect information for the report.

It is important to allow enough time for the collection effort. Often initial materials raise as many questions as they answer and secondary collection efforts must be mounted. Furthermore, the data collected must be verified and this may be time-consuming.

When embarking on a data collection effort, the dissemination of the requests for data (in survey or other form) should be done first. While the analyst awaits responses from the survey, other research can be done from agency files, criminal justice libraries, and other sources.

Data Collation

Data collation can be done in three different ways: by chronology, by topic, or by information. Historical reports may use time as their organizer. Reports with diverse topics (budgets, cases, arrest data, etc.) may organize the data by those topics. Reports that show the results of surveys may be organized around statistical tables (e.g., frequency distributions) showing the answers to each question asked.

When collating the data, it is important to remember that graphics are more easily understood by the average person than statistics or statistical tables. Wherever possible, graphics should be used in place of raw statistics.

Another key to organizing information is to experiment with its placement and format. The advent of word processing with its ease of juggling paragraphs and pages gives new freedom to the organizational process.

Writing and Editing the Report

Writing a report can be a difficult task, depending on its targeted size and the capabilities of in-house staff. With adequate internal resources, several staff persons may be assigned to write different portions of the report, while one person has overall writing/editing responsibility so that the tone of the report is smooth throughout. This finishing writer/editor may be a staff person or, if necessary, a consultant. If the report is a long one, several persons may be responsible for the writing and editing. Technical editing requires different skills from those of a researcher, or writer, or finishing writer; someone with grammatical expertise may be needed as well.

Some agencies use academic consultants or professional writers to produce the final draft of the report.

Graphic Design

Graphic direction is also important. Graphic design includes the way the cover looks as well as the way the inner pages are laid out, the typeface, and the pictures, charts, or drawings used. The size and layout of pictures, chapter breaks, headlines, and so forth, are all aspects of graphic design. While the layout of the report is not as important as the content, a poor layout can limit the reading appeal of the report to the degree that the content may be overlooked.

Agencies well known for their reports may have in-house design and production capabilities. Computer-aided design and desktop publishing software put this potential into the hands of almost every medium size to large agency. Alternately, there are freelance graphic designers who can develop title pages, layouts, and specialized graphic treatments at a relatively reasonable cost.

Legal Review

Legal review is the key to producing respectable public reports. Most agencies want to share enough of their work with the other agencies and the public to generate interest and support, but legal issues often narrow the types of information which can be imparted to the public. In most instances, cases under investigation or prosecution cannot be discussed. Persons shown as members of organized crime groups can only be named with sufficient corroboration or their reputations might be injured. Sufficient backup for allegations must be on file within the agency. The basis for naming persons often is their identification as organized crime members or associates by two or more independent sources, but this can present a problem as agencies may make wholesale use of each other's lists, thereby giving the wrongful appearance of actual corroboration.

Legal review follows the writing of the report and usually involves protracted discussion among lawyers, investigators, and writers. Ample time must be permitted to assure proper phrasing and fair descriptions of the persons or businesses included.

Management Approval

After the report has been reviewed and approved on legal grounds, a final approval from the management of the agency is necessary. In some agencies, a formalized approval process is required before the report is "officially" released. Again, ample time for its review by management is necessary.

Publication Logistics

Report publication mechanics include many details that must be handled. Someone must work with typesetters (or desktop publishing personnel) to make sure the copy is placed into an agreed upon layout, to read and reread galleys and page proofs to make them error-free, to work on choices of paper, use of color, thickness (and finish) of cover stock, deadlines for printing and binding, and so on.

A schedule of when copy will be forwarded to the printer and when the various stages of printing will be accomplished is often determined at the onset of the contract with the printer. A timeline or chronological table can assist the agency in establishing the schedule; working backward from a "must have by" date is often effective. These deadlines, however, may be missed by printers or originating agencies unless the interim deadlines on the timeline are met; thus someone's constant attention to expediting the report is required.

Indexing

Law enforcement reports, in particular public reports, are used by a wide variety of people including investigators, legislators, and academic researchers. Indexing supports the use, and thus increases the value, of the report. Indexing should reflect the needs of the potential audience of the report. If the report includes information on numerous individuals and will be used as a reference work, for example, then names should be indexed. The longer the report, the more the need for indexing becomes apparent.

The practicality of the indexing process demands that it is not done until the report is put into a page format. It should be remembered, however, that the indexing process may serve as an analytical process, uncovering connections in the material that may not have previously been noticed. These connections, once uncovered, should be placed into the report, even if only as a postscript.

Report Dissemination

The report's dissemination is a final consideration. If the report is a quasi-public document (that is, for law enforcement dissemination only and limited by virtue of a numbering system or other means of tracking the locations of copies), then the dissemination requirements under which it is being released must be met. If it is a public report, then dissemination is generally limited only by the number produced (limited by cost factors) and the method of dissemination. Postage costs can become a significant part of publication costs.

The agency releasing the report should have written dissemination policies which cover the types of reports they produce and what safeguards have been implemented to assure that reports are given out on the basis of those policies. Because reports which are disseminated to other agencies may inadvertently reach the eyes of the public, care should be taken in all reports not to compromise confidential data.

Report Follow-Up

When an agency disseminates a report with factual information and analytical conclusions, other agencies, legislative members, or the public may have an interest in that information and may request additional data from the distributing agency. In addition, other agencies with additional information on the subjects covered may be alerted to the disseminating agency's interest in a topic and may provide further documentation on the subject not previously held by your agency. In some instances, information which refutes or sheds a different light on occurrences written about in the report may be received.

Accordingly, the final copy of the report and all reference materials from the report should be archived and indexed to the page on which the information appears so that the staff can respond to any and all inquiries. These materials should be kept for at least five years.

PUBLIC REPORT EXAMPLES

Varied examples of public reports are those by organizations such as the Royal Canadian Mounted Police, the Pennsylvania Crime Commission, the Drug Enforcement Administration, the New York State Organized Crime Task Force, the New Jersey State Commission of Investigation, the New Mexico Governor's Commission on the Prevention of Organized Crime, and the Criminal Intelligence Service Canada.

The Royal Canadian Mounted Police (RCMP) published regular reports on drug intelligence through its Drug Directorate prior to 1991 when it reorganized its intelligence function into a central directorate. Its *National Drug Intelligence Estimate (NDIE)* is produced yearly and includes trend indicators for the following two years. It covers the major drugs and drug-money flow and is designed to present a "review of the origin, volume, trafficking routes, modes of transport and smuggling methods of all drugs on the Canadian illicit market" (Royal Canadian Mounted Police, 1990). Its purpose is "to coordinate the collection, collation analysis and dissemination of foreign and domestic drug intelligence of interest to policy makers" (Royal Canadian Mounted Police, 1990).

The *NDIE* of 1990, for example, analyzed all aspects of narcotics smuggling and distribution in Canada. It looked at common smuggling routes and means of transport, combined data on arrests and users with purity and price levels for the major drugs, and recounted seizures of drugs and drug laboratories. It spoke of drug distribution groups such as Jamaican posses, cocaine cartels, and Nigerian heroin couriers. The report noted increasing domestic production of marijuana and the success of asset seizure (Anti–Drug Profiteering) programs.

The *NDIE* made extensive use of tables showing statistics for trafficker investigations, seizures of drugs, source countries for drugs, narcotics arrests, drug cultivation, and pricing, all by specific controlled substance. Geographic distributions were also shown in the *NDIE*, depicting trafficking routes into Canada by drug and source country narcotic production regions. The movement of narcotics by mode of transportation was shown through bar charts. Of particular interest in the report was the section on trend indicators through 1992 which predicted increased shipments of heroin into Canada through 1991 as well as increased direct smuggling of cocaine from South America into Canada (Royal Canadian Mounted Police, 1991). It forecasted the increased use of diverted pharmaceutical drugs in Canada and greater cultivation of cannabis within its borders.

The Pennsylvania Crime Commission, which had a legislative mandate to investigate organized crime and public corruption and to report annually on the status of organized crime in the Commonwealth, was a leader in organized crime public reporting until its enabling legislation was changed in 1993. In addition to annual reports which blended organized crime facts with agency accomplishments, it has issued ten-year reports and case-specific reports. Its two landmark reports—*A Decade of Organized Crime: 1980 Report* and *Organized Crime in Pennsylvania: A Decade of Change: 1990 Report*—used a number of analytical techniques.

A Decade of Organized Crime: 1980 Report, which became a seminal volume for organized crime writers and reporters, used geographic distribution analysis, association analysis, general research, summarization, and descriptive analysis. It detailed the membership and activities of Mafia families in Pennsylvania and adjacent states. In addition, it recognized the presence of other organized crime groups (blacks, Greeks, outlaw motorcycle gangs). It placed particular emphasis on the infiltration of legitimate businesses by criminal elements. One association matrix from that volume showed the movement of employees among various pizza shops (Figure 3.1). The Crime Commission concluded that these employees were "illegal aliens (and) were purposely moved from shop to shop to avoid detection by immigration authorities" (Pennsylvania Crime Commission, 1980, p. 221).

The *1980 Report* also included biographical sketches of a number of organized crime figures in Pennsylvania. A summary of one of those sketches, on former northeastern Pennsylvania crime boss Russell Bufalino, is seen in Figure 3.2.

Organized Crime in Pennsylvania: A Decade of Change: 1990 Report reflected a more sophisticated analytical approach that included commodity flow analysis, association analysis, threat assessments, and event flow analysis in addition to the techniques used in the *1980 Report*. The report's chapters were

Figure 3.1
Examples of Employee Mobility 1974–1977

	SCOTTO PIZZA									FRANK'S PIZZA						MR. PIZZA					ANGELO'S			ROMAN DELIG.	
	MEDIA, PA	GREENSBURG, PA	HANOVER, PA	UNIONTOWN, PA	POTTSTOWN, PA	EXTON, PA	STEUBENVILLE, PA	NILES, OH	SANDUSKY, OH	VOORHEES, NJ	FAIRMONT, WV	MORGANTOWN, WV	TAMPA, FL	CHERRY HILL, NJ	WARMINSTER, PA	OXFORD, PA	UPPER DARBY, PA	DREXEL HILL, PA	ESSEX, MD	NORTHEAST, MD	ORELAND, PA	WILLOW GROVE, PA	FLOURTOWN, PA	WILMINGTON, DE	HORSHAM, PA
VINCENZO CIRINO								■													■				
SALVATORE SCOTTO DiMARCO	■	■																							
DOMINIC ESPOSITO		■	■																						
RAPHAEL SCOTTO DiMARCO						■					■														
MARIO LaROCCA					■	■					■									■	■				
GJOHNI BARD					■									■											
SALVATORE COPPOLA								■				■													
ANTHONY SCOTTO DiLUZIO													■		■										
JOE SCOTTO																									
ENRICO ROMANO																	■					■			
VINCENT SCOTTO D'APPOLLONIA																			■				■	■	
DOMENIC ORTADO																							■		■
JOSEPH MODICA																			■						

Pizza shop employees who work in shops associated with organized criminals often move from shop to shop. The Crime Commission, as shown in the table, found that it was common for pizza shop employees to work in several shops of a chain. Some were transferred to help set up a new shop. Others, however, were illegal aliens and were purposely moved from shop to shop to avoid detection by immigration authorities. Law enforcement investigations suggest that the illegal aliens may be smuggled into the United States to become prospective Cosa Nostra recruits.

Source: Pennsylvania Crime Commission, *A Decade of Organized Crime: 1980 Report* (1980): p. 221.

Figure 3.2
Biographical Sketch—Russell Bufalino

Rosario Albert Bufalino, known in the United
States as Russell Bufalino, was born on October 29,
1903, in Sicily. He became the head of the
northeastern Pennsylvania Cosa Nostra family when
crime boss Joseph Barbara Sr. died on June 17, 1959.

Bufalino was credited by federal authorities
for "arranging and attending" the 1957 Cosa Nostra
convention at Barbara's Apalachin, NY home...

He has been involved in a number of businesses
in northeastern Pennsylvania and New York,
predominantly in the garment industry...He has also
engaged in the selling and purchasing of jewelry,
especially diamonds...

Russell Bufalino has twice been tried for
extortion and was once convicted...on August 8, 1977,
Bufalino was found guilty and sentenced to four years
in prison...In the testimony of self-professed mob
hit-man Charles Allen, Allen claimed that Bufalino was
the leader of a group of men who participated in two
murders, three attempted murders, two acts of arson
and the embezzlement of union funds from 1973 to 1976.

Source: Pennsylvania Crime Commission, *A Decade of Organized Crime: 1980 Report* (1980): pp.
  51–52.

divided by crime groups—which were generally depicted as being ethnocen-
tric—rather than by the type of crime being committed.

One example of an analytical product from the *1990 Report* is an assessment
of motorcycle gangs in Pennsylvania. This used the conclusions drawn in the
summaries of the activities of several biker gangs in the state and combined
them into a summary (Figure 3.3). In this threat assessment, the Crime Commission commented, "Outlaw biker activity will continue to be a threat in the
Commonwealth, especially in the area of drug trafficking" (Pennsylvania Crime
Commission, 1991, p. 205).

In some respects these two volumes are indicative of the changes in analysis
during the 1980s. The *1980 Report* was done without analysts, with writers who
had no analytical training or particular knowledge of analytical techniques, and
yet it was analytical in nature. It contained rudimentary association matrices.
There were descriptive analyses and summaries of activities. The *1980 Report*
was analytical reporting (not surprising as the consultant/writers were all jour-
nalists) but did not draw conclusions from the information (Peterson, 1992).

The *1990 Report,* on the other hand, blended reporting data with analysis of

Figure 3.3
Outlaw Motorcycle Gang Assessment

By the end of the decade (1989), some law enforcement
personnel had written off the outlaw biker clubs as an
important organized crime threat, for several reasons:

> -Outlaw biker clubs lack the sophistication and
> are too oriented toward short-sighted hedonism to
> be highly-successful criminal organizations.
> -They lack the connections with law enforcement
> and/or the political power base to be major
> players in organized crime.
> -They have been severely weakened by the
> successful prosecutions of the 1980s, and they
> will continue to be paralyzed by the threat of
> RICO. . ..

Other law enforcement professionals are less sanguine,
however. They offer several reasons for treating
outlaw biker clubs, particularly the Pagans and
Warlocks, as a serious organized crime threat in the
1990s.

> -Most members of outlaw biker gangs are hard-core
> criminals who can never be rehabilitated...
> -The hierarchy of outlaw biker clubs tend to be
> fairly sophisticated and calculating. . ..Inter-
> gang conflict has lessened (but still exists) and
> various biker clubs now cooperate in joint
> criminal enterprise. . ..
> -The biker network of contacts provides a ready-
> made distribution chain for narcotics and stolen
> property. . ..

It is expected, therefore, that outlaw biker activity
will continue to be a threat in the Commonwealth,
especially in the area of drug trafficking.
Nonetheless, other groups such as LCN and Hispanic drug
groups are likely to pose a more serious organized
crime threat within the state during the 1990s and may
warrant more in the way of law enforcement attention
than do outlaw motorcycle clubs.

Source: Pennsylvania Crime Commission, *Organized Crime in Pennsylvania: A Decade of Change:*
1990 Report (1990): pp. 204–5.

data and threat assessments derived from them. The report's use of intelligence
analysis was a function of the integration of the analytical function into the
Crime Commission during the 1980s (Peterson, 1992). Yet both provide good
examples of analysis in historical public reports.

The U.S. Drug Enforcement Administration (DEA) releases a number of public reports. In addition to its intelligence mandate, it also performs a significant training role in the area of drug enforcement education. Some of its open distribution publications are *Intelligence Trends: From the Source to the Street, Drug Trafficking,* and *Drugs of Abuse.*

The *Intelligence Trends* booklet compiles current prices of various drugs and information on drug sources. This information is relayed by using analytical techniques of commodity flow charts, geographic distribution maps, and summaries.

The book *Drugs of Abuse* was first published in 1975 by the DEA Office of Public Affairs and has been revised several times since. It is an overview of the various types of drugs, their effects, what they look like, and laws relating to their use or sale. Color photographs of pills, powders, and source plants are used effectively along with summarizations of the narcotic involved, trade name(s), and scheduling of the drug. The primary analytical technique in this publication is the use of tables. One depicts trafficking penalties and regulatory requirements, while another highlights controlled substance uses and effects.

The New York State Organized Crime Task Force was established by the legislature to investigate and prosecute multicounty organized criminal activity and to assist local law enforcement agencies in their efforts against organized crime. It has released reports on particular investigations which it spearheaded. *Corruption and Racketeering in the New York City Construction Industry* (final report) was released in 1990. This in-depth view of corruption includes a descriptive analysis titled "Analysis of Why Racketeering and Corruption Have Been So Persistent and Pervasive in the Construction Industry" (New York State Organized Crime Task Force, 1989).

This analysis of the construction industry looked at industry characteristics which generate opportunities and incentives for profitable racketeering based on the concepts of "racketeering susceptibility" and "racketeering potential." It detailed the characteristics of the labor market which contributed to racketeering including the power of construction unions over the workers in the area and the power of the unions vis-à-vis their impact on the cost of the job (work stoppages and slowdowns, etc.). It also pointed out the susceptibility of the industry to racketeering because of the opportunity for illicit profits, the ease of generating and concealing cash payments, the ease of adding "no show" employees to the payroll to create "legitimate" racketeer income, the traditional role of the mediator the racketeer plays in the construction industry, and the lucrativeness of public construction as a target of racketeering (New York State Organized Crime Task Force, 1989). This is an example of a vulnerability assessment, showing how the construction industry is vulnerable to the influence of racketeers and what forms that influence takes.

This report by the New York State Organized Crime Task Force (OCTF) does not include any traditional products of analysis (i.e., charts). The descriptive analysis of the construction industry does assess the problems in it and arrives at specific conclusions and recommendations. The vulnerability analysis is an example of how indicators are derived from data and can then be applied to investigations in other areas.

The New Jersey State Commission of Investigation is similar in legislative mandate to the Pennsylvania Crime Commission. It also investigates organized crime and corruption and presents reports to the legislature and to the public. Among its recent reports are *Public Hearing Report and Recommendations on the Subversion by Organized Crime and Other Unscrupulous Elements of the Check Cashing Industry* (1988), *Solid Waste Regulation* (1989), *Video Gambling* (1991), *The New Jersey Garment Industry* (1991), *Afro-Lineal Organized Crime* (1991), and *Criminal Street Gangs* (1993).

The New Jersey State Commission of Investigation relies upon investigation, analysis, and public and private hearings to form the bases of its public reports. The primary form of analysis appearing in its reports is descriptive analysis, with some conversation analysis applied to the testimony covered. Of the reports cited, three, *Check Cashing, Solid Waste,* and *Street Gangs,* used traditional analytical products. A geographic distribution analysis, a table, a chart, and an activity flow chart of the check cashing industry were used in the *Check Cashing* report, a table and two charts were used in *Solid Waste,* and a geographic distribution analysis and several tables were used in *Street Gangs.* The graphic on the check cashing industry (Figure 3.4) shows the uses of the industry by criminal elements to evade taxes, to manipulate finances, and to aid fraud and con artists.

The New Jersey State Commission of Investigation also compiles yearly updates on organized crime which are published in its annual report.

The New Mexico Governor's Organized Crime Prevention Commission has a legislative mandate similar to that of the New Jersey and Pennsylvania commissions. Its geographic location and population variance from the eastern United States model reflect a different approach to organized crime, however. In New Mexico, the emphasis is not placed on traditional organized crime (i.e., La Cosa Nostra).

A recent report published by the New Mexico Commission is *New Mexico Street Gangs* (1991). This report highlights "Gang Member Identification Criteria," an analysis of the components of gang membership that lists indicators of gang membership. A geographic distribution analysis of Albuquerque in the form of a street grid map (Figure 3.5) shows the locations ("turfs") of specific gangs at a certain time. This map acknowledges its limitations (turfs change frequently as do gangs), but gives a comprehensive view of the pervasiveness of the problem.

The Criminal Intelligence Service Canada (CISC) is a law enforcement agency with federal, provincial, and municipal Canadian police members with full-time criminal intelligence units. Member agencies submit data to a computerized data base (Automated Criminal Intelligence Information System) which allows the exchange of intelligence data around the clock. The CISC

Figure 3.4
Check Cashing Industry

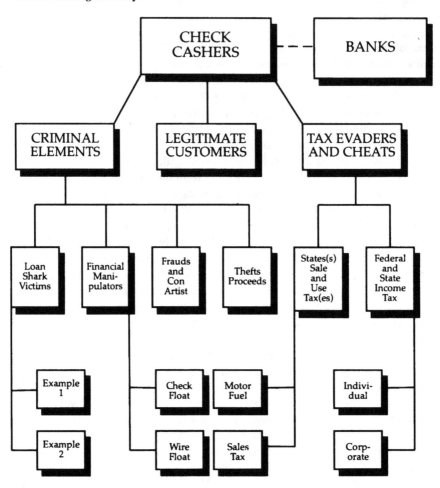

Source: New Jersey State Commission of Investigation, *Public Hearing Report and Recommendations on the Subversion of Organized Crime and Other Unscrupulous Elements of the Check Cashing Industry* (1988): p. 11.

covers criminal organizations, crimes of violence, drugs, economic crime, pornography, prostitution, gambling, hijacking, and smuggling. The CISC publishes an *Annual Report* which summarizes its work for the year. The *Annual Report 1985* included several analytical techniques and products, including geographic distribution maps, tables, charts, and descriptive analysis. It noted trends occurring in the various crime areas and broke down major criminal activity into geographic regions.

There are undoubtedly dozens of other agencies around the United States and

Figure 3.5
Albuquerque Street Gang "Turf Map"

Source: New Mexico Governor's Organized Crime Prevention Commission, *New Mexico Street Gangs* (1991): p. 30.

This map of Albuquerque depicts identifiable "turf" locations for street gangs. Each box represents the turf of a single gang.

other countries which produce law enforcement reports that reflect analytical techniques and skills. Many agencies produce annual reports which cover cases aided by analysis. Their lack of inclusion here is due only to limited space.

PREPARING STRATEGIC ASSESSMENTS

Strategic analysis and assessment are the cornerstones of some of the most significant work in law enforcement today. The strategic format allows us to take what is occurring or what has occurred in the criminal environment and use it to draw conclusions and to forecast what may occur in the future. These forecasts may be short-term (premonitory) or longer-term. Once a possible future is hypothesized, then law enforcement management can determine what steps, if any, should be taken to prevent that future criminal activity.

Strategic analysis and assessments are done on two levels—internal and external. Internal assessments may include sensitive, confidential, and speculative data. Those assessments destined for external distribution, even when that distribution is limited to law enforcement agencies, tend to be more general and deductive in their logic.

The process used to complete strategic assessments includes determining the topic to be addressed, devising a collection plan on the topic, collecting the data, organizing (collating) the data, performing the necessary analyses, writing a summary of the analyses, drawing conclusions based on the facts, making recommendations, and disseminating the report appropriately. A strategic assessment is usually completed on a particular crime group or a criminal activity. The topic for a strategic analysis must be narrow enough in focus to allow the study to be done in a reasonable amount of time, but not so narrow that the analyst will be unable to find data on it. Emerging activities or groups are often the subject of strategic assessments. The analyst may limit the topic by both group (or activity), location, and time, for example, "Have Jamaican posses been involved in significant 'crack' cocaine distribution in Philadelphia between 1988 and 1992?" The format may be organized either as a question or as a hypothesis to be proved or refuted (Sommers, 1986). Topics may be recommended by management, by investigators, or by the analyst. They are generally approved by management since their completion will require a significant dedication of agency time and resources.

The second step of the assessment process, the collection plan, includes the development of questions to be answered during the study, as well as the timetable for their completion. Sometimes the major portion of the collection plan is in survey form (Andrews, 1990), but it should also include the sources to be covered and the projected time frame of the collection effort (Sommers, 1986).

A blueprint for assessments was put forth by Sommers in 1986:

ASSESSING CRIMINAL GROUP ACTIVITY

Section A. Past and Present

1. Membership of group: all members with biodata available on them. Length of membership if available. Note any trends such as criteria for membership regarding number of members, geographic range of their legal and illegal activities.

2. Geographic data on group: headquarters, location of members, geographic range of their legal and illegal activities.

3. Hierarchy of group: past and present. Is there a known philosophy of current or past leaders relative to violence or criminal activities? Who appears to be rising through the ranks?

4. Criminal activities of group: all known or suspected illegal activities. Dates of criminal activity occurrences should be included to show possible changes or trends.

5. "Legitimate" business activities of group members: all known or suspected involvements with "legitimate" business including employment history, ownership of or investments in businesses, past and present. Look for hidden ownership through fronts and paper corporations. Again, look at possible trends or changes.

6. Financial health of group members: any information that shows evidence of financial condition of members or group—real estate, vehicles, travel, and other indicators of conspicuous consumption. Analyze tax and/or bank records of group leaders. Trends and changes should be noted.

7. Connections to other groups: is this group working with other criminal groups? Is the relationship between this group and another group equal, superordinate, or subordinate? Is "tribute" paid to another group? Does each group have an established territory? Have any changes occurred in these network connections?

8. Connections to the government structure: are there agencies or governmental bodies that regulate the general activity area in which the types of crime being committed occur (police, licensing, and regulatory agencies)? Do any known connections/relationships exist between group members and persons involved in these agencies or governmental bodies?

9. Previous work in the system: have any enforcement actions been taken against the group, for either criminal or civil violations, by any agency?

10. Has any agency conducted tactical investigative or strategic analysis on the group? If yes, what were the results?

11. What has been and is the social, economic, political, and criminal climate in the area(s) in which the group operates? Are there other groups perpetrating the same criminal activities? Is there a strong enforcement presence? Is there a strong community opposition to the criminal activity?

Section B. The Future

1. Future group membership.
2. Future geographic impact.

3. Growth potential for and direction of criminal activity.

4. Growth potential for and direction of "legitimate" business activity.

5. Future financial position.

6. Possible future changes in relationships with other groups.

7. Potential for future relationships with or corruption of government officials.

Section C. Enforcement Alternatives

Based on data developed in Sections A and B, evaluate feasible alternatives and make recommendations to the department regarding investigative deployment actions that could be taken to prevent further growth and/or success of this group. For each alternative, indicate the probable effectiveness of that action. (Sommers, 1986, pp. 34–36)

Collecting data may require an analyst to search a variety of information sources or to have intelligence officers conduct that search. Public records (deeds, licenses, etc.), investigative/intelligence files, other agencies' files, public information (books, articles, etc.), and government data (censuses, etc.) are potential sources of data.

The next step toward the completion of a strategic assessment is organizing or collating the data. While tactical products can often be broken down into computerized data bases, general strategic work is more dependent upon research techniques and descriptive formats. That is not to say that products usually considered "tactical," such as association charts or financial analyses, cannot be included in a strategic report, for they can, and the data which support their creation can be organized in the same manner to be used in tactical reports. But often a lot of public record data and other materials must be handled by using more traditional research methods which can be computerized in descriptive formats such as a computerized index card method, where the data, including their reference numbers, would be organized by topic or date. Reference numbers are the document numbers of the sources that are used. They can be numbers assigned during the document inventory process or numbers originally given to the documents by the organization which generated them. These reference numbers allow the analyst, investigator, or attorney to locate the sources of the information and verify its accuracy.

Varied types of analysis are completed, depending upon the data collected (Andrews and Peterson, 1990). For a group that is under assessment, an association analysis would be done. If criminal acts have occurred, an event flow analysis might be used to show their chronology. Statistical analyses could be completed to show trends in criminal occurrences. Descriptive analyses would also be made to summarize varied research information. In addition to completing individual analytical products, it is important to compare the products to prevent inconsistencies and to see whether they corroborate other products.

Writing a summary of the products' meaning is a crucial step in the assessment. This synthesizes the material which has been broken down previously for the purpose of analysis (Peterson, 1990). From these summaries solid conclusions and recommendations can be drawn to be presented to management in order to determine what actions, if any, should be taken.

The final step in the production of a strategic product is its dissemination. If it is a confidential product, a limited number of copies might be made available to key members of the agency's management. A less confidential report might be disseminated to many law enforcement agencies, but under prohibitions against the reproduction and further dissemination of the number-controlled report.

STRATEGIC ASSESSMENT EXAMPLES

The existence of internal assessments is generally known to persons outside the agency, but these are seldom officially seen outside the agency. It can be noted, however, that several federal and some state agencies have developed reputations for producing these assessments, including the Federal Bureau of Investigation, the Drug Enforcement Administration, the U.S. Marshal's Service, and the New Jersey State Police.

One assessment made by personnel in the New Jersey State Police Intelligence Bureau was later rewritten into an article for publication, "The Social Impact of Casino Gaming on Atlantic City" (Lettich, 1988). This article gave the sources of information on which the assessment was based. Tables of population and employment demographics were included, along with information on housing development, High School Proficiency Test scores, and crime rates. Descriptive analysis of the status of the local police department, city government, and instances of connections to traditional organized crime (Mafia) families was included. The closing remarks included summations of the problems found in the city and possible solutions. The article concluded that "the social environment in Atlantic City has steadily declined since the introduction of casino gaming" and that "a possible solution for Atlantic City is state takeover (of governmental functions)" (Lettich, 1988, p. 17).

The summarization of strategic conclusions into a public document can not only enhance the reputation of the agency completing the analysis but provide a valuable store of data to the analyst or investigator who is undertaking work on a similar topic. Information gains its worth by being shared. This article tells an investigator about possible areas to explore within a casino investigation, who may have intelligence data to share on casino-related crime (the agency who did the analysis), and what format to use for reporting the information.

A second example of a limited distribution report which resulted in a published work was the Western States Information Network analysis of clandestine laboratory activity in its region (California, Oregon, Washington, Hawaii, and Alaska), later reported by Karen Sanderson in the IALEIA *Digest* (Sanderson, 1987). The article detailed the steps taken to produce the assessment, including a collection survey, creation of data bases for the information, analysis of the data, and production of the report. The report and article used geographic distribution analysis, statistical analysis, tables, bar and pie charts, and descriptive analysis. Some bar charts are seen in Figure 3.6.

Figure 3.6
California Lab Seizures by Drug Type 1983–1985, Reported to WSIN

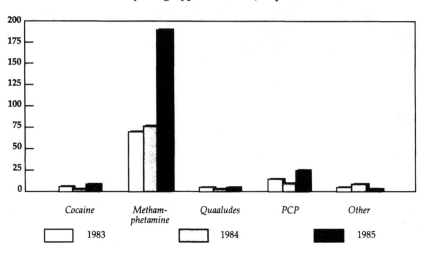

Source: Karen Sanderson, "An Analytical Response to the Clandestine Drug Laboratory Problem," *Law Enforcement Intelligence Analysis Digest,* Vol. 2, No. 1 (February 1987): p. 2.

General strategic assessments written for external distribution are obtained more readily, particularly within the law enforcement community. Examples are those of the Drug Enforcement Administration, the RISS projects (particularly MAGLOCLEN), the Florida Department of Law Enforcement, the Royal Canadian Mounted Police, the Revenue Canada Customs and Excise, and the Governor's Organized Crime Prevention Commission of New Mexico.

For example, the Drug Enforcement Administration (DEA), the lead U.S. narcotic agency, heads the National Narcotics Intelligence Consumers Committee (NNICC) and publishes a yearly report on the supply of illicit drugs titled *The NNICC Report.* The NNICC was established "to coordinate the collection, analysis, dissemination, and evaluation of strategic drug-related intelligence . . . that is essential to effective policy development, resource deployment and operational planning" (National Narcotics Intelligence Consumer Committee, 1990, p. iv). It provides an overview of the status of drug activities during a particular time frame, with suppositions (hypotheses) about why those activities occurred when they did.

The NNICC Report 1989 used the analytical techniques of summarization, descriptive analysis, and tables. One table, "Cocaine Use Indicators, 1986–1989" (Figure 3.7), for example, shows emergency room mentions of cocaine use (in various forms). The statistics show a 127 percent increase in emergency room mentions of cocaine between 1986 and 1989. The most significant increase is in the administration route of "smoking" cocaine (reflecting crack cocaine use), which increased by 227 percent. However, the accompanying text notes

Figure 3.7
Cocaine Use Indicators, 1986–1989

EMERGENCY ROOM MENTIONS *	1986**	1987**	1988**	1989***
All routes of administration	18,579	32,052	42,512	42,145
Intranasal snorting	4,316	4,705	5,702	5,251
Injection	5,460	9,041	11,471	9,346
Cocaine/heroin in combination	2,887	4,671	5,470	5,034
Smoking	4,174	10,274	14,332	15,743
Medical Examiner Mentions ****	1,269	1,808	2,334	1,723

Source: National Narcotics Intelligence Consumers' Committee, *The NNICC Report 1989* (1990): p. 11.

*Data from DAWN panel of 431 consistently reporting facilities.

**Data for 1986–1988 do not agree with data in 1988 NNICC Report because the emergency room data are based on a different consistent panel of hospitals.

***Medical examiner mentions are incomplete due to lag time in reporting for 1989.

****Excludes New York metropolitan area because of incomplete reporting.

that many 1989 figures were down from 1988, an indicator of decrease in cocaine use.

One important analytical aspect of this *Report* is that it integrates law enforcement data with nonenforcement data to arrive at conclusions. Its statistics are derived from the Drug Abuse Warning Network (DAWN), a hospital-based set of data which reflects emergency room mentions of controlled substances; from the National Household Survey and High School Senior Survey, both of which compile data on use of and attitudes toward drugs; the Drug Use Forecasting data base, which administers drug tests to arrestees; law enforcement statistics (arrests, seizures, etc.); and international intelligence gathering, including the International Narcotics Control Strategy Report. This broad look at narcotic activity is necessary to a more complete picture of narcotics use. Crimes do not exist in a vacuum and should be examined within their economic, social, and political milieux to be understood fully.

The Drug Enforcement Administration publishes several other documents which are strategic in nature. The El Paso Intelligence Center (EPIC) disseminates a "DEA Sensitive" publication which tabulates information on seizures during transport. The *EPIC Brief* includes articles on major seizures and cases as well as intelligence capsules and tables of seizures.

DEA also produces publications on narcotics source and transshipment countries. In 1991 they published the assessments *Cuba* and *Chile;* in 1990 they published *Argentina*. These country profiles give information on the political situation, drug abuse, drug enforcement, international banking and money laundering, and international illicit drug traffic. In relation to Cuba, for example, the descriptive analysis notes, "Cuba also figures prominently as a cocaine transshipment point in federal indictments handed down in . . . 1988 and 1989" (Drug Enforcement Administration, 1991, p. 3). The report *Argentina* notes that while that country remains a minor player in drug trafficking, "the potential for money laundering in Argentina is high because of the existence of a large, technically illegal market for foreign exchange which operates mainly with U.S. currency" (Drug Enforcement Administration, 1990, p. 9).

The Chile profile points to its role as a major producer of cocaine in the 1970s and states that it now is a large supplier of cocaine-essential chemicals to the neighboring countries Bolivia and Peru (Drug Enforcement Administration, 1991). It further points out Chile's lax regulation of monetary instruments, which creates an atmosphere conducive to drug profit money laundering (Drug Enforcement Administration, 1991).

All these were produced by DEA's Intelligence Division. Distribution was generally to federal law enforcement and intelligence agencies. The DEA Office of Intelligence also produces two annual overview publications entitled *Worldwide Heroin Situation* and *Worldwide Cocaine Situation*. These are distributed to state and local law enforcement agencies in addition to federal agencies.

The *Heroin 1990* assessment includes U.S. heroin availability data, illicit opium production estimates, and data on the heroin situation in Southeast Asia, Mexico, Guatemala, Southwest Asia, and Europe/Middle East. It includes analytical tables and charts. One example from the publication is "Heroin Availability in the United States," a series of pie charts (Figure 3.8). These pie charts clearly depict the shrinking reliance on Southwest Asian heroin in the United States from 1983–85 to 1989–90 and the dramatic increase in Southeast Asian heroin use here. This is particularly interesting since the trend in 1984–87 appeared to be toward domination by Mexican heroin, but in 1988, this trend reversed, leaving Mexican heroin with a smaller share than during any of the previous seven years.

The *Cocaine Situation 1990* assessment by DEA differs from the format of the *Heroin* assessment. While it includes prices and purity charts, it focuses on cocaine trafficking, broken down by DEA field divisions in the United States and by 32 foreign countries. This is done in a report format; each division has three to twelve paragraphs, in which it descriptively analyzes the region, the trafficking groups and routes used, any significant convictions made, and the availability of the drug. Primary geographic sources of locally used cocaine are

Figure 3.8
Heroin Availability in the United States*

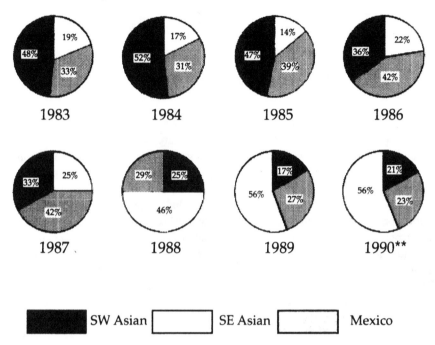

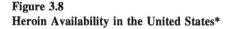 SW Asian [ ] SE Asian [ ] Mexico

Source: Drug Enforcement Administration, *Worldwide Heroin Situation 1990*, (1991): p. 3.

*Data based on analysis of 300–500 exhibits each year from DEA's heroin signature program. These exhibits include random samples of purchases/seizures as well as seizures made at U.S. ports of entry.

**1990 data is based on preliminary analysis of over 600 exhibits. 1990 figures are subject to revision.

referenced along with concealment methods of smugglers. A three-page section, "Significant Developments," summarizes overall smuggling routes and methods, availability trends, and conclusions.

The Middle Atlantic–Great Lakes Organized Crime Law Enforcement Network (MAGLOCLEN) is one of six regional information sharing systems funded by the U.S. Department of Justice, Office of Justice Programs. MAGLOCLEN has distributed over a dozen strategic assessments to its members from 1983 to the present. Topics of these restricted dissemination documents included the following:

La Cosa Nostra

Terroristic Acts Against the United States

Controlled Substance Analogs

Bunco Assessment
Cocaine Law Enforcement Perspective
Outlaw Motorcycle Gangs
Asian Organized Crime
Abortion Clinic Bombings
Jamaican Organized Crime
Colombian Cartels

These assessments, produced by MAGLOCLEN's analytical unit, generally followed a standard format. An executive summary was followed by a section compiling general research on the topic. This general research was gleaned from law enforcement publications, public records, or other nonconfidential data. This section was followed by the data of the report: the responses from a member survey or other data collection methods. It included specifics on criminal violators, persons identified as members of established crime groups, and, where applicable, information on specific criminal incidents. Each report contained conclusions based on all the data gathered, as well as recommendations for action by member law enforcement agencies.

MAGLOCLEN also disseminates a monthly newsletter to its members, called *Network*. *Network* is produced by MAGLOCLEN analysts and is a compendium of intelligence data submitted by members or gleaned from other law enforcement sources. Notices of persons with outstanding warrants may be included along with narcotics smuggling trends and notices of upcoming conferences. The other RISS projects (WSIN, ROCIC, MOCIC, RMIN, and NESPIN) produce similar publications, as do a number of state agencies including the Pennsylvania Attorney General's Office and the Ohio Bureau of Criminal Identification and Investigation.

The Florida Department of Law Enforcement (FDLE) has been considered a top state enforcement agency. Analysts play a significant role at FDLE and are employed at several locations around the state. One analytical assessment which was made public was *Crack Cocaine in Florida* (April, 1987). The report, based on a survey of law enforcement agencies in Florida, built on an earlier survey from the first half of the year. It asked law enforcement agencies questions such as "Do you perceive crack cocaine as a problem in your area?" "What percentage of your agency's total narcotics seizures would you estimate to be crack?" and "What percentage of crack arrests involved the seizure of weapons?" (Florida Department of Law Enforcement, 1987). Thirteen questions in total were asked. *Crack Cocaine* included several analytical products within the assessment and gave pie charts, tables, geographic distribution maps, bar charts, and indicators (methods of operation). Recommendations for action were culled from the survey responses, as well as new trends in crack distribution.

FDLE's analytical assessment of crack is an example of how agencies can detect significant changes in operational methods and availability of a drug by performing regular jurisdictional surveys. Rather than presenting a static picture of one time period, the survey compares two periods. These surveys over a period of years can give a more vibrant picture of the crime problem and can form a stronger basis for forecasting future occurrences.

The Royal Canadian Mounted Police quarterly *Drug Intelligence Trends* (previously disseminated monthly) has a magazine format with articles on recent drug-related activity in Canada, in the United States, and in narcotics source countries. An issue produced in the winter of 1991 included the sections "Domestic Drug Trends," "NIDA Survey Indicates Overall Cocaine Use Down, but Daily Use Up in U.S.," and "The Yakuza: Organized Crime in Japan" (Royal Canadian Mounted Police, 1991). That volume included the work of four RCMP analysts and reflected the analytical techniques of research, inference development, summarization, and forecasting. It has restricted distribution to law enforcement agencies in Canada, the United States, and some other countries.

The RCMP also distributed a special report, *Aerial Cocaine Smuggling into Canada,* to a limited audience. This report used descriptive analysis and geographic flow analysis to depict the significant impact of cocaine smuggling on Canada. It also presented a vulnerability assessment related to that smuggling (Royal Canadian Mounted Police, 1991). The specifics of the report cannot be quoted because of its protected dissemination status.

The Revenue Canada Customs and Excise (RCCE) is a federal Canadian agency which is responsible for securing the borders of that country. It includes an Intelligence Services Division. RCCE has produced *Intelligence Bulletin,* which is a restricted document, on a monthly basis. One issue of *Intelligence Bulletin* (91/02) included intelligence news, feature articles, immigration news, and significant seizure data for drugs, liquor, currency, and other items; also covered were pornography, narcotics, and the smuggling of children. The publication used summarization, descriptive analysis, and tables. The primary table showed significant drug seizures by date, airport or other port of entry, quantity, method of concealment, origin, person data, and indicators. Within the indicators, the most common factors were persons traveling alone, those traveling from a source country of narcotics, and those paying for their tickets in cash.

Finally, the Governor's Organized Crime Prevention Commission of New Mexico distributes confidential reports, among them *New Mexico Prison Gangs.* This report included information on various nontraditional organized crime groups operating in the prison environment and gave a statistical analysis of the demographic data on prison inmates as well as a threat assessment. Fifteen pages of charts on gangs were included.

STRATEGIC ASSESSMENTS AND PLANNING

Strategic analysis can and should be done to support law enforcement policy-making. The process enables police managers to evaluate the problems facing them as well as their capabilities to solve the problems. For example, decisions to initiate or discontinue enforcement programs should be the result of a thorough needs assessment.

But while strategic assessments have become an integral part of the analytic process in some agencies, few have used them to span the gap between operations and planning. Traditionally, planning is done by those with budgetary and administrative expertise; thus many "strategies" are, in actuality, plans for how to expend funds.

Strategic assessments have been tied to the receipt of federal funding in the United States through the Drug Control Systems Improvement Block Grant program which requires each state recipient to arrive at and submit a comprehensive strategy. In the format prescribed by the Bureau of Justice Assistance, the nature and extent of the problem, current resources, a strategy, and a strategy evaluation plan must be addressed.

An example of the use of strategic analysis to develop policy, programs, and grant funding is the *New Jersey Statewide Strategy for the FY '93 Drug Control and System Improvement Formula Grant Program* (1992). This document resulted from a strategic assessment in which data were gathered, by survey, from county and municipal agencies across the state and combined with data on narcotics arrests, drug users, drug-related crime, drug courier routes, treatment, and courts and corrections to form a comprehensive picture of narcotics activities in the state. From that, a narcotics mission was developed:

The narcotics mission of the State of New Jersey is to significantly reduce drug use. This mission is pursued through the overall strategies of narcotics abuse prevention and narcotics enforcement. . . .Specifically, New Jersey's narcotics strategy is to: develop co-operative education, prevention and public awareness programs designed to reduce the demand for illicit substances, to arrest any person who commits a controlled dangerous substance offense, and to provide a coordinated and integrated approach to narcotics issues. (State of New Jersey Department of Law and Public Safety, 1992, p. 18)

Concurrently, the Department of Law and Public Safety in New Jersey developed a *1993 Statewide Narcotics Action Plan* which detailed the roles and responsibilities of state, county, and local enforcement agencies in the fulfillment of the plan.

Both the strategy and the *Action Plan* were analytical products completed within the operational narcotics unit. The strategy document included a number of tables, charts, maps, and frequency distributions.

The overall strategic planning process has also been supported by the use of analytical techniques. In one example of strategic planning, the Milpitas (California) Police Department used a committee of its employees to develop a plan. The task of compiling and analyzing the data gathered in support of planning, however, fell to one individual. Within the resultant plan an expressed priority was to improve the information gathering and analysis capability of the department. This is not an unusual conclusion: good planning demands competent analysis.

CONCLUSIONS

The reporting function of a law enforcement agency is one which can best be done by, or with the assistance of, analysts. Analytical methods are readily applied to any type of data, from the agency's budget in an annual report to the treatment of violator information in a confidential strategic assessment. It is no accident that those agencies with a high public reporting profile—federal agencies and crime commissions—are the most likely to employ analysts. Accurate and interesting public and confidential reports are critical to modern law enforcement. They can engender better financing, broader political or community support, respect of other law enforcement agencies, and acquisition of federal grants. Assessments support law enforcement planning and the effective allocation of limited resources. Analytical support is key to reaching all of these goals.

CHAPTER IV

Violent Crime Applications

Violent crime includes robbery, homicide, serial violent crime, assault, and rape. It is differentiated from other crime by its violence and by its use of dangerous weapons and/or force. Many violent crimes are repeated crimes, which can be analyzed to uncover patterns, modus operandi, and criminal signatures. Some of them have profit as a motive while others involve revenge or fulfillment of a psychological drive. Another commonality to violent crimes is that they include various events and have the potential to leave physical evidence. For the purpose of this chapter, "violent crime" includes arsons and acts of terrorism, but does not include auto theft, which is covered in the chapter on street crimes.

Violent crime accounted for 5 percent of arrests for all offenses during 1992 (there were 742,130 persons arrested for violent crime and 1,932,274 violent crimes committed). Violent crime arrests increased 23 percent from 1988 to 1992. The 1992 clearance rate for violent crimes was 45 percent, even with 1991, but down from 46 percent in 1990. Aggravated assaults comprised 58 percent of the total violent crimes reported in 1992, robberies were 35 percent, murders were 1 percent, and forcible rapes were 6 percent (Federal Bureau of Investigation, 1993).

A statistical analysis of arrest/violation data on violent crimes in the United States shows several continuing trends:

- Violent crimes occur most frequently during the months of July and August with the fewest numbers in February. This trend of high rates in the summer and low rates in the winter has remained steady for several years.

- Men are commonly the perpetrators of violent crime. In 1992, 88 percent of all the violent crimes reported were done by males. Fifty-four percent of those arrested were white.

- Persons arrested for violent crime often fell into the twenty-five to thirty-four-year old age group. In 1992, 31 percent of the total known violent crime offenders were between twenty-five and thirty-four.

- During 1992, 31 percent of all violent crimes were committed by persons with firearms while 15 percent were committed by persons with knives. (Federal Bureau of Investigation, 1993)

Weiner lists over three dozen studies of violent criminals which have been done in the last three decades (1989, pp. 44–48) and notes that "relatively few members of general populations that are at-risk to accumulate official records for seriously violent behavior in fact accumulate such records . . . substantially larger numbers of people report having participated in seriously violent behaviors that failed to result in an official notation" (Weiner, 1989, p. 127).

Violent crimes may result in lengthy investigations if the assailant is unknown. The investigative process includes gathering, evaluating, and analyzing data and arriving at additional leads or hypothetical conclusions regarding the assailant. Evidentiary documents beyond the crime scene may also be gathered to provide background information on the victim or the alleged perpetrator. These, when analyzed, can provide insights into the persons involved in the crime which may speed the investigative process.

BACKGROUND

Violent crime investigation is often the responsibility of the major crimes section of a police or prosecutor's office. Investigators or detectives from municipal to federal agencies may be involved in the investigation of violent crime. While violent crime is often prosecuted at the municipal or county level, some factors can cause the case to be assigned to a multi-jurisdictional task force. Among them are the location of the crime, the potential of the crime to be part of a series of similar crimes committed by the same perpetrator(s), or the crime's connection to offenses prosecutable in a different jurisdiction or at a different level of government.

Detectives or investigators assigned to violent crime units respond to specific reports of crime which are generated by the victim or witnesses and may be lodged through a patrol officer who has gathered preliminary data from the scene of the crime or has made the location of the crime secure while awaiting the arrival of investigators and physical evidence technicians.

Crime scene evidence and statements of victims or witnesses are the two predominant sources of leads in violent crime investigation. Where violent crimes involve perpetrators who have committed similar crime before (or since), patterns and commonalities may be seen which will help solve the case. Reviewing data from the incident and comparing it to similar incidents are analytical functions.

Traditionally, violent crime bureaus have relied upon the weight of the physical evidence gathered at the scene and the analytical/investigative skills of their detectives or investigators to solve the crime. Physical crime scene investigation, evaluation, and forensic (scientific) analysis often yield the information to suggest, if not to convict, the perpetrator(s). More in-depth investigation and analysis may provide the weight of evidence that will allow for a successful prosecution.

Investigative techniques and the types of analysis that can be applied to the investigations differ among the types of violent crime. The following sections provide a specific look at robbery, homicide, sex crimes, serial crimes, arson, and terrorism to see how analytical techniques strengthen the investigative and prosecutive processes.

ROBBERY

Robbery is the taking (or attempt to take) of something of value from another person by force or threat of force or violence (Federal Bureau of Investigation, 1992). Robbery is a crime of violence which is primarily motivated by a desire for profit.

From 1990 to 1991, the number of robberies in the United States rose by 7.6 percent, but a decrease of 2.2 percent was posted between 1991 and 1992 (Federal Bureau of Investigation, 1992 and 1993). The latter figure does not mean the number of robberies is headed permanently downward, only that 1992 figures failed to reach the high established in 1991.

Robberies increased overall by 24 percent between 1988 and 1992. The rate for convenience store robberies fell by 2 percent from 1988 to 1992 while the rate for bank robbery increased by 44 percent, the rate for commercial houses rose by 27 percent, and the rate for street robberies rose by 29 percent (Federal Bureau of Investigation, 1993).

The total estimated national loss from robbery in 1992 was $565 million. The clearance rate—cases in which arrests were made—was at 24 percent nationwide (Federal Bureau of Investigation, 1993).

Over half of the robberies reported in recent years have been committed on streets and highways, while about one-fifth occur in businesses and banks. The most frequently robbed locations within businesses are commercial houses—such as check-cashing establishments—followed by convenience stores. Residential robberies account for about one-tenth of the total of all robberies (Federal Bureau of Investigation, 1993).

Because robberies involve violence or the threat of violence, weapons, including firearms and knives or other cutting instruments, are often used. Firearms were used in about 40 percent of all robberies during 1992 (Federal Bureau of Investigation, 1993).

Small businesses (e.g., gas stations, liquor stores, and convenience stores) are the most frequent targets of armed robbery. These businesses are chosen by criminals on the basis of their locations, hours, small numbers of employees, and periods with low levels of customers. All-night businesses and those with late evening hours are particularly vulnerable.

An analysis of the attributes of those arrested for robbery during 1992 yields a "typical" robber of male (91.5 percent), black (61 percent), fifteen to twenty years old (37 percent). An analysis of temporal and location attributes would indicate that the robbery had the highest chance of occurring in December, along a street or highway, in a metropolitan area in the southern United States.

Street Robbery

Street robberies are often crimes of convenience involving little planning or forethought, which makes these crimes difficult to analyze or solve. Its perpetrators may cruise the streets looking for a potential victim and commit the crime after a quick assessment of the victim's weakness and the potential profit. These types of crime are almost impossible to predict or interdict unless a patrol car fortuitously arrives on the scene and apprehends the perpetrator.

Because these crimes are opportunistic, often unreported and unorganized, only through repetitive occurrences can an offender description or modus operandi generally be developed that could lead to the perpetrator's arrest. The locations of the robberies may give some clue to where the robber lives or works. A pattern of locations, times of day, days of the week, victim types, things stolen, weapons, words said to the victim, or a combination of these may emerge to give the police an opportunity to interdict a future attempted robbery. This information is pieced together by a criminal analyst who looks for the patterns and then develops a potential profile or scenario based on the materials.

Without positive identification of the perpetrator, police can use analysis to identify potentially dangerous areas for patrol deployment targeting which may interdict or even deter street-level robbery. This emphasis on location is effective when it is determined that a particular area is the scene of a higher than normal number of street robberies.

Factors which can be collected and analyzed include the following:

- the presence of nearby parks or wooded areas,
- the amount of lighting along the streets,
- a large number of dimly lighted alleyways nearby,
- the presence of bars and clubs with late hours that might disgorge befuddled customers who would be less able to resist robbers,
- the presence of abandoned buildings,
- nearby senior citizen housing, public housing, or college dormitories (all of which house potential victims), and
- all-night convenience stores or other businesses which would attract customers to the streets late at night.

In addition to its use as a basis for deploying personnel, this information may become part of a public awareness campaign to lessen the availability of victims to the roving robber. The data can also be used to encourage other governmental departments to remedy some factors, for example, fixing poor lighting and demolishing abandoned buildings.

Business Robbery

The robbery of small businesses accounts for about 20 percent of all robberies in recent years. These small businesses include gas stations, convenience stores, and "commercial houses" (nonbanking establishments which cash checks, provide cash for goods, etc.). Commercial house robberies have increased by 27 percent since 1988, while gas station robberies have increased by 7 percent over 1988 and convenience store robberies have declined by 2 percent (prior to 1992, they had experienced an increase of 10 percent) (Federal Bureau of Investigation, 1993).

Various means are used to rob small businesses. These can range from typical strong-arm tactics (when the activity cannot be witnessed by others) to closing-time demands for goods or money, to customer ruses (O'Hara and O'Hara, 1980, pp. 435–36).

Planning is required to choose a profitable business and to determine when it is best to approach the business. Some robbers "specialize" in particular types of stores (e.g., liquor stores, fast-food restaurants, or convenience stores), while others may rob in "waves," committing three or four robberies in one night and not robbing again for days, weeks, or months. The frequency of the robberies may be in proportion to the monetary needs of the perpetrators and a high frequency may indicate the possibility that the proceeds are supporting a narcotics habit.

Because business robberies, by nature, are a series of crimes (they generally do not garner enough profits to retire on, nor are they generally crimes of opportunity as street robberies are), there is usually a body of information gathered from the different incidents which can then be analyzed.

An example of the information is shown in Figure 4.1, Pattern Example. This information, when analyzed, allows you to predict the date and day of the week of the next robbery, as well as the modus operandi of the group doing the robberies.

In addition to pattern identification through multiple business robberies, varied investigative methods and analytical techniques can be used to support their investigation. Police could initially focus on the crime scene—was there any transference of materials by robbers such as fibers, hairs, fingerprints, footprints, or tire marks left behind?

An event flow chart could be made of the activities leading up to the robbery. A table showing the suspects and their opportunity to commit the crime could

Figure 4.1
Pattern Example

A series of robberies has taken place in San Francisco
on the following dates and at the following locations.
Patterns and breaks in patterns occur. An analyst
would arrive at conclusions about the robberies:
whether they were all perpetrated by the same group, or
if not, which were and how breaks in patterns could be
accounted for.

Robbery 1: McDonald's, Union Street, 4/2/93, at 9:15
p.m. Four armed males wearing masks and gloves entered
restaurant through service door in rear and demanded
money from all registers. Gave a black sports bag with
tan straps to manager to put cash in. The one male who
spoke may have been African-American. Told all
employees and customers to lie on the floor. Left
within 4 minutes.

Robbery 2: Pizzeria Uno, Market Street, 4/9/93, at
10:25 p.m. Three armed males wearing masks and gloves
entered restaurant through back door and demanded
money. Used a sports bag to put cash in. Told
employees (no customers present) to lie on the floor.
Left within 3 minutes.

Robbery 3: Wendy's, Embarcadero Plaza, 4/13/92, 9:30
p.m. Two armed African-American males entered
restaurant through front door and approached registers
demanding money. Wore bandannas across their faces.
Gave a paper bag to employee to put money in. One
seemed nervous and kept glancing toward the door.

Robbery 4: Brother's Pizza, Grand Street, 4/23/93,
9:50 p.m. Four armed males wearing masks entered
restaurant through front door and demanded money. Told
employees to put money in plastic bag. Hit manager in
the face with gun several times and rendered him
unconscious. Left in 5 minutes.

be developed. Financial analysis on suspects could be done to determine who
might have a need for cash.

All available information, organized and analyzed, will provide the investigators and prosecutors with leads, hypotheses about who committed the crime,
and, ultimately, the solution to the crime.

Bank Robberies

According to some experts, the most highly skilled criminals specialize in
bank robbery (O'Hara and O'Hara, 1980, p. 418). The number of bank robberies

increased by 44 percent between 1988 and 1992 (Federal Bureau of Investigation, 1993). Bank robberies are most often the work of professional criminals. Professional bank robbers gather information and plan robberies carefully so the maximum amount of cash or negotiable instruments will be on hand when the robbery occurs.

Because of their complexity and planning, bank robberies require thorough investigation. The study, or analysis, of modus operandi is of great importance in major robberies (Internal Association of Chiefs of Police, 1975).

The "typical" bank robber's preparation for a theft would include the following decisions:

- selecting a target (often a branch office or a small savings and loan)
- choosing a day (Wednesdays and Fridays are favored) and time (openings, closings, and lunch hours are preferred)
- wearing disguises (sunglasses and hats are most common, followed by masks and hoods)
- using weapons (firearms in the majority of cases)
- planning an operating method (time to accomplish, approach to bank personnel, ways to deal with staff and customers, if present)
- choosing an escape route and method (generally an accomplice with a common model getaway car, stolen, rented, or having incorrect plates)
- deciding the size of the group to commit the robbery (usually two but can be more) (O'Hara and O'Hara, 1980, pp. 419–21)

An activity flow chart depicting the typical actions leading up to a bank robbery is seen in Figure 4.2.

The investigation of bank robbery usually focuses on witness information/identification of robbers as known bank robberies, the vehicle/method used to escape, and/or the possibility of an inside accomplice.

The escape vehicle may be rented or stolen and these activities may provide clues. The robbers may have left fingerprints on the vehicle or may have left behind a traceable personal item. The weapons used in the robbery may give fingerprints of the robbers.

In addition, the way in which the robbery was performed may give clues to the perpetrators. The method of operation used in the robbery, including day and time of robbery, number of robbers, physical descriptions of robbers, words used to commit robbery (written or spoken), method used to subdue bank employees and customers (including binding types and methods), receptacle used for robbery proceeds, type of vehicle, and weapons used may provide leads in the case.

All relevant information can be employed to outline a modus operandi of the robbers, which is then shared with other law enforcement officers to alert them to the potential for similar crime in their area.

Figure 4.2
Activity Flow Chart—Bank Robbery

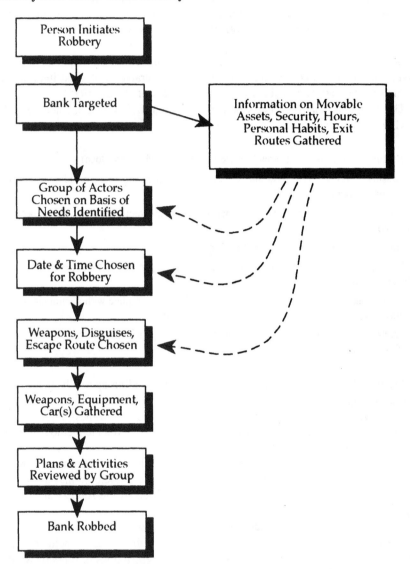

Several types of analytical techniques can be used in support of bank robbery investigation in addition to the crime analysis techniques discussed. Event flow charting, for example, can be used to detail the planning and execution of the robbery. Association analysis can be done to show the past and present relationships of all the conspirators involved.

The analysis of telephone records of one or more of the robbers can provide leads to other coconspirators and may provide probable cause for a wire intercept (Title III) on group members still at large. The subpoena and analysis of bank or personal records could show a sudden accumulation of wealth which might indicate the receipt of proceeds from the robbery.

In most jurisdictions, bank robberies are considered to be significant cases which warrant experienced investigators and priority attention. These cases also warrant analytical support.

HOMICIDE

The number of homicides in the United States reached an all-time high of 24,703 in 1991 and decreased to 23,760 in 1992 according to FBI *Uniform Crime Reports* (1992 and 1993). Homicides increased by 15 percent between 1988 and 1992.

Homicides occur most often in July and August and least often in February in the United States. The typical murder offender is male, black, and between the ages of fifteen and twenty-five. The typical murder victim is male, black, and between the ages of fifteen and thirty-five (Federal Bureau of Investigation, 1993). Overwhelmingly, white victims are killed by white offenders (83 percent) and black victims are killed by black offenders (93 percent) (Federal Bureau of Investigation, 1993).

Homicides are most often committed with firearms (70 percent), cutting instruments (14 percent), and blunt objects (5 percent). They most often involve people who are acquainted or related (78 percent of the identified offenders were known to the victim). Twenty-two percent of the homicides occurring in 1992 were related to some other felonious crime (Federal Bureau of Investigation, 1993).

While homicide generally has a high clearance rate (65 percent in 1992), the seriousness of the crime and its urgency have caused it to be the subject of many investigative techniques and advanced analysis. One reason for this has been the 32 percent increase (since 1988) in the number of murders committed with an unknown motive. Further, the number of juvenile gang-related murders—including drive-by shootings of innocent victims—has increased by 147 percent over that period.

The following investigative activities are required in a homicide:

1. recording the crime scene,

2. collecting physical evidence,

3. identifying the victim,

4. identifying the motive for the crime, and

5. interviewing witnesses and potential suspects. (Osterburg and Ward, 1992, pp. 511–13)

There is often much physical evidence available at the scene of the crime to be analyzed. Researchers note that the "characteristics of evidence and victims can reveal much about the murderer's intensity or planning, preparation and follow-through" (Burgess, Hartman, Ressler, Douglas, and McCormack, 1986, p. 252).

In spite of this, numerous homicides are unsolved for years. Some of these fall into the category of serial crimes; others are single crimes but have cloudy motivation which makes them difficult to solve.

Motivations for a homicide include revenge, anger, profit, interruption of the commission of another crime, sexual gratification, self-protection, mistaken identity, and removal of a witness to wrongdoing (Osterburg and Ward, 1992, pp. 514–18).

There are several analytical techniques used in working homicides, including criminal profiling, crime scene analysis, event flow analysis, and suspect tables. If profit is a possible motive, then the victim's and suspect's records should be analyzed to determine the potential for gain. Personal records could also provide documentation for motivations relating to quarrels or revenge. Some examples of the use of these techniques are shown in this chapter.

The Federal Bureau of Investigation has shown itself to be a leader in the area of violent crime investigation and analysis. It has established a National Center for the Analysis of Violent Crime (NCAVC) in Quantico, Virginia. At this center, it has pioneered work in the areas of crime scene analysis and the automated criminal profiling of homicides and sexual crimes. In this system, murders have been categorized in terms of motive, intent, number of victims, and type of victims.

An early example of the Bureau's homicide work was seen in 1982, when it was involved in a midwestern homicide. A twenty-five-year-old woman had allegedly been raped and murdered. The murder weapon, a hammer, had been left, washed, in the kitchen sink. The apartment had been ransacked and some jewelry was reported as missing. The local department had been unable to solve the crime and asked the FBI to participate.

Detailed crime scene analysis through photographs showed that there had been no struggle from the woman. The medical examiner stated that, in spite of the semiclothed manner in which the victim was left, there was no direct physical evidence of sexual assault.

The FBI agent/analyst reviewed the physical, crime scene, and psychological evidence to determine a profile of the victim and of the offender. He informed local police that the crime was a result of an argument with someone with whom the victim had been drinking. A sexual assault had been staged after the murder to give the appearance of a sexually motivated crime. The local police, after hearing the profiler's analysis of the crime, said, "You just told me the husband did it" (Douglas and Burgess, 1986, p. 13). The police reinterviewed the husband, giving him a polygraph test, which he failed. The husband admitted his guilt to the polygraph examiner.

The FBI's Violent Criminal Apprehension Program (VICAP) is a continuation of the original criminal profiling concept. It became operational in May 1985. VICAP is a nationwide data information center designed to collect, collate, and analyze specific crimes of violence. To do this, it requests the entry of data on solved and unsolved homicides, missing persons when foul play is suspected, and unidentified dead bodies (or body parts). State and local agencies are the sources of the data entered. By analyzing this information, VICAP staff determine whether similar pattern characteristics exist among cases in its system. This pattern (profile) identification is made by analyzing modus operandi, victimology, physical evidence, suspects' descriptions, and suspects' behavior patterns.

One product of a VICAP analysis is seen in Figure 4.3. This VICAP alert, which appeared in 1986, was the result of an analysis of three crimes connected with the perpetrator. On the basis of those crimes and the perpetrator's history, an alert was sent out in the hopes of helping local police identify similar unsolved homicides or sexual assaults which may have been done by this individual.

The profiling of murderers includes psychological profiling (determining what type of person a murderer is by his or her deeds) and criminal profiling (making a composite of the "typical" murderer). Psychological profiling is often the result of studying the characteristics of violators as a group. In 1986, for example, FBI and academic personnel published a report of a study on sexual homicide (Burgess, Hartman, Ressler, Douglas, and McCormack). In it, 36 sexual murderers, their behavior, and their experiences were analyzed, with particular emphasis on the role sadistic fantasies played in their murder acts. As a result, a "motivational model" of sexual murderers was constructed (see Figure 4.4). This model shows indicators of the potential for persons with certain types of behavior and background to be involved in sexual sadism or murder.

A system similar to VICAP was developed in the state of Washington under a grant from the National Institute of Justice: the Homicide Investigation and Tracking System (HITS). HITS is a data base which allows various types of data to be entered and analyzed. It supports the analysis of travel patterns, methods of operation, suspect descriptions, and chronological data.

In one case, HITS assisted in the identification of a suspect in a series of random killings in railroad yards. In another, two slayings in nearby counties were connected to potential suspects (Keppel and Weis, 1993).

Complementary systems are in use in other states, including California and New York. The Royal Canadian Mounted Police developed the Violent Crime Linkage Analysis System (VICLAS), based in part on the FBI's VICAP, which compares significant elements of each case and looks for similarities (Hill, 1992).

In Florida, the Manatee County Sheriff's Office has worked to develop indicators of potential family homicide with the idea of working with social ser-

Figure 4.3
VICAP Alert

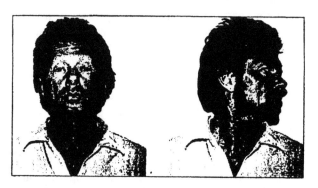

Benjamin Herbert Boyle

Race: Caucasian; DOB 7/22/43,
Hobart, OK; Height: 5'7";
Weight: 170 lbs; Hair: Red; Eyes:
Blue; Complexion: Fair; Build:
Muscular; SSAN 443-42-4965; FBI
No.: 405 757 EA8; Driver's License
No.: OK 443-42-4965
(Type: Chauffer).

Crime
Benjamin Herbert Boyle was
arrested on October 17, 1985, and has
since been in custody in Amarillo, TX,
charged with the murder of a white
female.

Background
Boyle was in the military from
August 1960 to August 1963, and was
discharged in Wheeler, IN. From 1969
to 1980, he indicated he lived in Colorado, where he owned an auto body
shop. He moved to Las Vegas, NV, in
February 1980, where he resided until
November 1981, during which time he
worked in an auto body shop. Another
move in November 1981, took him to
western Oklahoma. From that time
until his arrest in October 1985, he was
a truck driver for numerous trucking
companies, making both local and
cross-country hauls. During those
years, he lived in Oklahoma, Texas,
and Lousiana.

In addition to the murder charge in
Armadillo, Boyle was convicted of
attempted kidnapping in Colorado
Springs, CO, and a warrant has been
issued for his arrest in connection
with a rape in Colorado.

Modus Operandi
Described below is a crime connected
with Boyle.

On November 20, 1979, Boyle
attempted to kidnap a 28-year-old
white female as she was walking
along a residential area in Colorado
Springs, CO. He tried forcing her into
his personal automobile, but the
victim pulled a small knife from her
pocket, stabbed Boyle 5 times, and
fled. Boyle pleaded guilty to
attempted kidnapping and was given
a 5-year probated sentence.

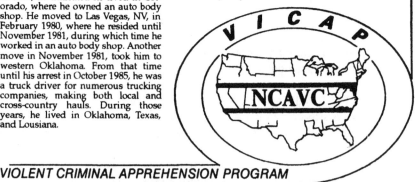

VIOLENT CRIMINAL APPREHENSION PROGRAM

Figure 4.4
Sexual Homicide—Motivational Model

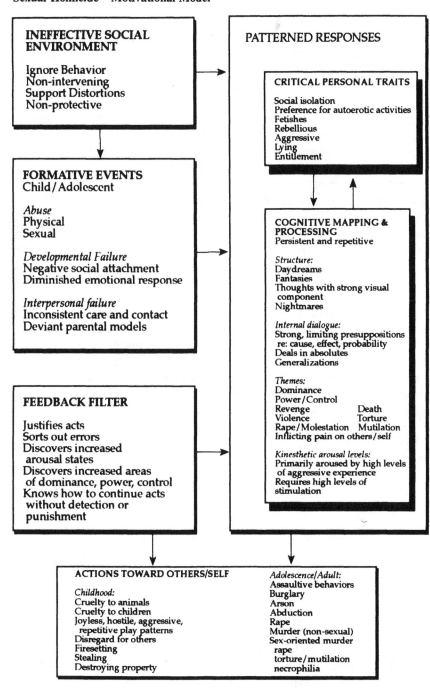

| INEFFECTIVE SOCIAL ENVIRONMENT | PATTERNED RESPONSES |

INEFFECTIVE SOCIAL ENVIRONMENT

Ignore Behavior
Non-intervening
Support Distortions
Non-protective

PATTERNED RESPONSES

CRITICAL PERSONAL TRAITS

Social isolation
Preference for autoerotic activities
Fetishes
Rebellious
Aggressive
Lying
Entitlement

FORMATIVE EVENTS
Child/Adolescent

Abuse
Physical
Sexual

Developmental Failure
Negative social attachment
Diminished emotional response

Interpersonal failure
Inconsistent care and contact
Deviant parental models

COGNITIVE MAPPING & PROCESSING
Persistent and repetitive

Structure:
Daydreams
Fantasies
Thoughts with strong visual component
Nightmares

Internal dialogue:
Strong, limiting presuppositions re: cause, effect, probability
Deals in absolutes
Generalizations

Themes:
Dominance
Power/Control
Revenge   Death
Violence   Torture
Rape/Molestation   Mutilation
Inflicting pain on others/self

Kinesthetic arousal levels:
Primarily aroused by high levels of aggressive experience
Requires high levels of stimulation

FEEDBACK FILTER

Justifies acts
Sorts out errors
Discovers increased arousal states
Discovers increased areas of dominance, power, control
Knows how to continue acts without detection or punishment

ACTIONS TOWARD OTHERS/SELF

Childhood:
Cruelty to animals
Cruelty to children
Joyless, hostile, aggressive, repetitive play patterns
Disregard for others
Firesetting
Stealing
Destroying property

Adolescence/Adult:
Assaultive behaviors
Burglary
Arson
Abduction
Rape
Murder (non-sexual)
Sex-oriented murder
 rape
 torture/mutilation
 necrophilia

Source: R.K. Ressler, A. W. Burgess, & J. E. Douglas, "Sexual Homicide Patterns and Motives," *Journal of Interpersonal Violence* (September 1986): p. 50.

vice agencies to implement prevention strategies. Some of the indicators are drug or alcohol use, previous threats against family members, previous violence against family members, a threatener who was previously a victim of violence, and previous contact with police about violence (Hagaman, Wells, Blau, and Wells, 1987).

The FBI also uses a criminal profile generating process (Figure 4.5) which can be adapted to other departments' work. It includes which data to collect and input, models, assessments, profiles, feedback, investigation, and apprehension. This information may or may not be computerized, depending upon its bulk. Requisite to this process is the use of analysis in developing the decision-process models, assessing the crime, and developing the profile.

Event flow charting can be used to depict the activities engaged in by the victim and the suspects leading up to the homicide and the suspects' activities after the homicide. This is an analytical technique which may produce further leads, may narrow (or widen) the suspect field, or may provide further details about the crime. One way to depict these activities is to create a multiline event flow chart with each line depicting a different suspect and the victim. The times and placement of the various players can then readily be compared during the time leading up to (and away from) the homicide.

Developing a suspect table is a fourth analytical method which can be applied to homicide investigations. Within a homicide case, the suspects are listed in a table format along with identifiers (social security numbers, criminal identification numbers, etc.). Their relationship to the victim, their possible motives for committing the homicide, and their opportunities to commit the homicide are shown in other columns of the table. This format provides an easy way of organizing the data when dealing with a large number of suspects and can help to eliminate potential suspects.

Unknown homicides provide a challenge to police departments around the world. The use of analysis in their investigation is critical.

SEX CRIMES

Sex crimes cover the range of indecent exposure to brutal sexual homicide. For the purpose of this chapter, we will focus on rape and sexual assault, pedophilia, and child pornography.

Only rape is reported in the *Uniform Crime Reports* as a distinct crime. Forcible rape is defined as "carnal knowledge of a female forcibly and against her will" and its reporting includes sexual assault (Federal Bureau of Investigation, 1993).

The reporting of forcible rape increased by 18 percent between 1988 and 1992. Two decades ago, rape was considered the least-reported violent crime, with four out of five rapes unreported. Rape occurs most often in July and August and least often in February in the United States. There was an increase

Figure 4.5
Criminal Profile Generating Process

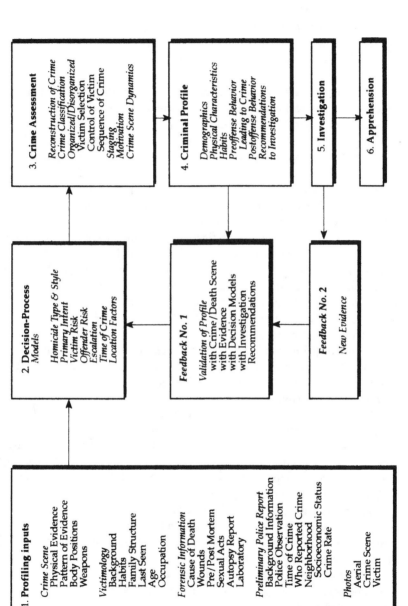

Source: John E. Douglas, Robert K. Ressler, Ann W. Burgess, and Carol R. Hartman, "Criminal Profiling from Crime Scene Analysis," *Behavioral Sciences and the Law,* Vol. 4, No. 4 (1986): p. 407.

of 2.3 percent reported between 1991 and 1992. Thirty-seven percent of the rapes reported in the country occurred in southern states (Federal Bureau of Investigation, 1993).

Child molestations are less frequently reported than rape. Children have been reported as being molested by immediate family members, by other relatives or family friends, or by strangers who may seduce them through promises and gifts.

In the case of rape or sexual assault/molestation, the investigation requires collection of physical evidence; sworn statements from witnesses, victims, and suspects; and records of the suspect(s).

It may be difficult to collect physical evidence in sexual crimes. Unless an examination of the victim has been done immediately after the incident, physical evidence of rape or molestation may be scarce. Also, the incident may have several crime scenes: where the victim met the perpetrator, where the crime occurred, and where the victim was left. The location of all of these sites may not be known to the victim or to police.

The most commonly used investigative technique in sex crimes cases is the interview of witnesses and interrogation of potential suspects. Preliminary interviews are done to get a physical description of the offender(s), the location(s) where the crime took place, the identification of possible witnesses, the circumstances leading up to the attack, and information on vehicles and weapons used (Osterburg and Ward, 1992, pp. 633–34). Follow-up interviews attempt to elicit more detail about the incident.

The goal of the investigation is to show that forced sexual relations occurred and to link the offender and victim to the location and activity of the crime (Osterburg and Ward, 1992, p. 638). The goal of analysis, then, would be to support those investigative aims.

While psychological and criminal profiling are major forms of analysis used in sex crimes, other traditional analytical methods can also be used. Sexual abuse incidents—rape, molestation, and so forth—are events which can be charted and subjected to event flow analysis. Analyzing several events in this manner may allow their ready comparison and result in the determination of a modus operandi for the perpetrator.

Conversation analysis or written text analysis may be key to constructing a profile of a sexual violator. Telephone calls, interaction with victims, letters written, and diaries can all give insight into the psychological makeup of the criminal. These can also reveal patterns in speech or writing which, when compared to other conversations or written materials, could indicate that one person is responsible for multiple offenses. It is not uncommon for sexual abusers to keep detailed records of their "conquests" in photographic and written form. These are often hidden in the suspect's living space and may require a thorough search of that area.

Rape

According to the FBI's *Crime Classification Manual,* there are four primary types of rapists:

* power-reassurance (fantasy-driven),
* exploitative (predatory),
* anger (aggression—misogynist), and
* sadistic (violent). (1992, pp. 194–95)

In addition, there is a "sexual ritual" which occurs in rapes and sexual assaults which is not a modus operandi, but which fills a need of the offender (Douglas et al., 1992, p. 196).

Criminal profiling of a rapist was done in a study by FBI personnel and published in the *American Journal of Psychiatry.* The study analyzed data pertaining to twelve rapes and rape-murders committed by one male adolescent over a four-year period (Ressler, Burgess, and Douglas, 1983, p. 24). This study included profiles of the victims, an analysis of the criminal incidents, interaction between the victims and the offender, and his behavior after the five rape incidents which included murders.

This analysis enabled them to see a pattern of escalating violence by the offender over the period of the rapes (five of the last six resulted in murder) in which he progressed from last-minute murder to premeditated murder (Ressler, Burgess, and Douglas, 1983, p. 25). Moreover, this and other analysis of rape incidents showed that rape and attempted rape are chronic and repetitive crimes. Many rapists who are caught for one act have committed several previous acts for which they were not caught (Ressler, Burgess, and Douglas, 1983). This type of information is important in rape investigations, as is the fact that rapists have a propensity for increasing violence toward their victims.

Analytical techniques which can assist rape investigations include psychological profiling, event flow analysis, conversation analysis, and association analysis. Information from the crime scene and victim information about the perpetrator should provide enough data to develop composite psychological profiles of rapists. After investigating hundreds of rape cases, Hazelwood and Burgess classified rapists as "selfish" or "pseudo-unselfish" and then went on to delineate six types of rapists: the power reassurance rapist, the power assertive rapist, the anger retaliatory rapist, the anger excitation rapist, the opportunistic rapist, and the gang rapist (1987, pp. 170–82).

According to Hazelwood and Burgess, the most common type of rapist is the "power reassurance rapist." He commits the rape to reinforce his power and control over women. This type of rapist often picks his victims in advance and engages in the fantasy that they are his willing conquests. He may apologize afterward, even calling the victim several days after the attack. If this attempt is unsuccessful, he may move on and find another victim that same day. He may keep detailed records of his victims (1987, p. 177).

One example of the use of analysis in a rape case was in Amherst, New York (a suburb of Buffalo). Investigators gathered information on the rapes of six females and the rape and murder of another female, to look for similarities. They produced an analytical bulletin, "Death of a Jogger," about the rapes to alert police officers around the area. The rapes occurred between 1986 and 1990, during the summer, and all occurred outdoors on a bicycle/exercise path or frequently used neighborhood shortcut (Amherst Police Department, undated). The bulletin listed case similarities (use of garrote, attack from behind, taping of victims, etc.) and a subject description. One similarity shown was the verbiage used by the attacker to threaten and direct the victim. The wide dissemination of this bulletin allowed the rapist to be caught.

Child Molestation

The investigation of child molestation is even more delicate than that of rape since the children may not be aware of what was done to them, that it is illegal, or how to talk about it. Children may also develop psychological problems after a molestation and may believe that they did something wrong, that it was their fault they were molested. Therefore, great care is necessary in the investigation, particularly when interviewing or relying upon the testimony of victims or juvenile witnesses.

As in adult rape and sexual assault, crime scene evidence and information about the perpetrator are of great importance. Physical evidence analysis is the first step toward solving a child molestation case. The second step is careful interviewing of the victim(s) and others who may have knowledge of the molestation or of the opportunity for molestation.

Those who prefer to engage in sexual acts with children are known as pedophiles. Kenneth Lanning, of the FBI, compiled extensive data on child molestation and pedophiles. Some of this was published in *Child Molesters: A Behavioral Analysis* (1986) and in *Child Sex Rings: A Behavioral Analysis* (1989). In the former, Lanning provides a listing of pedophile characteristics (Figure 4.6), which can be used as by investigators and analysts to compare with suspects' characteristics.

Pedophiles can limit their activity to one or two available children (sons or daughters, nieces or nephews, neighbors, etc.) or they can organize a ring of children who will not only fulfill their personal needs but be used to fill the needs of other pedophiles through photographs, videotapes, correspondence, or actual meetings. These are called child sex rings.

A profile of multidimensional child sex rings shows them as including multiple young victims (as young as 2 to 6 years old), numerous offenders (nearly half of whom are female), use of fear as a controlling tactic, bizarre or ritualistic activity, and multidimensional motivation (Lanning, 1989, pp. 17–19).

Figure 4.6
Pedophile Indicators

Background of sexual abuse

Limited social contact as teenager

Premature separation from military

Frequent, unexpected moves

Over 25, single and never married

Excessive interest in children

Limited peer relationships

Views children idealistically

Skilled at identifying vulnerable potential
            victims

Identifies with children

Has hobbies which attract children

Shows sexually explicit material to children

Photographs children

Collects child erotica or child pornography

Source: Kenneth Lanning, *Child Molesters: A Behavioral Analysis*, Washington, D.C.: National Center for Missing Children (1986): p. 13.

This book also includes a profile of historical child sex rings which shows that they include male offenders who are preferential child molesters and generally have male victims, are sexually motivated, have collections of child erotica and pornography, and exert control over their victims through seduction (Lanning, 1989, p. 11). These profiles are the products of both psychological and criminal profiling.

In addition to providing a picture of what to look for in sexual abuse of children, profiles help to identify the best person to approach for evidence. In a multidimensional child sex ring, for example, the victim who has gotten through the abuse but wants to protect younger children just coming in to the pattern is more likely to provide evidence against the abusers (Lanning, 1989).

Association analysis is another technique which can be adapted to some types of sex crimes. Child sex rings, in particular, can be charted to show the connections among suspects and victims.

Child Pornography

Child pornography can be viewed as a substitute for actually engaging in sexual activities with children or can be an extension of pedophile activity. Pedophiles always have a collection of child pornography, from commercial as well as private sources. The pedophile keeps photographs of his child sexual partners as mementos through which he can relive his actions. These photographs, along with letters and other memorabilia, can be used as evidence against the pedophile. Pornographic records, along with other records (personal phone books, travel records, etc.), may be of use in reconstructing the pedophile's illegal career.

In reverse sting situations, where the police arrange to sell child pornography or solicit sexual liaisons, the conversations, correspondence, or computer contact they have with the suspect can be significant in the prosecution of the case. These can be analyzed to provide a view of the ongoing nature of the defendant's participation in such activity and the degree of this involvement.

The analyses of criminal incidents have application to other cases as they allow for the development of indicators, profiles, and violation-specific investigative techniques. The information relayed in training and intelligence conferences is often the result of an analysis of what occurred in a case or set of cases that is then applied to a broader spectrum of investigations.

SERIAL CRIMES

Serial crime is the repetitive violation of criminal law over a period of time and often over a multijurisdictional geographic area. This is most often seen in homicides, rapes, and sexually motivated homicides.

The investigation of serial crime involves detailed evidence gathering, comparison, and analysis. Most of what we know today about serial killers is based on that process, and the models given earlier in this chapter are those used to help determine whether a crime is part of a series of similar incidents.

One of the telltale signs of a serial murderer, according to Douglas and Munn, is that the violent, repetitive offender often leaves a "calling card" or signature on the crime (1992, pp. 2–3). This signature does not relate to what is needed to complete the crime (which may change over time and circumstance), but is constant and is a reflection of the perpetrator's style. One example of this would be a pattern of wounds inflicted upon bodies after death. These wounds are not necessary to kill a person but reflect a psychological need of the perpetrator.

In serial crime it is important to remember that the perpetrator's method of operation can change over time as he gains more experience in the act and/or needs new levels of violence or activity to feed the psychological drive to commit the act. In this way, a series of rapes may evolve into a series of sexually motivated homicides.

The investigative steps used in homicide and rape investigations also apply to serial homicide and rape investigations. The difference is that there is more evidence from which to draw conclusions and there is some knowledge—at a certain point in the series—that the perpetrator is killing from a psychological motivation, rather than for profit or for revenge.

The use of analysis is a requirement in serial crime investigation. The factors of each incident must be carefully compared to determine similarities and differences (mindful of evolving modus operandi). All records available should be gathered and analyzed. Statements from witnesses, relatives, and friends must be cross-referenced and analyzed.

The best-known analytical method in serial crime investigation is the psychological profile. Figure 4.4 gives an outline of motivation for sexual homicide. Figure 4.7 gives a set of indicators of a sexual homicide suspect. This is used by collecting information on potential suspects and comparing it to the indicators on the left side of the page. These indicators, or characteristics, can be used to compare the "model" serial homicide suspect to actual suspects in a case to determine the actual suspect who most closely matches the "model" characteristics. In his recent book, *Whoever Fights Monsters,* Robert Ressler recounts case after case with killers who are psychologically motivated. He contends that many come from similarly dysfunctional families and that the seeds of their abusive adult behavior were sown on a common field (Ressler and Schachtman, 1992, p. 76).

A second analytical process—analyzing travel records—can also be key to an investigation of serial crime which is believed to have occurred over more than one jurisdiction. These records can include travel diaries, hotel receipts, gas receipts, toll receipts, bank card records of purchases, and collect or calling card calls from other cities.

In the investigation of serial murderer Ted Bundy, his travels were documented and entered in a timeline (chronological event listing) by the Multi-agency Investigative Team headed by the FBI. This showed the vehicles Bundy drove, dates and locations of gas sales, hotel stays, plane trips, car repairs, vehicle rentals, and medical treatments, as well as school and work activities (Federal Bureau of Investigation, 1992).

By reviewing this information, the Investigative Team was able to place Bundy in the locations of abductions and homicides in Washington, Oregon, Utah, Colorado, Idaho, and Florida.

Some serial crime investigations require that numerous analytical products be prepared. In another serial homicide case, MAGLOCLEN worked with the New Castle County (Delaware) Police Department and the Delaware State Police after they requested assistance. The analytical unit prepared a chronological summary (event flow chart) of the suspect's activities, diagrams depicting where the victims' bodies were found, a comparison of the victims' wounds, a map indicating the suspect's travels and the geographic relationship of his home, the victims' homes, the locations where the victims were last seen, and the locations where their bodies were found. A diagram of the suspect's van was also prepared. These diagrams were used during preparation of the prosecutor's case and in

Figure 4.7
Serial Homicide Indicators/Suspects Table

Indicators *	Suspects 1	Suspects 2
Caucasian		
Eldest Son		
Bright Intelligence		
Average (or better) socio-economic background		
Family History		
Criminal Problems		
Psychiatric Problems		
Alcohol Abuse		
Sexual Abuse		
Father Left Home by Age 12		
Unstable Family Residence		
Fair to Poor Academic Record		
Destruction of Property		
Fire Setting		
Cruelty to Children		
Assaultive to Adults		
Poor Body Image		
Chronic Lying		
Isolation as Child, Adolescent and Adult		

Source: A. W. Burgess, C. R. Hartman, R. K. Ressler, J. E. Douglas, and A. McCormack, ''Sexual Homicide: A Motivational Model,'' *Journal of Interpersonal Violence,* Vol. 1, No. 3: pp. 42–45.

the trial. The suspect was sentenced to two life terms for the murder of two females. He requested the death penalty and was executed in 1992.

Traditional analytical products, including association analysis, event flow analysis, activity flow analysis, telephone record analysis, and visual investigative analysis, can support serial crime investigations. A flow chart of a serial murderer's activities is shown in Figure 4.8.

One aspect of serial crime that has become paramount in some investigators' minds is the need for centralized collection and analysis of investigative data. To this end, the FBI has recently recommended that all serial homicides be coordinated through the VICAP data base in cases that

- involve abduction
- are random, appear motiveless
- are sexually motivated
- have missing persons and suspicion of foul play
- have unidentified dead bodies where the cause of death is unknown.

While state-level systems for crime identification and analysis are somewhat effective, the FBI believes a national system is best as it can gather and analyze information across a broader range of jurisdictions.

ARSON

Arson is the "willful or malicious burning or attempt to burn" of a building, vehicle, aircraft, or personal property belonging to another (Federal Bureau of Investigation, 1992). The motives behind arson may range from fraud to intimidation, revenge, or attention seeking to personal psychological gratification, to attempting to hide a crime.

The FBI reported 102,009 arsons nationwide in 1991, but that figure is low since it represents agencies reporting, which were 71 percent of all agencies in the United States. Thirty-two percent of all arsons reported occurred in residential structures, 27 percent in mobile conveyances (predominantly automobiles), and 20 percent in other property (e.g., crops, timber) (Federal Bureau of Investigation, 1993).

The 1992 clearance rate (cases with arrests made) for arson was 17 percent, with juveniles (under 18) responsible for 40 percent of the clearances. White males comprised 87 percent of all arson arrestees (Federal Bureau of Investigation, 1993). According to Osterberg and Ward, the conviction rate for arson is only 1 to 2 percent, which is a result of the limited number of trained investigators (1992).

The keys to an arson investigation are proving that a fire did occur, that its origins were intentional (willful or malicious), that a motive existed for the arson, and that there is sufficient proof against the defendant.

Some of the difficulties facing an arson investigation relate to the fire's ability

Figure 4.8
Event Flow Chart—John Wayne Gacy, Serial Murderer

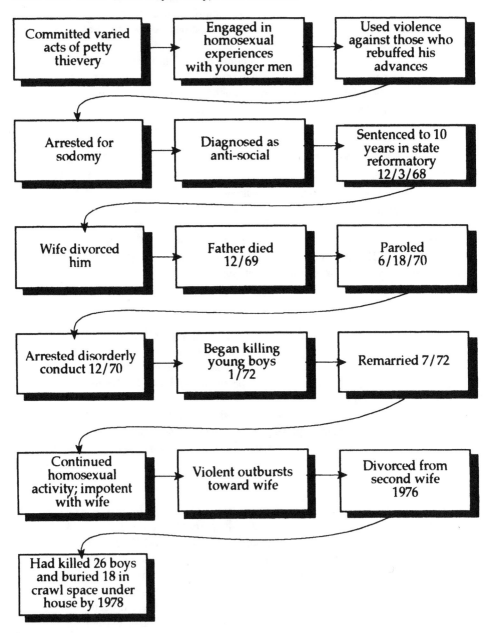

Source: Facts from Donald J. Sears, *To Kill Again.* Wilmington, DE: Scholarly Resources, 1991.

to consume evidence that is proof of intentional fire, the further potential of the destruction of evidence by efforts made to put out the fire, weather (extreme hot or cold) problems, and ability to use a time-release device to start the fire while the arsonist is covered by an alibi elsewhere (Osterburg and Ward, 1992).

The FBI, in its *Crime Classification Manual,* lists several types of arson:

- vandalism-motivated arson,
- excitement-motivated arson,
- revenge-motivated arson,
- crime concealment–motivated arson,
- profit-motivated arson,
- extremist-motivated arson,
- serial arson,
- spree arson, and
- mass arson. (1992, pp. 163, 164)

Arson has been used by organized crime figures to collect insurance money. In 1965, Joseph Migliazza, of Easton, Pennsylvania, ostensibly paid $5,000 to an arsonist to burn down his restaurant, the Stagecoach, in Easton so he could collect $90,000 insurance. He told this plan to an organized crime associate to show how he was going to repay a $12,000 gambling debt. The restaurant burned, Migliazza collected the insurance money, and no criminal charges resulted from the incident (Pennsylvania Crime Commission, 1980).

In another example of arson fraud, an individual purchased a house for $171,000 and burned it down nine months later. He claimed that a number of expensive items, including a luxury car, had been burned in the fire, but several items, including the car, were found in self-storage bins by the police. He was convicted and sentenced to eight years in prison (Federal Bureau of Investigation, 1992).

The physical evidence at the fire may indicate whether the fire was deliberately set. Burn patterns, levels of destruction in various portions, and evidence of accelerant and ignition devices all provide graphic evidence. The computer-aided drawing capability of the analytical unit can assist the crime scene investigators in preparing diagrams showing the location of the point of origin of the fire, the location of burn patterns, and the locations of evidence found, including ignition devices, fingerprints, and footprints.

The motivation for the arson, however, can seldom be ascertained by the physical evidence unless the fire was set for vandalism purposes by a person with little experience who left evidence such as fingerprints or footprints behind.

The investigation of a more sophisticated arson requires a detailed look at the possible motivation behind the fire and at the target of the fire. These can indicate who perpetrated the arson.

When a suspicious fire occurs, investigators should gather information on the financial condition of the owner of the property including loans, bank balances, and other possible sources of debts (gambling, etc.). This information should be analyzed to determine whether the owner was in need of substantial funds. The possibility of hidden ownership of the property should not be overlooked.

Insurance policies should be reviewed to determine whether any were recently purchased or expanded to give greater return when a fire occurred. This could be an indicator of arson fraud.

Other crimes such as homicide, larceny, and embezzlement may have been committed when an arson occurred. The arson provided a cover for the crime or destroyed evidence of the crime (such as records).

Analytical techniques used in arson investigation can be dependent upon the type of motivation for the arson. In all cases, an event flow chart showing the activities leading up to the arson and the arson can be produced. Another analytical product is a suspect chart, where the suspects, their possible motivation, and their opportunity to commit the crime are shown.

Arson for fraudulent purposes requires the analysis of various financial and business/personal records. Indications of occurrence of other crimes may also arise through a review of the individual's business records.

If the arson has involved a conspiracy with a hired arsonist, then an association chart showing the connections between the paid arsonist and the owner or person benefiting from the arson may be an appropriate analytical product. The analysis of telephone records would uncover these connections. An analysis of checking account records could uncover large cash withdrawals which could indicate payments to a hired arsonist.

Criminal investigative analysis—the comparing of suspects to analytically derived psychological overviews of arsonists—should be done particularly when a psychological motivation such as pyromania is possible. A psychoeconomic profile of an arsonist is shown in Figure 4.9.

Serial Arson

Serial arsonists are also called "firesetters." They often randomly choose targets which are targets of opportunity rather than targets of revenge.

Serial arsonists fall into two categories: those who commit arson close to their homes, who are often less educated and leave more evidence at the scene, and those who travel more widely to commit their arsons and are organized, use more sophisticated devices, and leave little to no evidence at the scene.

The Federal Bureau of Alcohol, Tobacco and Firearms and the Federal Bureau of Investigation have compiled psychological characteristics of serial arsonists and use those to compare to serial arson cases to assist local agencies in determining suspects. In doing this, they have

- identified common characteristics of serial arsons,
- looked at serial arson motives,

Figure 4.9
Profile of an Arsonist

          Male

          Not Married

          Not Well Educated

          Employed as Blue Collar Worker

          Renter of Property

          Low Socio-Economic Status

          Has Police or Fire Department
               Contact

Source: Adapted from J. E. Douglas, A. W. Burgess, A. G. Burgess, and R. K. Ressler, *Pocket Guide to the Crime Classification Manual*, New York: Lexington Books, 1992: pp. 63–64.

- looked at modus operandi used by serial arsonists,
- identified what common backgrounds serial arsonists may have, and
- developed a computer system based on this knowledge. (Icove and Horbert, 1990)

This is a form of criminal investigative analysis.

In one example of a serial arsonist, an analytical data base called the Advanced Serial Case Management System played an important role. The case had a task force of 150 state, local, county, and federal officers working on as many as 113 fires which had been set in a four-county area around Seattle, Washington. The data base was used to manage the information, keeping track of all the leads that each investigator followed, thus reducing duplication of effort. The data base also allowed investigators to pinpoint suspect, motives, and patterns by linking pieces of related data (*Law Enforcement News,* 4/30/93).

The data base gave investigators an overview of the perpetrator's modus operandi, including the days he set fires, buildings he preferred to fire and the time of day he set fires. Shortly after the composite was developed and widely released, information provided by his family led to the perpetrator's arrest (*Law Enforcement News*, 4/30/93).

TERRORISM

Terrorism has become a serious worldwide problem. While terrorism has existed for centuries, it is in the past 25 years that it has blossomed as a significant threat to the populace. Terroristic activity has included the massacre of Israeli athletes at the 1972 Munich Olympics, airplane hijackings, letter bombs, armed robberies, assassinations, and large-scale bombings such as the bombing of Pan American Flight 103 in 1988 and the World Trade Center bombing in February 1993.

Terrorism has been defined as "the unlawful use of force or violence against persons or property to intimidate or coerce a government, the civilian population, or any segment thereof, in furtherance of political or social objectives" (Federal Bureau of Investigation, 1992, p. i).

Terrorism is used to coerce policy change by drawing attention to a group (generally the perpetrators of the terroristic act) which espouses a certain political ideology. Public fear is key to the psychology of terrorism. Because the terroristic act is often unpreventable and is done in a public setting, innocent bystanders may be injured or killed. Terrorists may consider themselves "guerrilla" soldiers in a war. The difference is that guerrillas attack regular military forces, while terrorists often kill innocent civilians or put their lives in danger.

During the 1980s, "narcoterrorism" became a factor in the efforts to control the sale and distribution of controlled dangerous substances, particularly cocaine. Within Colombia, South America, where many cocaine processing plants are located and Colombian cartels are responsible for enormous cocaine distribution networks, numerous judges and public officials who opposed the drug trade were killed by narcoterrorists. At one point, there was even some concern that stepped-up antinarcotics efforts by U.S. law enforcement officials might lead to rash of assassinations in America.

There are three classifications into which terrorism has been broken down: domestic, transnational, and state-sponsored. Domestic terrorism is committed by terrorists operating within their own country against their own people. Transnational terrorism is international terroristic acts perpetrated by nonstate actors. State-sponsored terrorism is recruitment, financing, and directing of terrorist acts against nations or groups by nations.

Bombings and attempted bombings form the majority of terroristic acts that occurred in the United States during the past decade.

The terroristic activities require both proactive and reactive investigation. Large police departments in the United States, particularly those of Washington, D.C., and New York City, may have units specifically assigned to collecting and analyzing information on the individuals, locations, and activities of known terroristic groups as well as on groups or individuals suspected of being aligned with terrorists. Within these cities are locations (national monuments, international embassies, etc.) that are common targets for terrorism.

At the national level in the United States, the Federal Bureau of Investigation is responsible for investigating domestic terroristic activities. A 1992 publication, *Terrorism in the United States 1991,* was published by its Terrorist Research and Analytical Center, Counterterrorism Section, Intelligence Division. This publication is an analysis of the terroristic incidents that occurred from 1987 through 1991 and includes a threat analysis of domestic and international groups operating in the United States. Key to the investigation of terrorism are gathering, analysis, and sharing of information. One significant change in the operating procedures for the Olympic Games resulted from the terroristic activity at the 1972 games. It has been reported that there had been a warning issued by the international agency, INTERPOL, of possible terrorist activity at the 1972 games, but that the warning was ignored (Rackmill, 1992).

Now security is a significant part of the planning process. Investigators and analysts from major law enforcement agencies are assigned to the task of collecting data on potentially threatening groups or individuals and preparing threat assessments on the vulnerability of the various aspects of the Olympics. These efforts, usually in the form of multiagency task forces, have also been brought into play for other significant events such as the Pan Am Games and major celebrations.

Recent attention has also been given in the United States to the activities of groups now considered domestic terrorist groups including Skinheads, the White Aryan Resistance, and the Ku Klux Klan. These groups were considered by some experts to be the primary white criminal street gangs in the United States in 1993 and were responsible for much of the white street gang violence in some areas. These gangs are ideological racist gangs, rather than profit-motivated gangs. They resort to violence to further that ideology. Because of their domestic locale and the availability of weaponry, these gangs can pose a threat to various activities within the United States.

Analytical Applications

The types of analytical products which can be used in the investigation of terroristic activities depend on the proactive or reactive nature of the investigation.

Proactive terrorist investigations involve intelligence gathering, analysis, and assessment production. Because of the unpredictable nature of terrorism, it is imperative that an information gathering and analysis effort be maintained on all known groups at all times.

The types of information gathered fall under several general headings: group information, financial information, personnel data, and locational data. The group information includes the ideology of the group (political or social beliefs), the history of the group, and dates significant to group (may be dates of significance in the group's home nation, or dates upon which former leaders have been killed).

Financial information includes the sources of funds, which can include other suspected crimes such as armed robberies. The sources of funds can be a key to the ideology of the group as well. A sudden influx of funding into the group may be an indicator of preparation for a terroristic activity.

Personnel data for the group include its members and former members (possible sources of financing), its leadership (and changes therein), the capabilities of those members (weapons expertise, electronics expertise, etc.), and any personal connections between its members and other groups of similar or other ideologies.

Locational data can include the locations of the group's headquarters, "safe" houses (often rural farmhouses where people can hide from police), and "stash" houses (where weapons, bomb parts, or other supplies are kept; may be near location to be attacked and are often found in self-storage concerns in recent years), and so on.

Each of these pieces of information must be collected and analyzed to develop assessments of the potential threat to life and property posed to a jurisdiction by the groups' activities. As a result of these threat assessments, actions may be taken to increase security for events, individuals, or places. Information on groups has also led to arrests of members and seizures of large quantities of weapons and explosives that have prevented acts of terrorism.

Reactive terrorism investigations mirror the general investigative process, on one hand, but also benefit from the proactive assessments of the groups which are available.

One of the first questions asked after a terroristic event is, Who was responsible for the act? While some groups make their involvement known (e.g., through telephone calls taking credit or through ideological flyers left at the scene) as a way of publicizing their cause, others do not. Having an intelligence data base on terroristic groups and their affiliations may enable the investigators to answer that question and thus lead to the perpetrators of the act.

Terroristic acts differ from many other violent crimes in their complexity and planning. They often require significant financing, numbers of participants, and coordination. The investigation of the act unravels these activities and shows connections between the group and its members and other activities or groups. Each piece of data must be carefully collected and analyzed to give the investigators the most complete picture of the activity possible.

While intelligence gathering becomes part of the investigative process in reactive terrorism cases, more tactical analytical products are also involved. These can include the analysis of telephone and bank records of the group and/or its members, the charting of the associations of group members, and the chronological charting of the events leading up to the terroristic act. The complexity of these cases may require numerous analytical products to assist in developing further leads in the case and presenting the case in court.

CONCLUSIONS

Violent crime investigation has always been a priority for law enforcement. Homicides, for example, do not occur often in comparison to other crimes yet are immediately investigated and have the highest clearance rate of any crime committed. While the investigation of violent crime has always been supported by forensic analysis (bullet and gun comparisons, autopsies, and more recently DNA testing), its use of criminal analytical techniques has been less extensive.

Both crime and intelligence/investigative analytical techniques can be used to further violent crime investigation. This chapter has given a brief look at some of the ways violent crime investigation can benefit from the use of analysis.

CHAPTER V

Organized Crime Applications

In the past, organized crime and intelligence units have included analysts or the analytical function more often than narcotics or other investigative units. Many of the applications of analysis which have been developed spring from its uses in the organized crime setting. This chapter provides an overview of analytical applications to organized crime—traditional and nontraditional—investigations, corruption, and RICO investigations as well as the use of organized crime intelligence systems.

INTRODUCTION

It is no accident that the analytical function found its primary home in organized crime/intelligence units. Its initial techniques and assignments supported organized crime investigations and intelligence gathering. The 1967 *Task Force Report: Organized Crime* counseled that "organized crime units should have . . . one or more investigators who are trained and competent intelligence analysts" (President's Commission on Law Enforcement and Administration of Justice, 1967, p. 20). The revised edition of the *Basic Elements of Intelligence* (the early Bible of analysis) was prepared for the Organized Crime Desk of the Law Enforcement Assistance Administration (the Federal LEAA), now called the Bureau of Justice Assistance (BJA). *Basic Elements* began its discussion with the following comment: "An effective intelligence unit is one of the most important weapons the police department has in its fight against crime and especially against those criminals who, by organizing, seek to maximize their illegal gain. . . .The unit provides the chief of the department with an analysis of what is known of the particular group under review" (Harris, 1976, p. 1).

Likewise, Ianni had noted that intelligence and analysis, rather than individual case development, could dramatically improve the ability of the criminal justice system to study organized crime (1974, pp. 330–31).

History of Organized Crime Units

Decades earlier, the investigation of organized crime activity in the United States began. In the 1920s, the New York City Police Department's "Radical Squad" included a "Gangster Squad" (Bouza, 1976). The Radical Squad was the successor of the Radical Bureau, formed in 1912, which had changed its name to the Neutrality Squad in 1915. The Gangster Squad was assigned to inquire into the activities of criminal gangs and died with the end of Prohibition (Bouza, 1976). Organized crime groups, however, did not die. They used the huge sums of money they had amassed to organize rackets and infiltrate legitimate businesses (Harris, 1976).

In 1924, the Federal Bureau of Investigation was initiated within the United States Department of Justice, and by the time of Prohibition the Department of the Treasury was investigating Al Capone and his gangster cohorts in Chicago and other major American cities.

In the 1950s, the Justice Department, spurred by the Kefauver hearings (Special Committee to Investigate Organized Crime in Interstate Commerce, U.S. Senate, 1951), formed an Organized Crime and Racketeering Section. In 1956, the Law Enforcement Intelligence Unit (LEIU, a private organization of intelligence officers from law enforcement member agencies within the United States) was formed. In 1957, the famed Appalachin conference of Mafia bosses was held in upstate New York.

During the early 1960s, numerous investigations into organized crime occurred. As Attorney General of the United States, the late Robert F. Kennedy began an attack on the group known as the Cosa Nostra. The President's Commission on Law Enforcement and the Administration of Justice reported that cities should have organized crime units to collect information on criminal cartels and uncover organized criminal activity (1967).

Also during the 1960s, intelligence units were concerned with a broad range of "subversive" groups on the American scene from communists to pacifists, from the John Birch Society to the Students for a Democratic Society, from the Ku Klux Klan to the Black Nationalists. It was as a result of some agencies' zealousness in obtaining information on these groups that many intelligence systems were shut down or stymied. The line between engaging in potentially criminal activity and engaging in free speech became blurred in some police departments' collective minds; information was collected and maintained on persons who had done nothing more harmful than participating in a peace march.

During the 1970s, organized crime investigation continued. Special investigative and prosecutive units, including crime commissions, were created. The Mafia was the primary focal point of these investigative bodies, encouraged by violence which captured public attention, including the assassination of crime boss Carmine Galante on July 12, 1979. Organizations such as the Pennsylvania Crime Commission and the California Department of Justice were publicly reporting on organized crime activity in various businesses, including the pizza, pornography, and garment industries.

The beginning of the 1980s saw a shift in some agencies' focus relative to organized crime. The Pennsylvania Crime Commission, for example, created headlines when it proclaimed, "There's more to organized crime than the Cosa Nostra." Its *Decade of Organized Crime: 1980 Report* included outlaw motorcycle gangs, theft rings, the "Greek Mob," and the K&A (Kensington and Allegheny, a street corner in Philadelphia) Gang. The Bureau of Alcohol, Tobacco and Firearms was focusing on outlaw motorcycle gangs. A shift away from the preoccupation with La Cosa Nostra began. The 1980s brought several important forces to bear on organized crime. First, the investigation and prosecution by federal agencies of Cosa Nostra leaders was stepped up. Successful prosecutions of several La Cosa Nostra family bosses occurred. Public awareness was heightened as a result of public reports and televised reports on organized crime.

While these investigations and prosecutions continued into the 1990s, some of the organized crime focus has shifted in the past decade as a result of the emergence of the narcotics industry and its nontraditional distribution syndicates. Different organized crime paradigms have arisen. Organized crime is no longer viewed as the exclusive territory of men of Sicilian ancestry. Ethnic-based organized crime groups included in the 1990 Pennsylvania Crime Commission report, for example, included Sicilians, Colombians, Dominicans, Jamaicans, Puerto Ricans, Cubans, outlaw motorcycle gangs, Chinese triads and tongs, Vietnamese street gangs, and African-American groups (1991). This shift toward nontraditional organized crime group activity requires less narrow definitions of organized crime structure and models. Analysts can play a role in uncovering the new and varied faces of organized crime.

Definitions

Organized crime has been described as "an organization that produces or supplies those (illegal) goods and services (which the public demands), and corrupt public officials who protect such individuals for their own profit or gain" (Ianni, 1974, p. 17); and as an organization which seeks "to gain money and power without regard for law by utilizing economic and physical force, public and private corruption, in an extension of the free enterprise system" (quoted by Harris, 1976, p. 2, from Messick and Goldblatt, 1972); or as including characteristics of corruption, violence, sophistication, continuity, structure, discipline, multiple enterprises, legitimate business, and bonding (Maltz, 1990).

These definitions have some common threads: violence, corruption, and organization (structure). Some argue that the distinction between organized crime and opportunistic crime is seen in the continuity of organized crime. A spate of descriptions including "syndicates," "cartels," and "enterprises" has arisen to cover groups not clearly viewed as "organized crime."

Although the definitions of organized crime vary, there was a general agreement until the 1980s on what group was being referred to when the term was used: it was La Cosa Nostra or the Mafia. The Mafia was that group of predominantly Sicilian-American organized criminals who were made famous through the media as the purveyors of liquor, gambling, prostitution, stolen goods, and other criminal services. From the Kefauver hearings of 1951 to the latter 1980s, the spotlight of law enforcement activities was on the Mafia.

But as Ianni comments, "Organized crime as an American way of life persists and transcends the involvement of any particular group" (1974, p. 14). The carefully constructed model of organized crime as Mafia has since transmuted itself at least into a model of "traditional organized crime"—La Cosa Nostra—and "nontraditional organized crime"—all other organized crime groups. Some experts now suggest that there never was a "traditional organized crime model," outside the one created by the media. Further, they believe that the varied ethnic crime groups have always been active, but did not garner media or public attention because of the narrow and circular vision of Mafia watchers.

Analysis and Organized Crime

Organized crime investigation generally requires a significant amount of raw data (sometimes called "intelligence") to be gathered, then evaluated and analyzed. The process of interdicting covert hierarchies requires the ability to look at not only individual crimes and violations, but the aggregate criminal environment. Analysis, formal or informal, must be used to arrange the pieces of the organized crime puzzle in a cohesive and comprehensible whole.

The expansion of the use of analysis was, for many years, in direct proportion to the investigation of organized crime. New technologies used in organized crime investigation—electronic surveillance, for example—created the need for new analytical techniques such as conversation analysis. In 1985, the International Association of Chiefs of Police stated that the analysis of collected information is critical to the control of organized and sophisticated crime.

In the 1990s, the emergence of new organized crime groups creates a need for new analytical models. One of the challenges facing today's organized crime bureaus is to determine the structures and operating principles of these nontraditional crime groups in order to interdict them. It is only through a joint effort of analysts and investigators that this challenge will be met.

Corruption and RICO

Corruption and Racketeer Influenced Corrupt Organizations (RICO) investigations are often carried out in tandem with organized crime investigations. Corruption, as indicated earlier, is an integral part of organized crime activity.

And, as Walter Lippman stated, "An entirely objective view of political life . . . would show that corruption in some form is endemic" (Lippman, 1930, quoted in Douglas and Johnson, 1977, p. 334).

Public corruption with no ties to organized crime may also be investigated by those within the organized crime unit as the organized crime investigators have become the "experts" in this arena.

The investigation of racketeer influenced corrupt organizations (RICO) requires a team of experts including attorneys, asset investigators, and analysts. This level of investigation and prosecution demands a view of the organization which includes its illegal ongoing and pervasive activities, its organization and hierarchy, its business interests, and its assets.

The intent of RICO investigation is not only to uncover criminal acts, but to find criminal profits. The monies and properties which can be proved to have been accrued from illegal activity may then be forfeited to the state. This gives the government the potential ability to remove significant amounts of profit from crime.

Intelligence Systems

The final key to organized crime investigation has been the development of intelligence collection and analysis systems. An intelligence system is one which includes data commonly found in other police information systems (such as data from Criminal History Record Information systems) along with other data from investigative files including information on criminal associates, potentially illegal business involvement, crime group affiliation, and hangouts. The intelligence process takes all these and, through analysis, combines them into an overview of the suspect which is often termed an "intelligence product."

At its best, an intelligence system can predict and forecast crime problems (Dintino and Martens, 1983). At its worst, it provides benefit to no one if it collects data and collects them in a paper or electronic morass with little retrievability. Within this area of discussion, the limitations which should be placed on data systems are noted and common standards are discussed.

TRADITIONAL ORGANIZED CRIME

If organized crime investigation is the home of analysis, then the analysis of traditional organized crime is the inhabitant with the longest tenancy. Traditional organized crime—otherwise known as La Cosa Nostra or the Mafia—investigations dominated organized crime units from the 1950s to the late 1980s. For some time in some circles, "organized crime" was synonymous with "Mafia" (Martens and Cunningham-Niederer, 1985, p. 63). As of 1994, a number of credible law enforcement agencies still focus most of their organized crime investigations on La Cosa Nostra members or associates while ignoring all but the most flagrant nontraditional groups.

As of 1986, law enforcement reported that there were about twenty-four La Cosa Nostra families in the United States, headquartered in thirteen states stretching from California to New Jersey, and from Florida to Massachusetts and Michigan. These families included a hierarchy of a boss (or acting boss), an underboss, a consigliere (counselor), capos (lieutenants), and soldiers (members). For every member, some estimated that there were thirty to fifty non-member associates who were committed to the principles of La Cosa Nostra. Associates played an important role in the workings of the families since membership was limited to men of Sicilian ancestry. Legal and illegal enterprises were run for members by associates who could never gain entry to the family. The midpoint estimate for the adjusted net income from organized crime activities in 1986 in the United States was $36.4 billion (President's Commission on Organized Crime, 1986).

Since then, state and federal prosecutors have successfully prosecuted a number of Mafia bosses and other members of the hierarchies. According to the Pennsylvania Crime Commission, a few families in that state have been virtually disbanded (1991). Prosecutions and interfamily wars in New York City, long the stronghold of the Mafia in the United States, have noticeably thinned the ranks of La Cosa Nostra.

Analysis has played a vital role in the investigation and prosecution of traditional organized crime. Some forms which this has taken include association analysis, use of telephone record analysis and content analysis during electronic surveillance, support of undercover operations and confidential informant management by the use of analysis, and use of overview assessments of organized crime groups.

Association Analysis

Association analysis can be used to depict the size and membership of organized crime groups. Using data received through surveillance, testimony, confidential informants, and so forth, the analyst can show the links among the known and suspected members of the group and thus give some indication of the group's strength and influence.

Association matrices and link charts have also been used to show the extent of an organized crime group's infiltration into businesses. In another application, during the 1987 trial of John Gotti, defense attorneys Bruce Cutler and Susan G. Kellman used an association matrix showing "Criminal Activity of Government Informants" which listed seven key witnesses against Gotti and sixty-nine different crimes in which those witnesses had been involved. X's were placed in the boxes next to the long listing of crimes. The overall impression created was one of intense criminal activity by all those used by the government to give testimony against Gotti. In referring to their use of this association matrix as a courtroom graphic, author Edward Tufte commented, "Such displays are likely to be especially persuasive and memorable in situations where most information communicated consists of spoken words—as in a trial. . . .Visual displays of information encourage a diversity of individual viewer styles . . . reasoning, and understanding'' (1990, p. 31).

Association matrices and link diagrams are used to show criminal relationships to people, places, and entities (businesses or organizations). They can be developed and used as aids during the course of the investigation and as graphics to support the prosecution. In a number of states, analysts are now accompanying link charts and other analytical products into the courtroom and onto the witness stand as expert witnesses.

Telephone Analysis and Content Analysis Used in Electronic Surveillances

Few long-term organized crime investigations occur today without some form of electronic surveillance being employed. Evidence must be gathered to support charges of conspiracy and the organized crime group must be shown to have a pattern of racketeering activities. Quite often, this pattern emerges through the use of electronic and physical surveillances of the targets.

The ability to observe persons legally and covertly as they go about their criminal business is of great benefit to law enforcement. Electronic surveillance can entail wire or oral interceptions, electronic communications, consensual undercover recordings, beepers and transponders, or telephone/computer tracing (*18 USC* 2516). Devices used for intercepts include the following:

- Dialed number recorders or pen registers which record the times a telephone receiver is lifted or put in its cradle plus any numbers which are dialed (or touched) while the line is open. This is called a nonaudio wire intercept, meaning that it does not record conversation being held while the telephone is off the hook.

- A wiretap, which generally is used to mean the audio interception of telephone calls. A wiretap must be closely monitored by investigative personnel, who must take care to "minimize" (not record) conversations not relevant to criminal activity.

- A law enforcement wire, which is worn by an undercover police officer and records conversations and other audible activity held around the officer.

- A consensual wire, in which individuals (usually informants or cooperating violators) consent to having their conversations with target violators recorded and secrete the wire on their person or in some other covert spot under their control.

All of these techniques are governed by law and may only be initiated with the proper court orders.

The most basic form of electronic surveillance, the pen register or dialed number recorder, provides data on a printed-out tape or in a computerized format. The data are then entered into a computerized data base which allows them to be compiled by several factors, including number called, time of call, location called, length of call, number called from, and number billed.

Figure 5.1
Pen Register Data Base

Date	No. Called	Time Start	Time End	Length
3/27/91	555/237-0912	10:13:23	10:13:43	0:00:20
3/27/91	555/832-9749	10:25:08	10:28:19	0:03:11
3/17/91	555/932-6936	11:01:34	11:02:47	0:01:13
3/17/91	------	11:05:25	10:07:14	0:01:49

Pen registers operate on exact times phones are lifted from the cradle (''off hook'') and put back on the cradle (''on hook''); thus times and length are shown in hours, minutes, and seconds. Call 1 may be a ''no answer'' call as its 20 second length may be only the time elapsed for ringing. Incoming calls are also shown (call 4), as the phone is removed from the cradle, but no number connected to is known. The number of calls which may be collected in a pen register can range from a few dozen to a few thousand over the course of months or years.

Telephone record analysis is the process used to review these records and draw conclusions about the telephone activity. A sample telephone record analysis data base for pen register data is seen in Figure 5.1.

The same compilation and review are used on telephone toll records, with the primary difference that the pen registers record every call made, while the telephone toll records show only the calls made to numbers outside the local calling area (unless a cellular phone is involved, in which case both local and long-distance calls are ''toll'' calls). The products which result include tables showing all numbers contacted by the target, for example, or only the numbers contacted most frequently. A sample primary listing is shown in Figure 5.2.

Frequency distributions of calling hours and lengths of calls can be noted. A sample of the distribution of calls in a sports betting operation is shown in Figure 5.3. The geographic breadth of the target's contacts can be shown in a tabular format or on a map covering those areas. Foreign calls should be identified, along with those above the average in length or made at times of day or on days when calls are not normally made. Charts showing the numbers receiving calls most often, collect calls, and third party activity are drawn. (A sample multiple subscriber telephone chart is seen in Figure 5.4). Concurrently subscriber identification and criminal history checks are done on those persons to whom highlighted calls were made.

Within organized crime investigations, telephone record analysis is often used to support requests for an audible wire intercept. By showing that an individual is making calls to criminal associates or may be conducting criminal business by telephone, investigators may receive the court's permission to listen to the content of those telephone calls through a wiretap.

Telephone record analysis can also show the presence of certain types of criminal activities engaged in by traditional organized crime families such as gambling. A sports betting operation, for example, could show a flurry of incoming calls, immediately before a sporting event, by persons wishing to place

Figure 5.2
Telephone Record Primary Listing: 215/555-9738

Subscriber No. Dialed	Number Calls	Date Span	Total Length
609/555-4239	9	6/14-9/15/93	36
212/555-3131	7	6/15-9/15/93	21
202/555-7097	7	7/1-8/6/93	15
718/555-6956	5	7/15-8/1/93	9
305/555-7306	4	7/111-7/15/93	12

A Primary Listing shows the numbers contacted most frequently by someone whose telephone records (toll calls, long-distance calling service, cellular phone– or pen register–obtained) have been analyzed. This forms one portion of the written report of the telephone record analysis.

bets. Likewise a "numbers" betting operation might show heavy incoming calls immediately before the televised announcement of the state-sponsored "daily number" each evening.

Audible electronic surveillance is viewed as a way to prove, irrefutably, that an individual is involved in a particular form of criminal activity. In order to gather such evidence, however, often days, weeks, or months of surveillance are necessary as criminal activity is designed to not meet the public eye. In the case of audio intercepts (telephone and wire transmitters), dozens to hundreds to thousands of tapes may result from an investigation covering thousands of hours of conversation. Transcripts of those conversations are made from the tapes, transcripts which are later introduced in court. Both the tapes and the transcripts are then reviewed by attorneys, investigators, and analysts.

Further processing of the taped material must then be accomplished. Portions of conversation which are viewed as pertinent to the charges being brought against the suspect can be highlighted, summarized, and put into proper order for presentation to a grand jury or court.

The conversations captured by electronic surveillance may be analyzed in several ways. First, they can be reviewed to uncover clues as to the association between those speaking as well as those about whom they may speak. From those extracted pieces of information, an association analysis can be completed. Second, conversations can be reviewed to uncover clues as to the hierarchy of the criminal organization being investigated. An association analysis or a modified table of criminal organization can be made from that information. Third, conversations can include data about past or planned future events. The dates and times of the conversations, as well as the events referred to during them, may be depicted in an event flow analysis. Fourth, financial information, such as leads on legitimate businesses which have been infiltrated and other business-related data, may cause the analyst to develop financial analysis products after a review of wiretap tapes or transcripts.

Finally, conversations captured by electronic surveillance can be analyzed by a technique called content or conversation analysis. As Shuy explains, "Whenever a law enforcement agency tape records conversations of suspected persons,

Figure 5.3
Sample Distribution of Calls to Sports Betting Operation During Football Season

Hour	Sun	Mon	Tues	Wed	Thurs	Fri	Sat
9 am	1	6	7	-	-	-	2
10 am	1	8	10	1	2	-	15
11 am	12	5	1	2	1	2	26
12 noon	19	7	1	2	1	2	32
1 pm	37	4	1	1	1	1	53
2 pm	2	10	1	1	2	3	3
3 pm	3	18	2	-	-	2	6
4 pm	8	24	4	3	1	6	8
5 pm	10	31	3	1	3	7	13
6 pm	3	17	6	-	1	8	5
7 pm	2	62	4	2	1	6	4
8 pm	1	3	2	1	1	3	2
9 pm	2	2	4	-	-	2	1
10 pm	-	1	-	-	-	1	1
11 pm	-	6	-	-	-	-	-

The typical distribution of calls to a sports betting operation shows heavy telephone traffic before Saturday, Sunday, and Monday night football games with a second surge of calls after the games.

there is a potential for misunderstanding both in the production of the speech acts themselves as well as in the interpretation of the speech acts by other conversational participants, and later by listeners such as juries'' (Shuy in Andrews and Peterson, 1990, p. 117).

Within content analysis, there are a number of subtypes of analysis, including phonological analysis, syntactic analysis, and discourse analysis. Phonological analysis deals with the meter and syllables of a particular portion of a tape which may be muffled and can help to uncover the words spoken. Syntactic analysis relates to the object of a sentence, which may be ambiguous—''I want you to do it''—as directed to several people, any (or all) of whom may be the addressee of the declaration (Andrews and Peterson, 1990).

Discourse analysis, considered by Shuy a subset of conversation analysis, comprises topic analysis, response analysis, topic flow analysis, language function analysis, and contrastive analysis. Shuy uses the *U.S. vs. John DeLorean* case as an example. In analyzing a taped conversation between DeLorean and the government undercover agent James Hoffman, Shuy shows that of all the topics raised by both during the conversation, only one topic raised by DeLorean related to the drug business in which he was accused of participating. That comment, ''It would be dangerous,'' is an oblique one. Shuy says that Hoffman, on the other hand, kept making references to the drug business but got no clear supportive statements from DeLorean in return. DeLorean was later acquitted (Shuy, in Andrews and Peterson, 1990).

Seasoned investigators of organized crime know that crime figures are sophisticated about the probability of being overheard on their telephones and in their residences or hangouts and often speak in code to prevent law enforcement officials from comprehending their conversation. One reference to the dangers of not speaking in code was seen in the tapes used in the trial of John Gotti. On January 24, 1990, Gotti was taped saying the following:

Figure 5.4
Telephone Record Chart—Multiple Subscriber

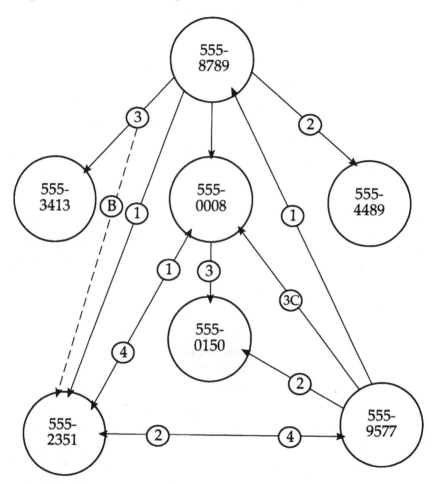

This chart depicts phone calls among six coconspirators. The small circles show the number of calls, the type of calls (C = Collect), and thirty party calls (B = Billed to). Arrows show the direction of the calls.

And from now on, I'm telling you if a guy just so mentions "La," or if he wants to say, "La, la, la, la." He just says "La" . . . he don't have to say "Cosa Nostra," just "La" and they go. . . . Look, I heard other people's—I heard nine months of tapes of my life. . . . I was actually sick . . . sick for this "thing of ours." Sick for that—how, how naive we were five years ago. This was '85. . . . And, I'm, I'm sick that we were so f——— naive . . . this (is) how we get into trouble—we talk. (*The Gotti Tapes*, 1992, pp. 121–22)

Clearly, there is a wealth of information presented in audio and videotapes of allegedly illegal activity. It is in the defense bar's interest to discredit such tapes; it is in the prosecutor's interest to have them carefully analyzed so that they may withstand any attempts made to discredit them.

Undercover Operations

The purpose of an undercover officer is to gain proximity to the suspects and, through that closeness, have access to information that could eventually convict the organized criminals and their hierarchy for crimes committed. As organized crime operations are, by nature, secretive, there are sometimes no other ways to obtain information necessary to convict except through covert operations such as undercover operations or use of confidential informants.

The types of information which can be gained through undercover work include determining whether crimes are being planned or committed; identifying witnesses, informers, and persons involved in criminal activity; checking on the reliability of informants; and identifying the locations of criminal activities or contraband storage areas.

An undercover officer collects data through observation and through participation in or overhearing of conversations among criminal associates. The information thus gained is passed on to investigative supervisors and analysts so that it can be collated and analyzed. This process can provide insights into the structure of the organized crime group, into the habits of the group's members, and into their personal environments. Undercover work can obtain leads to support continuing or expanded investigation into uncovered assets, coconspirators, or related criminal activities.

The types of analytical products which can be completed from undercover officer data include association charts, event flow or commodity flow analysis, tables of organization, and content analysis of recorded conversations. An undercover officer who has successfully become a prospect ("wannabe") of an outlaw motorcycle gang, for example, may gain knowledge of the hierarchy of the gang: who its chapter president and other officers are, what the locations of other chapters are, and how extensive its membership is. This information is readily convertible into an association chart, table of organization, or geographic distribution map.

Event flow or commodity flow charts may be drawn from data related to specific criminal violations occurring over time or to the flow of contraband gathered by the undercover officer. Hijacking proceeds of a gang, for example, can be shown to flow from hijackers to storage, or to a fence for sale to merchandisers, or to the public.

It is common for undercover officers to wear "body bugs" (hidden wires which relay conversations to a concealed taping operation). This is done to record incriminating conversation engaged in by the suspects. These recorded conversations are reviewed and analyzed as detailed in the discussion of electronic surveillance.

It should also be noted that when law enforcement officers operate undercover there is a risk to their safety. Data relating to the criminal culture and the environment in which the officer has been placed must be constantly collected from corroborative sources and analyzed to alert supervisors to danger which may be surrounding the officer. Raw data collected by the officer should be compared and combined, by an analyst, with other current data on the criminal environment to maximize the officer's ability to do the job and to maintain personal safety.

Confidential Informants

Another aspect of organized crime investigation is developing, cultivating, and managing confidential informants. Confidential informants have been central to many traditional and nontraditional organized crime investigations. While confidential informants can come from any sector of society, the most effective are those who have been in the criminal group under investigation or are criminal associates of the group.

Criminal informants are difficult to control and are not known for the dependability or reliability of their actions or their information. When data from them is received, it is evaluated on the basis of the reliability of the source and the validity of past information provided by them. Generally accepted evaluation rankings for reliability of sources and validity of information are shown in Figure 5.5.

Some agencies use field officers to evaluate the sources and the information on intelligence reports; others use analysts. Those who choose the former believe that the officers have more personal hands-on knowledge on which to base their evaluations; those who choose the latter believe that the analysts have a more objective view of the sources and data at hand.

Analysts serve as information managers and must work closely with the data received from confidential criminal informants. They are in a position to have close knowledge of the files on the investigation or crime group and be in a position to readily answer the question "Is this information corroborated by other previously collected information?"

It is for this reason that they can be of use when an officer is working with informants. The analyst can keep files on what intelligence has been received from the varied sources which will point out inconsistencies in information continually being provided by an informant, as well as corroboration or noncorroboration of the information with data received from other sources. And, with the broad knowledge of the other sources of similar data gained by the analyst's being conversant with the files, he or she can also point the investigator in the direction of other sources of information which may, when approached

Figure 5.5
Source Reliability and Information Validity Evaluation Levels

<u>Source Reliability</u>

"Reliable" - No doubt of source's authenticity; past
        information has been reliable in all instances.

"Usually Reliable" - some doubt of source's
        authenticity; past information has been reliable
        in most instances.

"Fairly Reliable" - Some doubt of source's
        authenticity; past information has been reliable
        in an average number of instances.

"Not Usually Reliable" - There is doubt of source's
        authenticity; past information has been reliable
        only on occasion.

"Unreliable" - There is great doubt as to source's
        authenticity; past experience has proven it to be
        unreliable but it may still now be reliable.

<u>Information Validity</u>

"Confirmed by Other Sources" - Information
        substantiated or confirmed by one or more
        independent sources.

"Probably True" - Information which appears to be
        accurate but is not confirmed.

"Possibly True" - Information which is neither
        confirmed nor contradicted; not capable of
        confirmation at this time.

"Doubtfully True" - Information believed to be
        unlikely but is not definitely contradicted.

"Improbable" - Information contradicted by other
        intelligence; disagrees with general body of
        knowledge on subject.

by the investigator, be able to provide corroboration (or not) of the data in
question.

   The area of inconsistencies within an informant's data is particularly important if the informant is to provide testimony about criminal activities in a grand
jury or trial setting. The analyst can be of assistance to the prosecutor by providing synopses of factual statements made by the informant at particular dates

and times and analyzing them for inconsistencies so that they may be cleared up before the informant, as a government witness, enters an adversarial setting.

Overview Assessments

Overview assessments of organized crime groups or activities entail the detailing of those groups or activities for either intradepartment or public view. The types of information on crime groups included in these assessments vary from author to author; some generally accepted topics are the following:

* membership of the group,
* geographic boundaries of the group,
* types of criminal behavior engaged in,
* types of legitimate businesses involved in,
* leadership and structure of the group,
* longevity of the group, and
* relationships of the group to other criminal groups. (Sommers, 1986; Andrews and Peterson, 1990)

It is obvious that the investigator must collect data to support the compilation of these types of assessments and often knows more about the individual group than appears in a written document. These assessments can be of assistance to investigators nonetheless. While investigators may be "experts" on the group they are following, they may know little about a related or competing group from a contiguous geographic area, the activities of which may impact on their group. Therefore, the analyst, and the assessment, serve as the bridge between expert investigators and allow them access to information on groups outside their immediate investigative mandate.

Assessments are also used by management to prepare reports on the status of crime and criminal groups in their area for elected officials and appointing authorities. Having this overview ("big picture") knowledge is important to the highest levels of law enforcement management.

La Cosa Nostra (LCN) has been a common topic of assessment and reassessment by organized crime investigators and analysts. Thus, in *Organized Crime in Pennsylvania: A Decade of Change: 1990 Report,* conclusions were drawn about the future of LCN in Pennsylvania:

While La Cosa Nostra may be battered and ailing, it is premature to write LCN's obituary. Overall, the decade of the 1990s may see a Cosa Nostra that is restructured to exclude high-profile "Godfather" crime leaders (like John Gotti) who are easily targeted and prosecuted. It may see a Cosa Nostra that is more decentralized and more entrepreneurial than ever, taking lessons from the RICO prosecutions of the 1980s and from the successes of the drug entrepreneur groups. It may see an even more secret core organization, engaging in wider use of non-Italian associates, and guiding the provision of illegal services and legitimate goods. It may see the LCN evolving into an even more diversified multi-national conglomerate than it presently is. (Pennsylvania Crime Commission, 1991, p. 188)

Ralph Blumenthal commented similarly in his foreword to a book on the tape-recorded conversations of John Gotti: "Yet it was precisely by courting celebrity that Gotti would sow the seeds of his own undoing. He forgot that criminals work best in the shadows. By flaunting his outlaw status, he set himself up as an irresistible target" (*The Gotti Tapes*, 1992, p. xi).

In response to these conclusions, a seasoned investigator or manager might initiate an investigation into the businesses and enterprises of those remaining LCN family members to determine whether, in fact, they were shifting to low-profile activities that were even more financially remunerative.

NONTRADITIONAL ORGANIZED CRIME

Nontraditional organized crime covers a broad range of criminal groups and criminal activities in the 1990s. To some, nontraditional organized crime is almost synonymous with drug syndicates, since the most widely known non-traditional groups are those who have derived most of their profits from the distribution of drugs. These have included the Colombian cocaine cartels, the Jamaican posses, and other ethnic-based drug groups including persons of Dominican, Costa Rican, Cuban, Nigerian, Pakistani, Vietnamese, and Chinese nationality. Nontraditional organized crime can also include outlaw motorcycle gangs, street gangs, and other groups of organized criminals including the Junior Black Mafia (in Philadelphia), the Yakuza, the Mexican Mafia, the Russian Mafia, and the Israeli Mafia.

There are distinct problems in investigating and analyzing nontraditional organized crime activities. First, law enforcement does not have the decades of information on the members and structures of groups outside the Cosa Nostra paradigm. There is no historical basis, therefore, for assessments, investigations, or prosecutions. Second, it is harder to prove that there is an ongoing group at work in nontraditional settings as the membership is often fluid and decentralized while its leadership may reside in another country. Third, the members of the ethnic community from which a nontraditional group is drawn may be unfamiliar with American customs and distrustful of American police. Certain foreign customs (e.g., Chinese practices of casino gambling and extortion of businesses) are illegal in the United States but may be found in every Chinatown in America. These activities may be indicative of Chinese organized crime or normal Chinese customs. As Kelly, Chin and Fagan note, "In the Chinese communities in New York, and probably elsewhere, the pervasiveness of extortionate crime suggests that . . . a culture of extortion exists. . . " (1993, p. 21). Finally, the languages spoken by these varied international groups necessitate the use of

Figure 5.6
Indicators of Organized Crime Influencing Government

- Support by top-level echelon of law enforcement for organized crime.

- Weak or absent enforcement campaign.

- Enforcement budget cuts by legislature.

- Lack of vigor in prosecution or sentencing.

- Personnel decisions (transfers, etc.) within police department that support criminal activity.

- Unusual speed in granting licenses and variances.

- Frequency of hidden ownership cases with liquor control authority.

- Irregularities in licensing, health, and fire code regulation.

Source: Roger W. Davis and Charles H. Rogovin, "Indicators of the Impacts of Organized Crime" (unpublished, funded by grant 80-IJ-CX-006, National Institute of Justice).

interpreters or undercover police operators from that same ethnic background. Ethnic officers or undercover operators can be at a premium, particularly in light of the foreign groups' general unwillingness to cooperate with police.

Analysis has a distinct and important role to play in the investigation of nontraditional organized crime. Newly emerging groups must be researched by contacting other agencies or accessing materials published on the group. Raw data must be gathered, evaluated, and analyzed to form a picture of the group.

Analysts must be familiar with indicators of organized crime so they may apply those criteria to distinguish the level of organization present and assess the potential range of influence of that organization and potential threat to the community. For example, indicators of the impact of organized crime on government can be seen in Figure 5.6.

Analysts, then, bridge the gap between individual criminal activity and organized group activity by uncovering the links between the actions and comparing those actions to models of criminal group activity.

The Use of Confidential Informants

The use of informants and the collection of informant data are among the most critical elements of almost any nontraditional organized crime investigation because these groups are often organized along ethnic and/or racial boundaries which cannot be crossed by an individual not of that ethnicity or racial background. The next best thing to police undercover infiltration of a group is having an informant who is accepted by it.

The data received from an informant, however, can be suspect. Informants may provide information for revenge, for financial remuneration, or in exchange for a lenient sentence. Informants are, not infrequently, persons who have committed a substantial number of crimes. The reason they are valuable is also the reason they are suspect.

Informant data should be catalogued, compared, and analyzed to test its veracity and its constancy overtime. It needs to be included in the intelligence process and compared to other known or factual data, such as surveillance or public records, to see whether it can be corroborated. These are particularly important points when the informant data are to be used as evidence.

CORRUPTION INVESTIGATIONS

The three primary definitions of organized crime noted at the beginning of this chapter contain similar elements: organization, profit, and corruption (Ianni, 1974; Maltz, 1985; Harris, 1976). Some would contend that, absent corruption, crime is disorganized or opportunistic, rather than endemic.

Organized corruption takes many forms. It can be reflected in patrol officers who turn their backs on the local organized "craps" game, in bribes to police officials, in graft to elected officials, or in kickbacks in return for the award of government contracts.

In the late 1960s, it was estimated that $2 billion was given by organized crime figures to public officials each year (Key, as quoted in Pennsylvania Crime Commission, 1980). As of 1980, that figure was believed to have tripled. At this writing, one must assume that it has at least doubled from the 1980 figure, bringing it to $12 billion per year in bribes and kickbacks. The reason for these bribes was put forth by Cressey, who noted that the "Cosa Nostra functions as an illegal invisible government . . . its political objective is a negative one: nullification of government" (1969, p. 248).

Corruption investigations are often done by organized crime investigators, presumably because corruption and organized crime go hand-in-hand but also because organized crime investigators are familiar with the techniques necessary for a successful corruption investigation. The same techniques of undercover operations and confidential informants are heavily used, as well as physical surveillance and financial investigation.

Likewise, the analytical function can support corruption investigations. The applications of analysis to undercover operations and confidential informant data have been noted. Financial investigations, which are to a large degree financial analysis, are covered later. The analytical component of physical surveillance includes the simple, yet necessary, cataloging of surveillance logs, tapes, and photographs as well as the construction of analytical products including event flow charts from this data. Visual investigative analysis (VIA) charts can also be drawn up from surveillance information.

An association chart can be used to explain the relationships between persons with political power and their ties to illegal activities. In the *Organized Crime in Pennsylvania: A Decade of Change: 1990 Report*, the Pennsylvania Crime Commission depicted the business and political connections of John Nacrelli, a former mayor of Chester (Figure 5.7). It showed that certain businesses which Nacrelli represented or was in partnership with were influenced by persons involved in illegal gambling, loansharking, extortion, and racketeering. It also detailed his influence over the school district, the local Republican Party Executive Committee, and a waste energy conversion project.

RICO INVESTIGATIONS

The Racketeer Influenced and Corrupt Organizations (RICO) statute is considered by some to be the single most important piece of legislation enacted against organized crime. At the federal level, the RICO law was passed in 1970; since then many states have passed laws which mirror the federal language. The concept behind RICO is to prove the existence of an organization which has conspired over an extended period to commit illegal acts for profit. The "pattern of racketeering activity" is defined as two or more violations of any of over forty different federal and state laws within a ten-year period (*18 U.S.C.* 1961–68). Participation in an organization must be shown; the participants then become liable for all the acts of the organization regardless of their personal participation in an individual violation.

RICO penalties are severe. Convictions allow for the forfeiture of assets gained as a result of criminal behavior or assets used to further criminal behavior. Lengthy prison sentences and fines are also levied.

The convictions of major La Cosa Nostra families in New York are indicative of RICO charges. Federal agencies have garnered over one thousand convictions of LCN members and associates. Members of LCN hierarchies in nine states have been prosecuted.

Analysis is crucial to RICO investigations. The patterns of racketeering and associations between members of organized groups are shown through analytical products. A significant amount of data gathering, investigation, and analysis is required to uncover the assets of a RICO group. Libonati and Edelhertz state, "The existence of an intelligence base that reveals the potential property interests of the subjects ... is crucial ... such intelligence ... could determine whether RICO preliminary remedies should be sought and whether criminal or civil remedies, or both, should be pursued" (1985, p. 50).

Nontraditional organized crime RICO investigations are problematic. While decades have been spent identifying and "structuring out" LCN groups, the more fluid cartels and syndicates of today can defy lengthy analysis or inves-

Figure 5.7
John Nacrelli: Chester Power Broker

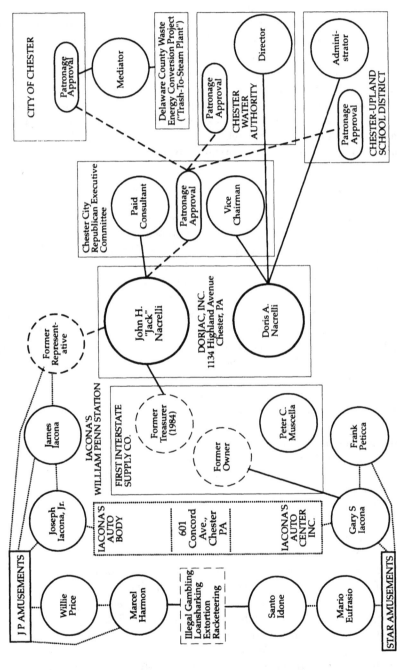

Source: Pennsylvania Crime Commission, *Organized Crime in Pennsylvania: A Decade of Change: 1990 Report* (1990): p. 321.

tigation. RICO has successfully been used against outlaw motorcycle gangs, and it may be a matter of time before enough intelligence has been gathered and analyzed to support RICO convictions of other nontraditional groups.

FINANCIAL INVESTIGATIONS

Drugs, theft/fencing, white collar crime, and illegal gambling may garner $224 billion a year for organized criminals. Blakey comments "No sane society can long permit such large sums to be acquired by criminal means and still hope to maintain its basic integrity" (1985). Financial investigations have become a routine companion to all organized crime investigations. The financial investigation itself requires a thorough and careful uncovering of hidden assets in various locations. It includes financial analysis methods such as net worth analysis, bank record analysis, and business record analysis, which are most often done by intelligence analysts or by accountant/investigators.

Net worth analysis is the compilation and review of financial data on an individual to determine whether the person has income from illegal sources. All legal sources of income are reviewed, determining expenditures for a particular year and ascertaining any significant differences between the two. This is done over several years to show changes in net worth which may reflect illegal income. Net worth analysis is key to many organized crime investigations because it helps to uncover the profits of the crime rather than just focusing on the criminal act.

Net worth analysis is done in an accounting format developed by the U.S. Department of the Treasury, Internal Revenue Service (Nossen, 1982). The standardized protocols call for information on assets, liabilities, reported income, and yearly expenses, including loan payments and living expenses (food, rent, etc.). When the form is tallied, the "bottom line" shows potential illegal income. Charges including tax evasion might stem from this type of investigation but are not pursued unless the "bottom line" is large enough to ensure a significant return from a prosecution. A second format, termed Source and Application of Funds, lists the expenditures, increases in bank account balances, reductions in loans, and living expenses and then shows sources of legitimate funds (Nossen, 1982). Again, the "bottom line" shows potential income from illegitimate or illegal sources.

Because of the confidentiality surrounding financial information reported to the IRS, most local investigators do not have access to a target's income as reported to the IRS but may be able to access comparable information through other means such as state income records, employer records, or credit applications. Much of this information may only be accessed through the subpoena process. A sample Sources and Applications of Funds format is shown in Figure 5.8.

Bank Account Analysis

Bank account analysis compiles, reviews, and analyzes the records of one or more bank accounts to provide information on the financial status of the owner

Figure 5.8
Sources and Applications of Funds

FUNDS APPLIED (EXPENDITURES)	1989	1990	1991
Increase in Checking Account Balance	$ 840	$1,432	$2,845
Increase in Savings Account Balance	700	5,470	7,860
Securities Purchases:			
500 shares XYX Corp.	15,000		
1,000 shares LM Corp.			35,000
Purchase of Condominium		151,000	
Purchase of Automobiles			
1988 Honda CRX	8,000		
1991 Porsche			45,000
Purchase of Diamond Ring			5,000
Reduction of Mortgage on Condominium			50,000
Personal Living Expenses	30,000	40,000	53,000
TOTAL FUNDS APPLIED	$54,540	$197,900	$145,705

SOURCES OF LEGITIMATE FUNDS			
Automobile Loan	$5,000		
Mortgage on Condominium		$100,000	
Salary	40,000	44,000	48,000
TOTAL SOURCES OF LEGITIMATE FUNDS	$45,000	$144,000	$48,000

Potential illegal income for 1989 would be $9,540, for
1990 would be $53,900, and for 1991 would be $97,705.

of the account(s). It looks at the overall flow of funds into and out of the account,
the specifics of payments, and the resultant financial position of the account
holder. It can be used in conjunction with commodity flow analysis or to help
ascertain the living expenses for a net worth analysis.

Within an organized crime investigation, bank account analysis might result
in information relating to

- money laundering,
- the use of corporations and accounts to hide interest or ownership,
- potential tax violations,
- skimming of profits,
- the presence of illegal income,
- the presence of payments for illegal goods or services,
- assets owned by the target of the investigation which might be seized as part of a RICO investigation,
- the use of nominees or "paper" corporations to hide illegal profits.

The types of products which might emerge from a bank record analysis include various financial summaries, commodity flow charts, and association charts. The financial summaries could include monthly or quarterly summaries of income and expenditures, primary payees (persons/entities to whom checks were made out), unusual payments, large cash deposits or withdrawals, and so forth. Commodity flow charts could show the flow of funds into and out of the account or, more commonly, the flow of funds among related accounts, such as those used in associated businesses such as paper corporations.

Business Record Analysis

Business record analysis is an overall category that entails the analysis of varied business records, including sales and order receipt books, journals and ledgers, bank records, employee wage reports, business filings, sales tax filings, and corporate records. Historically, researchers have documented the involvement of organized crime in business ventures (Cressey, 1969; Ianni, 1972; Kwitney, 1979; Anderson, 1979; Pennsylvania Crime Commission, 1980; Reuter et al., 1983; Haller, 1991).

The analysis of business records to determine the involvement of the business in criminal activity or the beneficiary role of the business in criminal activity is at the forefront of many criminal investigations today. Some of the information a thorough analysis of business records may uncover is the following:

- actual ownership of hidden assets;
- use of nominees, fronts, or other devices to hide the ownership of assets, businesses, or bank accounts;
- actual business profits;
- use of businesses and business accounts to launder funds received from illegal activities;
- use of business accounts to underwrite personal expenses without declaring the funds as business or personal income;
- interconnection of seemingly independent businesses;
- use of businesses to provide ''legitimate'' sources of income for persons not actually employed by them (''ghost employees'');
- presence in the business of ''silent partners'' whose obvious presence might prohibit the business from being licensed because of their past criminal activities;
- presence of vertical or horizontal integration in the industry of persons associated with organized crime.

The types of products associated with business record analysis include financial summaries, commodity flow diagrams, event flow diagrams, association charts, and written reports.

Economic Analysis

Economic analysis can also be done in an organized crime milieu. Who owns what, how legal and illegal business interests are disbursed through the crime groups, who gets the profits or sustains the losses are all part of the economic picture of organized crime. Economic analysis is done as part of public reports on organized crime or as separate reports. An example of the former is in the Pennsylvania Crime Commission's *A Decade of Organized Crime: 1980 Report,* which included a chapter on organized crime's infiltration of legitimate business. One analytical product contained in that chapter was an association matrix showing the connections of members of the Russell Bufalino La Cosa Nostra family in various garment industry companies (Figure 5.9).

The Reuter, Rubinstein, and Wynn report, *Racketeering in Legitimate Industries: Two Case Studies* (1983), looked at the waste disposal and vending industries and the involvement of vending in them. The waste industry study was, in large part, an economic analysis. It pointed out, for example, that

racketeers will probably play an important role in markets which have particular characteristics . . . strong incentives to create a cartel . . . but impediments to its formation . . . low status backgrounds (of the entrepreneurs) will ease contacts between entrepreneurs and racketeers; thus low status industries where the firms are owned by poorly educated entrepreneurs are more likely to involve racketeers. (Reuter et al., 1983, p. 6)

It goes on to discuss other factors, or indicators, of what industries might be vulnerable to racketeer control.

In another example of an economic analysis of organized crime, Haller wrote about the Bruno La Cosa Nostra family:

Each of the active members carried on his money-making activities within relatively independent clusters of business partners and associates who cooperated in a variety of enterprises. Sometimes only one participant in the cluster was a member of the Family. . . . Scalleat in Hazleton . . . formed partnerships with various relatives and outside businessmen to run the garment factories and beer distributorships . . . (while) the Bruno Family provided a quasi-government within which members and associates operated. (1991, p. 17)

In his analysis, Haller created an overview of the business interests of a particular crime family while drawing some conclusions about the structure of the organized crime family in general.

INFORMATION SYSTEMS THAT SUPPORT ORGANIZED CRIME INVESTIGATIONS

Information systems which support organized crime investigations are commonly called "intelligence systems." An intelligence system goes beyond the

Figure 5.9
Past and Present Bufalino Family Members' Garment Industry Affiliations

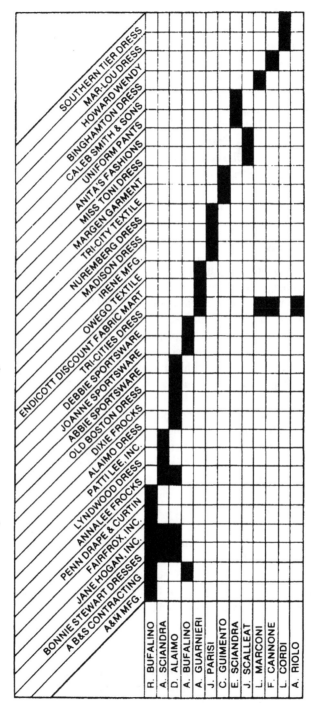

Source: Pennsylvania Crime Commission, A Decade of Organized Crime: 1980 Report (1980): p. 235.

basic criminal history records collected by law enforcement to search for all relevant data (Dintino and Martens, 1983). That is to say, intelligence systems may include not just information on criminal arrests but also on persons reasonably suspected of being involved in criminal activities or on groups which primarily engage in criminal activities.

Sometimes these information systems take the form of "expert systems" which support decision making related to criminal targeting. In others, the systems are "pointer indexes" which provide information on which agency or department has data on a particular criminal or crime group. In still others, a computerized index is linked to detailed files on microfiche or other storage media. Finally, a number of systems are based on "relational data base" structures which allow for the compilation of a criminal profile from a number of files throughout the data base.

Expert Systems

Expert systems are computer programs that simulate the way experts solve problems (Ratledge and Jacoby, 1989). One of the best known examples of expert systems in law enforcement is the VICAP (Violent Criminal Apprehension Program) at the Federal Bureau of Investigation (see Chapter 4). An application of expert systems to the organized crime area is the identification, evaluation, and analysis of organized crime networks to determine the strength of the linkages (relationships) within that group and identify groups which could be infiltrated or groups with members who might become government informants.

These expert systems use the computer technique known as "artificial intelligence" in which searches of computerized information are made to determine matches to predetermined criminal criteria. Carrying the criminal group network concept forward, an investigator examine a crime group for an individual who is reasonably visible within the group, is not particularly well reimbursed for his group efforts, is not a long-time member of the group, yet has access to the upper echelon of group management, has a family that does not include long-term members of the group, and has committed crimes which could net him significant prison sentences, as someone who might be vulnerable to "turning." The development of fine-tuned indicators would result from researching the backgrounds and motivations of numerous individuals who had become government witnesses. The application of the indicators, through computer analysis, would be the basis of an expert system.

Pointer Indices

Pointer indices provide a centralized location for the names, group affiliations, criminal activities, and other identifiers for persons reasonably suspected of being involved in known organized crime groups or organized crime activity.

These skeletal files also include the identification of organizations which are currently investigating these individuals.

The concept is that an agency which initiates an investigation into an organized crime individual or group contacts the pointer index location and asks for information on the individual. The index holder then "points" the requester to the agency(ies) that has submitted information on the alleged criminal. A system which limits access to the index is necessary to ensure the security of the information.

The primary example of a pointer index is found among the Regional Information Sharing System projects. These federally funded projects include all fifty of the United States. This system, established in 1980, is covered by the Code of Federal Regulations (*28CFR* 23.20), known as Criminal Intelligence Systems Operating Policies. These regulations place certain safeguards on the system, including the requirements of audit trails, written procedures, definitions of "need to know" and "right to know," levels of access, and security audits. In addition to their application to the RISS projects, these policies also govern all state or local level multijurisdictional computerized information sharing systems which have been funded, in part or in total, by federal funds.

Mixed Media Systems

The third type of computerized intelligence system combines a computerized index to the files with other forms of data storage. Some systems continue to rely on paper files with varying degrees of retrievability depending upon the depth of the indexing involved. If only suspect names, criminal activities, and locations are indexed, retrievability is minimal. If all names in a report, along with dates, AKAs, descriptors, locations, and MOs or other criminal identifiers are indexed, there is a much greater prospect for retrievability.

Computerizing entire case files and all investigative memoranda is not always advisable in the current computer environment. Few computers can quickly search through massive amounts of data, and storage devices are not often sufficient to this task. The advent of CD-ROM disks which contain entire encyclopedias gives an indication of what law enforcement data storage may use in the future.

Relational Data Base Systems

The final type of computerized intelligence system is one which allows for access to and compilation of all materials available in varied data bases. The concept behind relational data bases is that various types of information are collected in the course of an investigation and require different types of data bases to computerize them. Surveillance logs, telephone call records, financial records, criminal history information, testimony, and crime scene data may all be used in an organized crime investigation. In some computer systems, access to outside data bases (including commercial information systems) can be integrated with access to varied internal data bases for an all-source approach to intelligence production.

The key to relational data bases is to construct (through programming) the varied data bases necessary for these different types of records and, while doing so, construct a linking (or ''stringing'') capability among them so that pieces of data may be searched and selected from the different data bases and placed into a report which includes all known information on the suspect individual. This type of computer system is supportive of ongoing investigations and helps to collate, in preparation for analysis, data on the criminal actors.

CONCLUSIONS

Traditional and nontraditional organized crime investigations are significantly enhanced by the application of analytical techniques.

In past decades, intelligence, organized crime, and analysis have been closely related; that is not expected to change in the future. Analysis is an integral part of the complex conspiracy investigation. As organized criminals become more sophisticated in their illegal and business enterprises, analysts will be challenged to devise new methods of uncovering those dealings.

CHAPTER VI

Narcotics Applications

Organized crime was the first focus of intelligence and analysis; narcotics, in spite of the characteristics it shares with organized crime, was not strongly linked to intelligence analysis until the late 1980s. The primary reason for this may be, Pagano and Martens suggest, that making narcotics arrests is often like shooting ducks out of a pond: numerous arrests can be made without complex investigation or the intelligence process (1986).

In the late 1980s and early 1990s, however, both national and state narcotics strategies focused on the use of intelligence to interdict networks and conspiracies. Emphasis on quantity of arrest was replaced in some agencies by quality of arrests. The analytical component was expanded in many agencies to support narcotics investigations, particularly at federal and state levels. A 1993 survey of analysts indicated that of 1,288 analysts in 106 agencies in the United States, 743 were employed by the federal government (Peterson, 1993).

Intelligence is used to investigate the three primary levels of narcotics work: street-level transportation and distribution, midlevel distribution networks, and major narcotics syndicates. It also supports RICO investigations, drug money laundering cases, clandestine laboratory investigations, and prescription drug diversion investigations. Further, analysis helps in making assessments of the narcotics threat and developing narcotics strategies and action plans.

BACKGROUND

In some states the 1980s was termed "the drug decade" (Pennsylvania Crime Commission, 1991). The period reflected a dramatic escalation in the demand for narcotics, as well as an escalation in the public's knowledge of, and concern about, drug abuse. Some of this concern was the result of drug-related violence, as shoot-outs and drive-by shootings harmed innocent bystanders as well as members of the drug subculture.

Violence in illegal drug networks is considered systemic and is used to protect or expand territories, to intimidate competitors, or to retaliate. Studies in New York, Miami, and Washington, D.C., showed that between 24 and 53 percent of homicides were drug-related (Bureau of Justice Statistics, 1992). Violence is also used by drug traffickers against police and judges.

Another concern is related to the increase in drug-related crimes; some contended that these crimes were committed because the violator was under the influence of drugs or needed money to support a drug habit. Surveys of prisoners in the 1980s showed that 75 to 80 percent admitted to using drugs previously (Bureau of Justice Statistics, 1987, 1988, and 1992). One-third of prison inmates surveyed in 1979 admitted use of heroin (Bureau of Justice Statistics, 1983) while 60 percent of the males arrested and tested through the Drug Use Forecasting system in 1990 had positive results that indicated drug use (Bureau of Justice Statistics, December 1992).

The role of the drug-dependent offender in recidivist activity is also significant, since 52 percent of all recidivists tested are "drug dependent" (Rand Corporation, 1988). The Bureau of Justice Statistics reported that active drug users commit offenses at high rates, and a national study of youth found offense rates rose with more serious drug involvement (1992).

The U.S. Parole Commission's opinion, given in the *Federal Register,* was "Drug abuse is so pervasive (in the prison population) that all released prisoners under supervision should be subject to an immediate drug test whenever ordered by their U.S. probation officer" (1990, p. 862).

Drug use and sale can have a serious and negative effect on a community. Fear levels rise. Disorder—graffiti, litter, abandoned houses, and so on—intensify. Drug sellers and drug users become targets for violent crime.

The Office of National Drug Control Policy (ONDCP) has tried to give some focus to antidrug efforts by developing a national strategy against drugs. Their strategy statements have contained national priorities set by the ONDCP which included support for the use of intelligence and analysis in the "drug war." The 1991 *National Drug Control Strategy,* for example, stated: "Within law enforcement agencies, intelligence functions must be adequately funded . . . we must . . . maximize the sharing of . . . information. . . . This information must be synthesized into various intelligence products, regularly updated, and disseminated. . . . Dismantling drug trafficking organizations requires intelligence. . . " (The White House, 1991, p. 115).

The 1992 *Strategy* lists intelligence under its "National Funding Priorities for Fiscal Years 1993–95"; among its goals are to "improve strategic and operational intelligence capabilities and products and continue to automate information systems" (The White House, 1992, p. 142). The El Paso Intelligence Center in Texas, managed by DEA, has been expanded and enhanced and the DEA's

Narcotics and Dangerous Drugs Information System (NADDIS) is being expanded to allow federal, state, and local law enforcement electronic access to the new NADDIS-X (p. 175). The major focus of the National Strategy's intelligence effort, the National Drug Intelligence Center (NDIC), opened for use in the summer of 1993, over six years after the start of the "drug war."

Despite efforts to make the use of intelligence and analysis a routine part of drug investigation, resistance continues. Most seasoned narcotics officers still believe that the two most effective ways to generate drug arrests are through confidential informant data and physical surveillance. Texts focusing on drug investigation such as the DEA *Drug Enforcement Manual* devote a chapter each to informants, surveillance operations, raid operations, and other traditional means of law enforcement, yet they provide only one paragraph about the use of analysis or intelligence in drug operations. Basic drug investigative courses given by federal and state agencies, in the main, have not included intelligence and narcotics as topics in drug officer training.

On the other hand, an increasing number of investigators involved in counternarcotics efforts have been trained in analytical techniques through the efforts of agencies including the Federal Law Enforcement Training Center in Glynco, Georgia, and various multijurisdictional task forces around the country.

Although numerous drug arrests can be made without planning or analysis in any city in the United States, the need for analysis persists. Such arrest have no real impact on the drug trade in the cities, raising questions about what the goal of a narcotics enforcement program is. Routine arrests generally bring low-level users and dealers to justice. These arrests result in high statistics, but do little to reduce drug trafficking or use. With the aid of intelligence and analysis, higher-level arrests of key traffickers can be made. This higher level of arrests generates asset seizures and forfeitures of property including cars, real estate, currency, jewelry, and other personal property.

For every arrest made of street-level dealers, several others step forward to fill the breach, suggesting the need for a new approach to include analysis, strategic targeting, and problem solving. As Andrews and associates commented in 1981, "The future of drug enforcement is dependent upon . . . prioritizing the drug problem . . . full enforcement . . . must give way to the selective and judicious allocation of finite police resources."

STREET-LEVEL NARCOTICS OPERATIONS

Street-level narcotics operations include actions against users, low-level dealers, and low-level narcotics gangs. The bulk of all narcotics arrests are made by patrol officers when apprehending someone for other criminal violations. These "incidental" arrests often involve drug users rather than drug sellers (or, they involve drug sellers who, because of the small amount they are carrying or other variables, have their charge reduced from distribution to possession).

The second-largest number of narcotics arrests are more deliberate and involve users or smaller-quantity dealers.

Low-level arrests can be viewed as part of a comprehensive narcotics strategy or as statistic generators. As part of a comprehensive narcotics strategy, they may form a component of directed enforcement and yield data that may indicate the presence of larger narcotics networks. Purely as statistics generators, they increase the number of drug arrests but are not used to target or gather intelligence.

Street-level narcotics enforcement has included a planned and coordinated approach in recent years. Federal funding has supported numerous programs, and experiences have been shared with other jurisdictions through federally funded technical assistance programs.

Three of these programs, in Denver, Miami, and Los Angeles, were highlighted in the Narcotics Street Sales Enforcement program developed by the Institute for Law and Justice for the U.S. Bureau of Justice Assistance. The enforcement methods used in these locations included reverse stings, street sweeps, gang task forces, intelligence gathering and sharing, undercover operations, and buy-busts.

"Reverse stings" are enforcement programs designed to snare drug users and act as a deterrent to casual drug use. They generally involve undercover police officers posing as drug dealers. These officers "sell" drugs to users who are then arrested for possession of a controlled dangerous substance. In Denver the substance sold was a crack cocaine look-alike made of wax, plaster of paris, flour, and coloring. One four-day effort in 1988 netted Denver Police sixty-five arrests and the seizure of fifteen vehicles and three bicycles.

"Street sweeps" are done in areas with known drug activity. They involve the arrest of all violators in a particular geographic area such as a block, a street corner, a public park, or a multifamily dwelling. These are effective in breaking up the illegal activity in the location through intermittent sweeps of the area. At times this causes the location of the narcotics sales to shift from the targeted location to a nontargeted area nearby. Street sweeps were used as part of an overall program in Denver. Confidential informants (CIs) and undercover officers (UOs) are used to identify and target high drug areas. Detectives and uniformed officers make the arrests on the basis of information about who was "holding" drugs from the CIs and UOs.

A "gang task force" is a consortium of law enforcement and education/social welfare professionals who deal with juveniles. These consortiums have banded together to intervene and deter gang activity by using a variety of tactics including nonenforcement programs to intervene in gang activities.

In Los Angeles one pilot program identified approximately 500 gangs with over 50,000 members who committed 13,618 crimes during 1986 and developed a number of enforcement, educational, and jobs programs to discourage reliance on gangs.

A number of programs have also used intelligence gathering, analysis, and dissemination as integral parts of their work against street-level narcotics. Information from informants, undercover operators, and patrol officers is compiled, evaluated, and analyzed to identify target individuals and areas for enforcement operations. Information systems tailored to specific program needs are developed.

Undercover operations have long been a mainstay of narcotics investigation. They involve police officers acting in a role which enables them to associate with violators to obtain incriminating evidence against them.

Buy-busts involve officers posing as drug buyers who, upon obtaining drugs in return for money, arrest the drug seller. These arrests support street-level programs or target drug dealers who may be able to provide information on higher-level distributors or organizations.

Analytical methods and techniques can be used to support each of these police tactics which investigate narcotics violations.

Street Sweeps

Pagano and Martens were referring to the street level of narcotic work in their comments about the perceived lack of a need for intelligence in narcotics enforcement: "Opportunistic enforcement . . . is sufficient in producing both arrest and seizure statistics—the standard measures of productivity for a narcotic unit" (Pagano and Martens, 1986).

Indeed, the late 1980s showed that these statistics increased by substantial percentages when patrol officers availed themselves of all opportunities to arrest violators. In New Jersey, for example, 1987 and 1988 drug arrests soared over the 1986 level, particularly for possession/use offenses (New Jersey State Police, 1990). These arrests sometimes occurred during a "street sweep" in which officers chose a particular corner or block for enforcement and arrested every individual who appeared to be committing a crime within that location or during specific enforcement action against known drug market areas.

Street sweeps can generate arrests for drugs, prostitution, curfew violations, carrying a concealed weapon without a permit, vagrancy, or other charges. Yet these street sweeps may do little to end drug crime and may place an impossible burden on the court system and on the jails. Most arrested face only disorderly person charges and are back on the corner the next day.

In response to an influx of cases, the courts often downgrade narcotics offenses, particularly in the larger cities. Sales of drugs may result in only a disorderly persons arrest. Drug dealers may also be back out on the street before the arresting officer has the paperwork completed, leading to loss of faith in the system among the public and the police.

The locations of the street sweeps in the model programs cited were selected rigorously, with analysis of potential areas for directed arrests. The sweeps were part of an overall strategy to clean up a particular area to allow for the initiation of community policing or other related programs. As such, they were more of a "directed enforcement" effort.

Directed Enforcement

The conventional "street sweeps" gave way in the early 1990s to "directed enforcement." The purpose of directed enforcement was to interdict drug networks and dismantle them. This is a longer-range investigative effort which often results in fewer arrests. In New Jersey, for example, the "body count" of drug arrests dropped from the 1989 high by 24 percent in 1990 and by another 12 percent in 1991 (New Jersey State Police, 1992).

Possession/use arrests dropped most, by 29 percent from 1989 to 1990 and by 14 percent from 1990 to 1991. Sale/manufacture arrests, indicative of longer-term investigation, also dropped, but at half the rate of the use/possession rates: by 14 percent between 1989 and 1990 and by 7 percent from 1990 to 1991 (New Jersey State Police, 1992).

In directed enforcement, various indicators and intelligence are gathered to determine locations of open-air drug markets or "crack" houses. These locations are then targeted for an enforcement sweep with the dual purpose of arresting violators and deterring the use of that location for drug sales. In the instance of crack houses, the properties are seized, when possible, and can be forfeited and returned to the municipality for renovation and sale under certain conditions.

The "directed" aspect of enforcement includes intelligence targeting. Choice of the location for the enforcement is based on the analysis of all available information. The sources of information may include tips from community members, arrest records, informant data, field reports filed by patrol officers, public records showing the ownership of the location or locations being considered, intelligence reports on gang activity, and other information. The data may be compiled and compared so that the targets chosen for the enforcement effort will be those which have the greatest positive impact on the community.

This heightened impact may include the arrest and conviction of violators with several previous violations (thus garnering longer sentences for this violation), the arrest and conviction of violators with weapons (which currently allows for enhanced prosecution under federal statutes), and/or the arrest and conviction of violators who own the property on which the violations occurred (which may make the property qualify for seizure and forfeiture). The intent is to maximize the possibility of arresting those habitual offenders who, by virtue of their past and present actions, pose the most serious threat to the community and will garner a significant jail sentence as a result of their criminal activity.

The concept of directed enforcement is the basis of some innovative programs occurring now in narcotics enforcement in the United States. One program is the Drug Market Analysis program, which was funded as a pilot project by the

Bureau of Justice Assistance, Department of Justice, in several cities around the country including Jersey City, New Jersey, and Hartford, Connecticut.

The Drug Market Analysis program is a computerized system used to identify particular locations for enforcement targeting. The program allows varied information to be collated into MapInfo, a computer mapping program which identifies "hot spots" for enforcement. The information includes calls for service, locations of arrests, locations of field reports, data from community surveys, arrest records, types of drugs sold by location, and sales techniques used by location. On the basis of this identification by analysts using the computerized program, enforcement managers can then target areas for stepped-up enforcement and patrol. In addition, the drug markets uncovered in Jersey City have been divided into traditional and innovative enforcement strategies to determine the effectiveness of nontraditional strategies on the drug markets (National Institute of Justice, 1993).

Another program using directed enforcement is the federally funded Weed and Seed program, which included Trenton, New Jersey, and Kansas City, Missouri, as its initial pilot cities. Weed and Seed was a multidisciplinary program which brought together enforcement, education, recreation, housing, community organization, and other leaders to develop strategies which would reclaim drug-torn neighborhoods. It included a Violent Offender Removal Program (VORP) component, to stabilize criminal occurrence in the program area so that community policing and community empowerment programs could take root.

Participants in the VORP program were federal, state, county, and local police and prosecutive agencies. Analysis was used in support of Weed and Seed to compile data on potential targets from previous arrest records and intelligence sources, to do background (criminal history) checks on potential targets, and to track the results of the enforcement activities for reporting to participants and the grantor agency.

The Denver street-level narcotics program used analysis to create a list of indicators of suspected drug trafficking:

- A lone male or female may attempt to rent the residence; if a lone female, she may state that her "boyfriend" may stay with her on occasion.
- The prospective tenant will prefer a corner apartment on ground floor or a higher-level apartment overlooking the street.
- The tenant will pay deposit and rent with cash.
- The tenant will provide little information on past employment or residential references, giving only general and unverifiable data.
- The tenant will move in with little furniture. (Denver Police Department, September 1987)

A listing of these indicators, along with suggestions of how to screen tenants for verifiable information, was made available to property owners and managers as part of a community outreach program.

Crime analysis has also been used to determine the presence of drug networks or drug territories. Many factors—including type of drug, sale location, drug packaging, drug purity, and use of beepers, stash houses, runners, and lookouts—can show connections between violators which elevate the drug activity from a simple crime of opportunity to a conspiratorial crime. If the goal of the law enforcement agency is to interdict drug networks, then crime analysis, followed by a detailed network analysis, will work toward that goal.

Drug gang territories can also be identified by an analysis of drug arrest records, surveillance reports, and field interview reports from patrol officers. This will support an evaluation of the relative strength of the gangs and their targeting by law enforcement, as well as an assessment of the likelihood of their becoming involved in territorial disputes with neighboring gangs.

Some law enforcement officials have found youth gangs to be heavily involved in drug trafficking. Others, such as those in the Los Angeles area, believe that focusing on gangs is an effective way to decrease street-level drug trafficking and developed a plan to eradicate street narcotics sales and gang-related activities in the city. They commented that ''one of the most serious narcotics trends . . . is the increasing involvement of violence-prone street gangs who are actively involved in narcotics trafficking, particularly with rock cocaine (crack)'' (Los Angeles Police Department, 1988, p. 2). Gang programs and analytical support for them are discussed in more detail in Chapter 8.

An analysis of past narcotics arrest records may also help identify real estate which has been used repeatedly to support narcotics activity. In some states and at the federal level, this property can then be seized, forfeited, and sold, with the proceeds going to support additional law enforcement effort. Intelligence analysts or asset investigators may complete record searches which will identify other possible assets for seizure and forfeiture.

A generally successful tactic in street-level narcotic enforcement has been the use of informants to identify dealers or other individuals for arrest. These informants provide raw data (which some erroneously call ''intelligence'') to the narcotics officer, who, in turn, must evaluate the reliability of that data before acting upon it. Narcotics informants, unlike other informants, are often not very dependable, perhaps in part because of their use of narcotics (Pagano and Martens, 1986).

One way to assist the investigator in determining the reliability of an informant is through the data collection, evaluation, and analysis process. That process uses analysis to compare the informant's data to other information gathered, to past information given by the informant, and to the reliability of past information given by the informant. Many major police departments require the evaluation of information for reliability of the source and accuracy of the information. Generally standardized scales have been developed (see Chapter 5). While some departments use investigators to do this evaluation (on the basis of their expert knowledge of the case and the informants), others use analysts to allow a more objective view of the data.

Narcotics Courier Interdiction

The interdiction of narcotics couriers has been an important part of narcotics enforcement. This has been done in areas near border crossings, such as "Operation Pipeline" in the Southwest, at international airports, or along transportation corridors in areas with high drug use, such as the Washington/New York corridor.

Narcotics couriers use various means to transport contraband. Road vehicles stopped with narcotics have included automobiles, leisure homes, tractor-trailer trucks, and automobile carriers. Narcotics are imported by train, by ship, and airplane. Narcotics are carried into the country in luggage or on the courier's person. They are shipped into the country hidden in a variety of containers, from hollowed-out books, to foodstuffs, to machinery.

Intelligence, and therefore analysis, plays a significant role in narcotics interdiction. This intelligence can be gathered from informants within the smuggling ring or from nonparticipants. Sometimes the data received are specific, telling of a particular shipment arriving on a certain date by a certain means. This is often one-shot information, tactical in nature, but it needs to be evaluated and analyzed in light of previously gathered data to determine the likelihood of its veracity.

In other instances, the data are more general and when compiled can provide information on potential narcotics couriers. The process for compiling this information to develop indicators is an analytical one, with a basis in crime analysis and frequency distribution.

One example of this type of analysis involved the analysis of a computerized printout on individuals from a particular country stopped on entry to the United States, at which time heroin was found. The data, collected in the mid-1980s, covered a four-year period and related only to airports. The types of information available on the individuals involved in the more than one thousand narcotics interceptions included the following:

- destination address,

- age,

- sex,

- port of entry,

- date,

- methods of concealment,

- country of flight origin,

- courier nationality,

- courier name.

From information gathered in the heroin seizures, indicators of heroin couriers of that particular nationality were developed. The composite showed that the flights originated in a particular country and arrived principally at Kennedy and Newark airports (both in metropolitan New York) in the United States and that the couriers were predominantly males between the age of 26 and 35 who were destined for New York, New Jersey, Maryland, Washington, D.C., Texas, California, or Illinois and carried the narcotic inside their bodies. A number of the heroin couriers gave certain New York City hotels as their destination.

Of the persons arrested in the one thousand-plus seizures, 86 individuals were shown to have been intercepted three or more times and were designated as "frequent" couriers. Multiple destinations given by these frequent couriers gave rise to geographic distribution analysis which showed the span of geographic contacts by the couriers.

This courier analysis provided information for agencies responsible for interdiction at airports. A significant amount of intelligence resulting from the analysis was disseminated to law enforcement agencies in the geographic areas which included heroin courier destinations. This information could be used to corroborate suspected heroin activity in those areas or could provide leads for investigation into previously unknown heroin activity.

In another example using analysis in interdiction, data relating to 553 packages which had been seized between 1983 and 1986 and were found to contain heroin or opium were analyzed. The data included address, addressee name, date, state, port of entry, narcotic type, and method of concealment. A temporal analysis of the incidents showed that in 1984 and 1985 the largest number of packages was seized, presumably the result of strong enforcement effort. The most popular methods of concealment used wood, books, or magazines for heroin, as well as cloth with the drug sewn in or saturating the fibers. This information was used to produce intelligence bulletins which were disseminated across the country. The identification of addresses to which packages were sent provided local investigators leads for potential action.

Transit interdiction has also been successful against street level dealers. Suburban drug dealers often replenish their supply of drugs through urban drug markets. Drugs can be carried back on public buses, trains, or rapid transit systems in small amounts to lessen punishment if caught. Numerous trips can be made by paid couriers or members of the drug group. Enforcement groups can target particular transit stops and use interdiction methods (drug dogs, random sampling, etc.) to uncover the presence of drugs.

This can result in numerous arrests and seizure of drugs, drug money, and weapons. It can also provide information relating to the sources of drugs entering the jurisdiction, the possible presence of drug networks, and the destinations of the drugs. This information, when assembled and analyzed, can support targeted enforcement efforts.

An extension of transit interdiction is the targeting of hotels and motels near airports and major transportation centers for their use as meeting places for drug couriers and distributors. Work has been done in this area to analyze data and identify possible indicators of narcotics traffickers and to alert hotel personnel to these indicators.

Public Housing Interdiction

During the 1980s, publicly subsidized housing was identified as a significant source of drug distribution and violence in the United States. Crime rates within the housing areas were higher. Residents were held captive by a criminal environment which supported vandalism, violence, and drug use and sales.

One strategy used to combat public housing crime was increasing patrols by the housing police or having the housing authority contract for increased patrols by local police. Another strategy was to combine increased patrols with reconstruction of the vandalized areas and support for tenant associations. By working closely with tenants, the police could gather information that would identify the most flagrant violators and violation locations. The data gathered from the residents would be evaluated and analyzed. These serious offenders, often recidivist violators, could thereby be identified and targeted for enforcement action.

In Knoxville, Tennessee, for example, the Knoxville Police Department initiated an Inner City Drug Enforcement Program which focused on repeat offenders and housing projects which it termed "high-risk drug areas." An analysis of the situation in Knoxville led the Police Department, working in conjunction with the Knox County Sheriff's Office, to join forces with city agencies responsible for housing, licensing, street lighting, zoning, and community development to provide a holistic approach to the problems of the housing projects.

They used four strategies—apprehension and prosecution, resident education, tenant leadership development, and interagency coordination of services—to impact on the housing areas. To support these strategies, they also developed a system to capture both investigative and statistical data for analysis and dissemination.

An analysis of street-level narcotics operations usually shows that few narcotics dealers are isolated, entrepreneurial operators. Most have connections to narcotics groups, and all have connections to higher-level narcotics suppliers. Polydrug distributors, in particular, have access to a number of drug sources and are thereby connected to several groups. Analytical and investigative review of the data on street sales and arrests can provide information which will lead to midlevel or upper-level narcotics distributors and syndicates.

MIDLEVEL NARCOTICS ORGANIZATIONS

The goal of most narcotics enforcement units is to identify, gain entry to, and prosecute the higher echelons of narcotics distribution networks. Analysis can assist in the identification of distribution networks through the review and com-

Figure 6.1
Narcotics Network Indicators

```
1.  Organizational structure
         - runners
         - lookouts
         - money collectors

2.  Communications ability
         - cellular phones
         - pagers

3.  Poly-drug distribution

4.  Exclusivity of territory
         - violence
         - coercion

5.  Immunity from prosecution
         - corruption of enforcement

6.  Sophisticated logistics
         - stash houses
         - rental vehicles

7.  Steady supply of contraband

8.  Distinctive packaging
         - taping
         - "brand" name
```

pilation of data received in street-level arrests, the integration of informant data, and the use of information gathered from other sources such as the patrol function or community watch groups. Analysis can also compare the activities occurring with those which are common indicators of narcotics network activity as shown in Figure 6.1.

Entry to the network may be done by "flipping" (turning a criminal into an informant) a street-level dealer, by using that dealer to introduce an undercover officer into the narcotics organization, or by arranging for the purchase of ever-increasing amounts of contraband which must be bought from persons higher in the distribution network. Through close contact with the networks' members, sufficient evidence can be gathered to prosecute the organization.

When entry has been gained, there are a number of ways in which analysis can support the operation. As mentioned, data provided by an informant, particularly over an extended period, can be catalogued, compared, and evaluated by an analyst or an investigator. An undercover officer or informant might be involved in consensual recordings which need to be transcribed and analyzed to ascertain the facts included and the overall meaning of the conversation. Data from a number of sources (physical surveillance, statements, electronic surveillance, etc.) must be integrated and compared.

Once targets have been identified, other records may be obtained through proper means which will require analysis. Telephone records, for example, have been collected from suspected drug dealers which showed direct calls from the target to drug-producing/manufacturing countries and to cities, including New York, Miami, and Los Angeles, which are common ports of entry and thus are the locations of large-quantity drug distributors.

In one example, collect calls to a suspected dealer showed a series of phone calls to his number from various pay phone locations along interstate highways beginning in Florida and ending in the Mid-Atlantic states. This indicated that a courier might be checking in during the drive northward. By tracking these locations and approximating the local arrival time, the shipment being transported was interdicted shortly before it reached its destination.

The analysis of the telephone call records of an individual can provide the basis for a request for an electronic intercept of the individual's phone which can lead investigators to obtain damaging spoken evidence from the target. It can also help to identify out of area contacts of the target which may indicate that a broader conspiracy or network is present.

Other records which may be subpoenaed and analyzed are utility records, bank records, and business records. Utility records are key to uncovering locations which may house illegal narcotics growing or processing plants. In recent years, marijuana growing under lights has become more common in the United States. An analysis of the charges on bills for heat and light may corroborate a suspicion that marijuana growing is occurring. Similarly, a clandestine narcotics laboratory which manufactures drugs such as methamphetamine or PCP could show unusual use of electricity or water.

The presence of mid- to upper-level dealers in an area may result in the creation of a multiagency task force including federal, state, and local level enforcement personnel. These task forces have been shown to be effective against narcotics syndicates in many areas of the country. They often use analysis in support of their cases, assigning an officer or analyst (if available) to this task. Common products developed in support of these cases include telephone record analysis, association analysis, event flow analysis, and financial analysis.

The Regional Information Sharing Systems (RISS) projects produce a number of analyses that support such cases. The Western States Information Network (WSIN), for example, supports over 120 tactical narcotics cases per year. In one WSIN case, analysts assisted a tricounty task force including federal, state, and local personnel. Evidence had been gathered that the defendant had been cultivating a sizable marijuana garden for several years. Analysts have prepared link charts that summarize the connections between the defendants and a map which summarized their illegal activity over the region. After defense attorneys studied the map and charts, the three defendants pled guilty to manufacturing a controlled substance.

One common use of analysis in midlevel drug investigation is to identify the source of the narcotics to expand the investigation to the major narcotic syndicate level.

MAJOR NARCOTICS SYNDICATES

Major narcotics syndicates operate nationally or internationally to smuggle and distribute large quantities of narcotics into a geographic region and are often involved in the laundering of large-scale drug profits. In recent years, these major groups included Colombian cartels (cocaine), Asian and Middle Eastern smuggling rings (heroin), outlaw motorcycle gangs (methamphetamine), and Jamaican posses (marijuana).

The investigative techniques used against these groups have been similar to those used against the more traditional organized crime groups with some differences due to the varying structures and makeup of the narcotics syndicates.

Undercover police officer placement, for example, is more difficult in Asian gangs because of a scarcity of Asian American police officers in the United States. Many drug syndicates are based not only on ethnic ties but on blood-family ties; thus they are harder to infiltrate. Informants are more likely to be used in these settings than undercover officers.

Electronic eavesdropping on drug groups can also be problematic if the people being tapped are speaking a foreign language. Many departments have noted the lack of bilingual or multilingual officers on their staff and have had to rely on contracted interpreters. At least one college which has developed an analytical degree program (Mercyhurst in Erie, Pennsylvania) requires proficiency in Spanish for a degree.

The structure of the narcotics syndicates also makes investigations more difficult. Where the organization and methods of La Cosa Nostra have been repeatedly and publicly detailed, the narcotics cartels do not operate similarly. Their members do not fit into the hierarchical model shown by the Mafia. Instead, their subgroups may be independently operating, loosely connected, and interchangeable. A link chart depicting this nonhierarchy is seen in Figure 6.2.

Most major cases are combined efforts of several agencies and often cover several states; as a result a number of agencies are collecting data. Major cases also usually include the subpoenaing of numerous records, including bank records, telephone records, and corporate records (if any). Major cases require major case management, which includes the use of analytical techniques to manage the information and documents which are collected and to analyze the documents to assist the investigation and prepare for court. Major cases can cause an analyst to produce a full range of analytical products, including link analyses, event flow and commodity flow analyses, telephone record analyses, financial analyses, and visual investigative analyses. For this reason, major cases may have several analysts assigned to them.

Major cases may also be international and often require cooperation with the

Figure 6.2
Diagram of Hispanic Organization

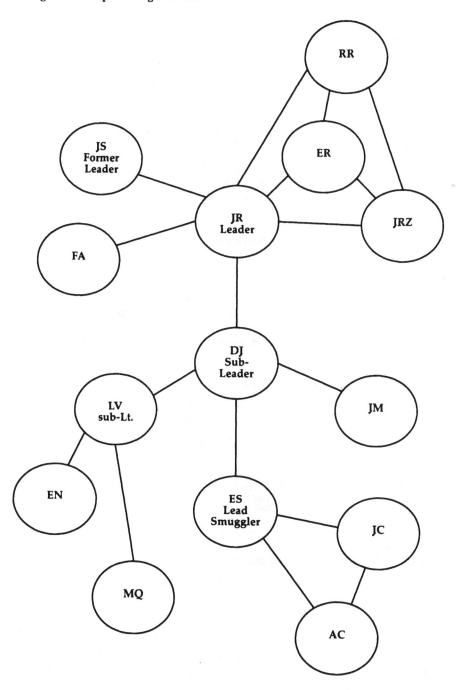

Figure 6.3
Selling Prices for the Equivalent of One Kilogram of Southeast Asian Heroin at Successive Stages of Trafficking (75–95% Purity)

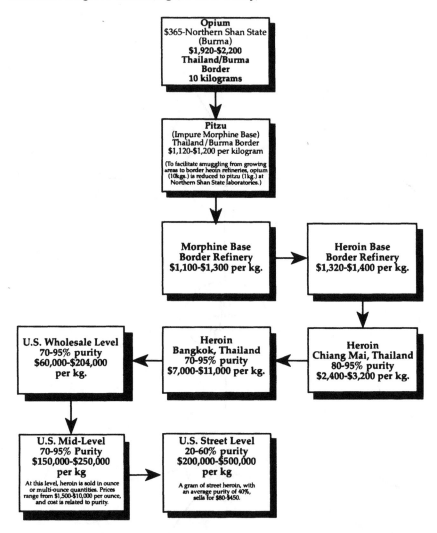

Source: Drug Enforcement Administration, *Intelligence Trends*, Vol. 17, No. 1 (1990): p. 9.

Drug Enforcement Administration and enforcement in other countries. Some of these cases involve tracing the drugs back to the source in an effort to interdict the drugs before they reach drug users. One analytical product that supports this process is a commodity flow chart. Figure 6.3 is a heroin flow chart which shows drug purity and pricing from the fields to the streets.

One major case involved a multistate effort against the Hells Angels outlaw motorcycle gang called "Operation Cacus." Operation Cacus began in 1985 when a member of the Anchorage chapter of the Hells Angels became an informant. Subsequently, the FBI was called into the investigation, and, in February 1987, WSIN was asked to provide analytical assistance. It began the analysis by gathering case reports from four different FBI offices. The reports were collated, numbered, and summarized in a computerized file. Later this file was used by prosecutors in developing cases and made it easier to find original case reports that substantiated information. When it came time to draw charts, the computer file was sorted by the crime type and a chronology of criminal activities was printed. Over fourteen charts were drawn and used in the investigation and prosecution. In November 1987, thirty-eight Hells Angels were arrested in California, Alaska, Kentucky, North Carolina, and South Carolina. Approximately $3.5 million in cash was recovered along with twenty-five pounds of gold and forty pounds of methamphetamine. One WSIN product from Operation Cacus, a VIA chart, is shown in Figure 6.4. As a result of its analytical work in the case, WSIN received $300,000 of the seized assets.

DIVERSION OF PRESCRIPTION LEGEND DRUGS

The diversion of prescription legend drugs (PLDs) is another, less publicized threat within the narcotics realm. Some narcotics investigators have maintained that this poses a more serious problem to the American public than cocaine. Others cite a concern for the betrayal of public trust by health care professionals (doctors, nurses, veterinarians, dentists, and pharmacists) who distribute prescriptions for controlled dangerous substances in return for cash.

The traditional means of investigation of health care professionals who are illegally dispensing drugs is by identifying the practitioner or pharmacy and sending in an undercover officer to purchase the prescription drugs. The evidence thus gathered is presented to the practitioner, who then often pleads guilty to an accusation, thus avoiding the court process and publicity.

Action against the practitioner, which may include fines, suspension of a license, community service, and/or drug treatment, is also taken by the appropriate regulatory agency. Because this method deals with individual practitioners and limited amounts of drugs being dispensed, it has a limited impact on the overall PLD problem.

Another investigative method is to gather extensive information on prescriptions and analyze it to find significant distribution points. This is particularly effective in states which have laws requiring multiple copies of each prescription written.

One analysis of prescription data was made in Ohio during the mid-1980s when 30,000 records were reviewed to determine whether excessive amounts of controlled dangerous substances were being prescribed by the same doctors or prescriptions were being filled by the same pharmacies. The information on the

Figure 6.4
Narcotic Activities of Charles Manganiello

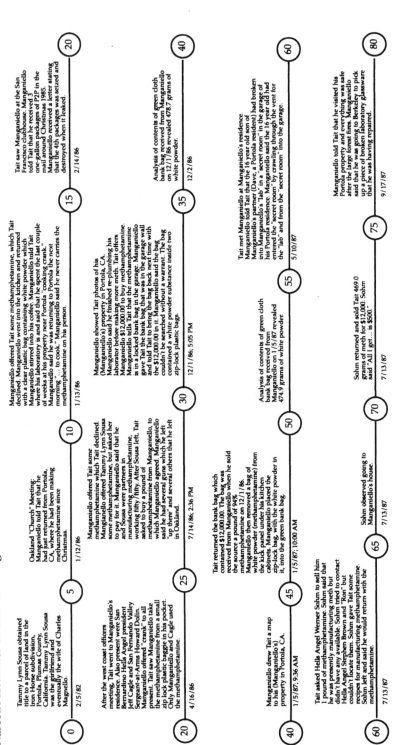

Source: Chart completed 12/87 by analyst Karen Sanderson, Western States Information Network.

prescription form, including the patient's name and address, the doctor's name and address, the type, dosage strength, and unit number of the drug prescribed, and the pharmacy's name and address, was reviewed.

This review uncovered individuals who were "doctor shopping" as well as doctors who were dispensing prescriptions for payment and pharmacists who were illegally dispensing drugs. Out of hundreds of doctors and pharmacists in the Ohio analysis, the most serious doctor and pharmacy violators were targeted for investigation and prosecution. The analysis preceding investigation led to effective targeting of these violators and most potentially successful prosecutions.

As more states enact laws requiring pharmacists to submit a copy of each prescription blank filled, more data will be available to support prescription legend drug investigations.

CLANDESTINE LABORATORY INVESTIGATIONS

Substances including methamphetamine (speed), PCP, LSD, and "designer drugs" are manufactured in clandestine drug laboratories. These laboratories may be in the trunk of someone's car, in a hotel or motel room, in a rented apartment in the city, or in a remote farmhouse. The people involved in the manufacture of these drugs are usually called "chemists" and may or may not have some scientific background. Cultivated drugs such as cocaine are also processed in laboratories, some of which are in the United States and others of which are in cocaine producing/processing countries.

The requirements of chemicals, glassware, water, and electricity vary from drug to drug. California has been the state with the highest number of drug laboratories (with approximately 225 labs discovered in 1985 as opposed to fewer than 40 in five other states which reported drug laboratories). A geographic distribution analysis which shows that comparison can be seen in Figure 6.5.

Clandestine laboratory investigations can be either reactive or proactive. In a reactive investigation, information is received about noxious odors or suspicious activity at a particular location. The site is quietly surveilled to determine whether it is a drug lab. If the assessment of the situation reaches a positive conclusion about a lab, then an entry team and environmental specialists are assembled to seize the lab and arrest the violators.

Because of the danger of the chemicals used in clandestine labs and the propensity of the lab chemists to "boobytrap" lab entrances, strict safety protocols are followed, including use of protective clothing and breathing apparatus. The U.S. Drug Enforcement Administration has trained thousands of state and local police to follow specific safety guidelines in clandestine laboratories and certifies these individuals as qualified to participate in lab interdiction.

It is often the case that the materials from the lab are recovered without arrests. This is true when the lab has been abandoned after the manufacturing

Figure 6.5
Clandestine Laboratories, 1985

Source: Karen Sanderson, "An Analytical Response to the Clandestine Drug Laboratory Problem," *Law Enforcement Intelligence Analysis Digest*, Vol. 2, No. 1 (February 1987): p. 40.

process has been concluded or when the chemist has been tipped off that an enforcement action may occur and leaves the lab. In this instance, the chemicals and glassware are carefully collected and analyzed to provide leads to the identity of the chemist or other financial backers of the lab.

Figure 6.6
Clandestine Laboratory Location Indicators

- Noxious odors associated with
          chemical/industrial use--ammonia, ether,
          solvents; strong or prolonged odor

- Exhaust fans on house or outbuilding
       constantly running or running in cold weather

- Windows sealed and/or painted

- High electric and/or water bills

- Deliveries frequently being made by parcel
       services of glassware, chemicals, etc.

- Purchase of large quantities of chemicals from
       hardware or other stores such as:
       - acetone in multigallon lots
       - sodium hydroxide products (e.g., "Drano")
       by the case

- Purchase of lab supplies or equipment

- Purchase of key chemicals (ether, etc.) or
       glassware from or through local companies

- Abnormal use of electricity and water

- All windows darkened or covered

Source: New Jersey State Police, *ALERT,* West Trenton, NJ, 1990.

The location is thoroughly searched for other leads about the identity of the violators. These leads may be found in trash, telephone records, personal records, or personal papers left behind. By contacting the owner of the property, utility companies, or other connected entities, additional information may be uncovered.

The chemicals and glassware may be traced to their sources to provide further leads. Telephone records and financial records, if obtained, can be analyzed to provide additional data.

Through analysis of numerous cases, certain indicators of clandestine laboratory locations have also been developed (see Figure 6.6).

Proactive clandestine laboratory investigations also occur. These can be generated from data gathered from suppliers of chemicals, glassware, or other paraphernalia used by the labs. The data on sales of particular chemicals or glassware are collected and analyzed to determine whether, by virtue of amounts purchased or combinations of ingredients and glassware purchased, certain buyers are potentially involved in clandestine laboratories. This analytical process can identify individuals and/or locations that may be connected to clandestine labs. An investigation into the possible violators then ensues. The Drug Enforcement Administration has had a precursor chemical tracking program for several years.

ASSET SEIZURE AND FORFEITURE

The strategy of asset seizure and forfeiture has been frequently used in narcotics enforcement, working toward the goal of taking the profits out of narcotics trafficking. Asset seizures have ranged from the seizure of cash carried by a drug courier to an in-depth asset investigation which uncovers houses, boats, bank accounts, jewelry, and other tangible assets which may be liable for forfeiture.

The immediate seizure of assets on hand during a road stop require little follow-up analysis. But the forfeiture of larger or more distant assets generally requires significant financial analysis, first to uncover the income from illegal activities that is present, and second to show that the assets have been acquired by using that illegal income or are in other ways connected to that illegal income.

The income from illegal activities is often extrapolated from the amount of drugs the person is known to sell during a period (day, week, or month) and multiplied to determine a ballpark annual gross income from drug sales. The known price of drugs sold from the level above the violator can be estimated, thus giving a more "net" profit amount, notwithstanding the costs of couriers, runners, stash houses, beepers, vehicles, and other accoutrements of the drug trade. In some instances, bank records may be available to be analyzed for deposits (primarily of cash) and withdrawals, but narcotics is primarily a cash business so the presence of bank records cannot be relied upon. In some instances the drug distributor may have a job which gives the distributor some reportable income. This, too, should be noted.

Given an estimated disposable income per year, the assets which the violator amassed (jewelry, vehicles, real estate, etc.) during the period can be analyzed to compare them to the income to determine whether the assets were only obtainable through the presence of illegal profits. If so, these assets are potentially forfeitable.

One example of the use of financial analysis in drug cases was shown in a New Jersey case where an individual had pled guilty to conspiracy to manufacture and distribute cocaine and methamphetamine, racketeering, and tax evasion. His assets were under threat of civil forfeiture but he appealed. A Source and Application of Funds schedule was completed to bolster the state's case by showing that his expenditures were substantially higher than his legitimate sources of income. The forfeiture was upheld (Nossen and Norvelle, 1993).

Certain indicators have been developed by analysts in an attempt to identify

Figure 6.7
Indicators of Potential Forfeiture of Assets from Narcotics Enterprises

1. Large quantities of narcotics sales.

2. Regular (daily or several times weekly) sales.

3. Large network of distributors.

4. Diversity of criminal activity present.

5. Target involvement in "legitimate" business.

6. Sophisticated method of operation in narcotics distribution.

7. Expensive transportation methods.

8. High-level financier or leader of network by investigation.

9. Group indicates strong ties to other crime groups.

10. Evidence of monopolistic drug enterprise is seen.

11. Group deals directly with foreign suppliers.

12. Group deals directly with large out-of-state suppliers.

13. Group oversees the manufacturing or processing of drugs as well as their distribution.

14. Group shows evidence of corrupting government officials.

possible narcotics investigations which might produce sizable assets for seizure and forfeiture. They are shown in Figure 6.7.

MONEY LAUNDERING

The Office of National Drug Control Policy estimated that illegal drug consumers in the United States spent $18 billion on cocaine, $12 billion on heroin, $9 billion on marijuana, and $2 billion on other drugs during 1990 (Bureau of Justice Statistics, December 1992).

This estimated $41 billion per year industry in the United States is nontaxed and uncontrolled. Money laundering—the concealment of income and its conversion to other assets to disguise its illegal source (Karchmer, 1986)—is done to move and use these illegally gotten funds.

Money launderers convert cash into financial assets or move the funds to where they can be converted into assets. Several techniques are used in money laundering, including "smurfing," business fronts, layers of wire transfers, transfers of funds to countries with bank secrecy laws, and the conversion of cash into certain financial instruments.

"Smurfing" involves the conversion of cash in amounts under $10,000 (the threshold that requires Currency Transaction Reports) into bank accounts or other negotiable instruments. Drug traffickers can use several individuals and accounts to make the transactions. They have also bribed bank officials to place them on a list which exempts them from having to report. One Miami bank laundered $94 million in cash while taking bribes not to forward the required report forms to the IRS.

Business fronts—usually businesses which have a large flow of cash through them such as restaurants and bars—can launder money by providing a "legitimate" source for the funds. Illegal dollars are mixed in with the receipts generated by the business and are thus "washed" for use. Businesses are also used as paper corporations into which illegal profits can be placed for "loans" back to the violator or his businesses to allow the violator to invest the funds "legally."

Wire transfers and other forms of financial instruments are used to muddy the sources of drug money. Cash can be taken into a financial institution and converted into a wire transfer. The money can then be wired through several accounts without a paper trail of signatures other than those of bank officials. This "layering" of wire transfers makes the source of the funds difficult to uncover.

Banking institutions are sometimes chosen for business by money launderers because of their location or connection to other locations. The Drug Enforcement Administration identified twenty-six locations around the world as being money facilitation centers; eight were in North America, six in Central and South America, seven in Europe, and three in the Far East (Bureau of Justice Statistics, December 1992). Banks in countries with bank secrecy laws are preferred because of the legal preclusions against providing information on bank account holders. Banks with international branches are also targeted because of their ability to transfer money from country to country.

Negotiable financial instruments, such as cashier's checks, are also used to launder funds. These are preferred because they can easily be exchanged for cash.

In one example of money laundering, a scheme called La Mina laundered $1.2 billion in cocaine profits over two years. The currency was transported to a jeweler in California, who had it deposited into banks that filed the Currency Transaction Reports (CTRs), but suspicions were not raised because gold is a cash market. The money was wired to New York to a collaborative company in payment for counterfeit gold (lead bars painted with gold). The collaborative company then transferred the funds to South American banks where the cocaine syndicates could access them (Bureau of Justice Statistics, December 1992).

The uncovering of money laundering trails is a complex and painstaking task. When major or midlevel drug distributors are arrested, all records which may provide information on their financial status should be seized, including bank records, stock transactions, real estate transactions, loans received, major purchases made, cashier's checks purchased, gambling casino visits made, and any dealings with check cashing facilities.

Financial analysts and accountant/investigators have received specialized training which allows them to review these records and extract information which may lead to the hidden locations of the funds laundered. Even transactions which appear legal on the surface should be double-checked to ensure their legitimacy.

Once this is completed, the appropriate seizure of assets and forfeiture efforts can be made, along with prosecution for appropriate charges including money laundering (which, in the United States, is generally prosecuted under federal law as few states have money laundering statutes).

Financial analysis is the key to uncovering complicated money laundering trails. Agencies involved in these investigations should have at least one person with analytical expertise on their staff.

NARCOTICS ASSESSMENTS

Narcotics assessments are continually being developed at the state and federal levels. These range from criminal bulletins to multipage assessments or estimates of narcotics activity. The criminal bulletins which are developed cover a wide range of topics from smuggling areas of vehicles, to new drug types, to major drug syndicates' activities.

Intelligence briefs can be one paragraph to a page or more. Photographs are used to show narcotics or weapons seized or the hiding places used for narcotics in a car, in wearing apparel, or in other objects. Modus operandi, or operational profiles, are often included in brief narcotics assessments to alert officers to activities which may resemble some which they have witnessed. Data on drugs, smuggling, or drug-related activities can also be disseminated in the form of a crime bulletin or "BOLO" (Be On the Look Out).

Another level of narcotic assessment is a multipage format prepared by state governments or RISS project members. One example was developed in Florida, where the Department of Law Enforcement (FDLE) Investigative Analysis Bureau completed an assessment of the crack problem in 1987 (when "crack" was still a relatively new commodity). This assessment gathered information from police chiefs, county sheriffs, medical examiners, and crime laboratories. It provided a warning to the police departments who received it about the increase in "crack" use and sales. It also compared some of its results to the results of a survey completed a year earlier, to show the change in the spread of crack arrests over the year.

Analytical products used in the Florida assessment included a geographic distribution analysis, pie charts, tables, and descriptive analyses. The questions asked in the survey ranged from "Do you perceive crack cocaine as a problem in your area?" to "Within the past six months, how many crack arrests has your agency made?" to "Please describe any similar physical characteristics, habits, methods of operations, specific organizations, new or significant trends involving crack or other narcotics in your area" (Florida Department of Law Enforcement, 1987).

From the questions, information such as "Dealers change clothes after each sale" or "Buyers swap stolen goods for crack" or "Money and property received by some dealers are reportedly funneled through local businesses and transported to Haiti" (FLDE, 1987) was obtained. Dissemination of the assessment allows other local departments to watch for similar developments in their areas.

A full-blown example of a narcotics assessment is that produced by the National Narcotics Intelligence Consumers Committee (NNICC) in the United States, which comprises representatives from all federal agencies that deal with narcotics. This yearly narcotics assessment is prepared with information from various countries and departments. Its contents are a series of charts and tables, along with a discussion of the charts and tables.

One significant aspect of the *NNICC Report* is that it combines all-source data to provide as thorough an overview of the narcotics situation as possible. For example, it combines drug trafficking indicators (drug seizures, major prosecutions, drug lab seizures) with drug use indicators (user surveys, Drug Use Forecasting, Drug Abuse Warning Network hospital emergencies, drug purity and pricing) and drug production levels in source countries. A recent volume of the *Report* included twenty tables of data which provided not only comparison of the data, but comparison to other years to show changes and trends. The *NNICC Report* provides a strategic assessment of overall drug trafficking and use in the United States.

DEVELOPING NARCOTICS STRATEGIES

Strategic analysis is the use of analysis to determine the situation, the alternatives available, and the alternative likely to be most effective. The narcotics effort since the late 1980s has been the primary arena for law enforcement strategy development, possibly because the narcotics threat is seen as a long-term problem and analysis and computer technology have concurrently emerged to support the development of strategy.

One of the difficulties in developing strategy has been the lack of distinction most law enforcement personnel draw between a strategy and a tactic: that is, they confuse tactics with strategies. Another is the fact that most law enforcement agencies do not have analysts or do not use them to develop the strategic assessments required for the development of effective strategies.

At the U.S. national level, one example of a published narcotics strategy has been the *National Drug Control Strategy* released by the White House (the President's Office). A document similar to the current *National Strategy* has been released since at least 1984; however, it was not until the late 1980s that emphasis shifted from a federal strategy, encompassing federal agencies only, to a national strategy encompassing federal, state, and local agencies.

The *National Drug Control Strategy* released in 1992 had one principal goal: to reduce the level of illegal drug use in America. The strategy document included a number of charts, tables, and graphs showing the various indicators of drug use and their change over time. Summaries of information and trends were included along with progress reports on the achievement of the nine objectives listed in the *Strategy*.

The strategies to be used to achieve the goal of reducing illegal drug use are found in chapter headings including "Deterring New and Casual Users," "Freeing Current Users," "Focus on the Organization," "Focus on Supply Networks," and "Focus on the Street Dealer." These approaches to resolving the problem include a number of tactics, including interdiction, prevention in the schools, drug treatment, and targeting of illegal financial operations (The White House, 1992).

Intelligence is seen as a tactic which supports several strategies, including that of interdicting narcotics networks. The *Strategy* states that

most interdiction operations are "intelligence driven." ... Improved intelligence capabilities increase the odds of successful interdiction operations by ensuring that interdiction forces are concentrated in areas where traffickers are expected to be. In turn, successful interdiction operations can lead to the collection of strategic intelligence about the infrastructure and operations of drug trafficking organizations. (The White House, 1992, p. 102)

Another example of a nationwide narcotics strategic assessment was done in Australia during 1991 by the Attorney-General's Department and was titled *Australia's Illegal Drug Problem: A Strategic Intelligence Assessment.* The goal of this assessment was to "provide Ministers and other high-level policy makers with a basis for deciding upon future ... strategies, priorities, resource deployments, organizational requirements and training needs" (Wardlaw, McDowell, and Schmidt, 1991, p. iii).

This *Assessment* included patterns of illegal drug use, a drug trafficking overview, an estimate of the extent of illegal drug use in Australia, and chapters on specific drug production, importation and distribution. It reviewed and evaluated current drug law enforcement strategies and made recommendations for improvements in law enforcement activities. A key recommendation was to improve information gathering and analysis capabilities within law enforcement agencies with the goal of producing yearly estimates of drug availability, distribution, and use (Wardlaw, McDowell, and Schmidt, 1991, pp. 141–56).

Statewide strategies have also been developed for narcotics enforcement. The primary intent of the Drug Control System Improvement (DCSI) grant program, funded by the United States Department of Justice, Bureau of Justice Assistance, was to support the creation of comprehensive narcotics strategies in each of the states. Each year since 1987, the states have been called upon to complete a "needs assessment" in their jurisdictions and submit a narcotics strategy to BJA as part of their request for DCSI funding.

In late 1992, the grant application guidelines for fiscal year 1993 funding by BJA commented that few states had been providing analysis and strategies in their applications; they had merely been submitting plans on how they would spend the millions of DCSI dollars.

The Bureau of Justice Assistance was looking for states to apply analysis to strategy development. The 1992 application for DCSI funds from the state of New Jersey met this standard by using an experienced tactical and strategic analyst to develop a needs assessment survey and to gather and compile all the data for the problem statement and strategy. The resulting document included a strategy statement, nine strategic goals, four prevention objectives, and four enforcement objectives for accomplishment under the fiscal 1993 Drug Control Systems Improvement grant. Moreover, it reflected the interrelationships of the state's strategy vis-à-vis the federal strategy and county and municipal strategies within the state.

The State of New Jersey Department of Law and Public Safety released this *Statewide Strategy* (1992) in concert with the *Attorney General's 1993 Statewide Narcotics Action Plan*. This document set forth varied tasks for state, county, and local law enforcement to accomplish in support of the achievement of New Jersey's narcotics strategy. The research and compilation of data for this document were also primarily done by analytical personnel assigned to the narcotics function.

Similar documents are, or should be, made in every state which receives this DSCI funding. Their development should include the analysis of multisource data reflecting drug trafficking and use in the state and should contain strategies to respond to the drug situation there. The best way to develop strategic plans is to use analysts.

CONCLUSIONS

The support of narcotics investigation by analytical methods and techniques grew several-fold in the late 1980s and early 1990s as a result of the national focus on narcotics and the increase in funds available to combat it. State, federal, and task force operations generally include some analytical support. Analysts can be effective in supporting street level, midlevel, and major network investigations. Analytical expertise in the financial area is mandatory for completing money laundering and asset forfeiture investigations. The range of narcotics work in the department, from street-level arrests to strategic planning, can be supported by analytical skills.

CHAPTER VII

White Collar Crime

White collar crime is a multibillion-dollar illicit industry in the United States. It includes fraud, bribery, tax evasion, arson for profit, racketeering, and environmental crimes. It may be the most underreported felony crime in the United States.

In spite of its widespread occurrence, few law enforcement agencies make it a priority. This is a result of the public's (and law enforcement's) perception that white collar crime, being nonviolent, is not as serious as other crimes. It has also had a lower priority because many who perpetrate white collar crime are otherwise "upstanding business people" and some believe they should not be punished for "bending" laws to increase corporate profits.

A 1983 study showed that 74 percent of white collar crimes prosecuted were convicted, a higher rate than for violent crime (66 percent). However, only 60 percent of white collar criminals were sentenced to prison and only 18 percent were sentenced to more than one year of incarceration (National Institute of Justice, March 1988). It has also been noted that white collar crime is often not reported because its victims do not want to be shown as vulnerable to crime.

The lack of emphasis on white collar crime in enforcement agencies has bred what Ronald Goldstock refers to as "systemic fraudulent behavior throughout the economic sphere" (in Edelhertz and Overcast, 1992, p. i). The underground economy now operates under the dictum "The only crime is to get caught" and has in its numbers legions of our neighbors, friends, and relatives.

Because of other priorities and funding restrictions, white collar crime is often the last area to which analysts are applied. Instead, "fraud examiners" and "accountant investigators" have carried the burden of performing analysis in white collar crime cases, supported by substantive accounting training but often with little analytical training.

Key questions must be asked when performing a white collar crime investigation:

- What kinds of illegality were involved?
- When did the offense begin and where was it located?
- What was the duration of the offense?
- How many offenders were there?
- What are the characteristics and social position of the offenders?
- Are there enumerable victims, and how many?
- What are the characteristics of the victims?
- How were the victims recruited? Was there victim-precipitation?
- Were the victims aware of their victimization?
- What were the methods of the offense?
- Was there a cover-up, and if so, what did it entail?
- What is an estimate of the amount of money involved in the violation or some other indicator of harm or impact?
- Were there other violations associated with the offense—i.e, tax fraud, mail fraud, regulatory violations, etc.? (Shapiro, 1980, p. 30)

White collar crime investigation is an area in which the application of analysis can be most fruitful. An analyst can perform some of the duties otherwise left to the investigator while also supporting the role of the white collar crime prosecutor.

DEFINITIONS

White collar crime has been defined as "an illegal act or series of illegal acts committed by non-physical means and by concealment or guile, to obtain money or property, to avoid the loss of money or property, or to obtain business or personal advantage" (Edelhertz, 1970, p. 3, Edelhertz and Rogovin, 1980, p. 4).

The Federal Bureau of Investigation defines white collar crime as "those illegal acts characterized by deceit, concealment, violation of trust, and not dependent upon the application or threat of physical force of violence. They are committed to obtain money, property, or services; or to avoid the payment or loss of money, property or services; or to secure personal or business advantage" (General Accounting Office, March 1979, Appendix 1, p. 1).

It should be noted that the Bureau documented 3,718 white collar crime convictions during FY 1979 with $4.8 million in fines levied, $60.1 million in funds recovered, and $921.4 million in potential economic loss prevented (U.S. Attorney General, 1980, p. 2a).

Finally, the U.S. Attorney General's White Collar Crime Committee defined it in 1977 as "those classes of non-violent illegal activities which principally involve traditional notions of deceit, deception, concealment, manipulation, breach of trust, subterfuge or illegal circumvention" (U.S. Attorney General, August 1980, p. 5).

White collar crime is also called economic crime or fraud. The term "white collar crime" originated because certain perpetrators of such crime were in professional ("white collar" as opposed to "blue collar") positions.

BACKGROUND

White collar crime is viewed as an "intellectual" crime rather than a crime of violence or a conspiratorial crime. Whereas organized crime and narcotics trafficking require groups or networks to be involved in the criminal activity, a white collar crime can be conceived and executed by one person. The success of this type of crime often depends upon the ability of the criminal to plan carefully and execute the plan, sometimes without involving anyone else and sometimes in concert with others. Conversely, it may be that when the white collar criminal becomes overconfident about his or her ability to outsmart the police he or she is most easily caught. They perceive themselves to be in a battle of wits with the authorities and often believe that they can bluff their way out of the role of suspect.

Various forms of fraud are considered white collar crimes. They include bank fraud, check fraud ("kiting"), utilities fraud, mail and wire fraud, insurance fraud, bankruptcy fraud, credit card fraud, welfare fraud, stock and commodities fraud, and business fraud. Tax evasion is an economic crime, as are "skimming" (removing profits from a business before recording them and thus avoiding tax exposure) and money laundering.

Pornography distribution is sometimes considered a white collar crime, as is the smuggling of goods (such as cigarettes or liquor) to avoid the payment of taxes on them. Also included in this category are forgery, computer crime, counterfeiting, arson for profit, and embezzling. Labor racketeering, antitrust violations, and environmental crime have also been included under the general umbrella of white collar crime (U.S. Attorney General, August 1980).

Frauds perpetrated against the government include social security fraud, welfare and food stamp fraud, procurement fraud, loan fraud, bribery, and grant fraud.

White collar crime is also found in conjunction with organized crime. As Edelhertz noted about organized crime cases he studied: "Operations of both legal and illegal businesses (by organized crime) involved the maintenance of false records, . . . collusion between customers and suppliers, commercial bribery, kickbacks, vertical and horizontal monopolies, and—as might be expected, omnipresent tax violations'' (1992, p. 168).

In fact, there is little organized crime which exists without the symbiotic relationship of white collar crime. Drug profits must be laundered. Illegal income must be shielded from taxes through evasion. Organized criminals are entrepreneurial and will adapt many new schemes to their benefit. As is noted later in this chapter, organized crime individuals have frequently been involved in bankruptcy fraud. Health care fraud and labor racketeering have also been seen to involve organized crime. Criminal involvement in creating monopolies in waste hauling businesses has long been a concern in a number of eastern states.

The annual cost of fraud in the United States during 1976 was estimated (Jack Key, as reported by the Pennsylvania Crime Commission, 1980) at the following:

Consumer fraud	$21	billion
Securities fraud	4	billion
Commercial bribery	7	billion
Embezzlement	3	billion
Insurance fraud	2	billion
Arson fraud	2	billion
Credit card fraud	1	billion
Computer crime	3	million
Bankruptcy fraud	1	million
Total	39.4	billion

In comparison to all other forms of revenues, white collar crimes comprised approximately 30 percent of the criminal profits estimated in 1979. While this may not be true today because of the high profits from narcotics trafficking, it remains a substantial source of funding for criminals across the United States. New forms of fraud continue to emerge, such as cellular phone fraud, which is estimated to cost between $100 and $300 million a year (Clede, June 1993).

The figures estimated by Jack Key were acknowledged as questionable when they were compiled in 1979 and were later questioned in 1984 by the President's Commission on Organized Crime. That Commission funded a study by the Wharton School of the University of Pennsylvania to determine a more precise figure of illegal income to organize crime groups. The estimated criminal income figures (President's Commission, 1986, p. 461) (in billions) were as follows:

Fraud arson	.012 to 1.001
Bank embezzlement	.324
Counterfeiting	.068
Cigarette smuggling	.193 to .388

It was also noted that 100 percent of the cigarette smuggling proceeds, 50 percent of the fraud arson proceeds, and 30 percent of the counterfeiting proceeds were presumed to be going to organized crime (President's Crime Commission, 1986, p. 463).

These figures, however, cannot be deemed to depict the income from white collar crime accurately as they only reflect four types of white collar crime and only relate to criminal income going to organized crime groups rather than to any perpetrators involved.

The success of fraud is dependent upon people's desire to make easy gain. "Scams" of all kinds are found across the United States, with victims ranging from senior citizens on limited incomes to doctors, dentists, and lawyers who are looking for a good investment return. One example is fraudulent loan schemes ("advanced fee loan schemes") in which people are promised unsecured loans from $1,000 to $20,000 if they pay an "application fee" of a few hundred dollars. One 1990 version of this involved twelve thousand people in thirty states and caused losses in the millions of dollars (Stern and Abelson, 1991).

There are several elements common to white collar crime. They include "intent to commit . . . disguise of purpose . . . reliance on carelessness of the victim . . . voluntary victim action to assist . . . and concealment of the violation" (Edelhertz, 1970, p. 13). Regarding intent, the person must be deliberately committing the wrongful act. Disguise of purpose arises from the person's pretense that the activity is lawful and legitimate. It is seen that the victim plays a major role in his or her defrauding, often becoming careless about checking the credentials of the defrauder because of the strong lure of profits. Concealment of the violation is a necessary ingredient. White collar crimes are often subtle and undetected, even by the victims, who may be led to believe that the loss of funds was beyond the control of the defrauder.

A principal technique of fraud investigation is the fraud theory approach (Wells, 1993). This approach closely mirrors the analytical process: a hypothesis is developed on the basis of available data and is tested against further data collected until it is proved or disproved.

The analysis of records is key to the investigation of white collar crime because it involves complex financial dealings which must often be unraveled by following paper trails. As Wells stated, "Fraud is rarely a single act . . . and most frauds are not readily apparent" (1993). In fraud, more than any other type of crime covered here, it is often impossible to gather sufficient evidence that a crime occurred without a detailed analysis of various records. Wilson and Matz have noted, "The 'proof' (in a fraud case) consists not merely of a relatively few items of evidence but of a large roomful of often obscure documents" (1977, p. 633). In some agencies, this records analysis is completed by accountants or investigative accountants, a number of whom have had the benefit of analytical training. In other agencies, analysts who may not have accounting backgrounds perform the financial analysis in the white collar crime unit. The ideal would be to have both analysts and accountants as participants on the investigative team.

Analysis is also key to developing white collar crime strategies and priorities. Morrill states, "A substantive analytic element [is needed to be] designed to illuminate the nature of the problem being addressed; . . . and to select or establish a process for selecting the best available course of action" (in Edelhertz and Rogovin, 1980, p. 86).

Certain general indicators of white collar crime have been developed by using an analytic approach to this branch of crime. These composite indicators of white collar crime are as follows:

* The presence of illegal income
* The presence of large cash transactions
* The presence of multiple bank accounts with significant movement of funds among these bank accounts
* The sudden ownership of one or more businesses
* Multiple businesses at one address, particularly if the address is one not able to support the operations of a business at it
* The presence of several corporations with little to no physical assets or apparent work product (paper corporations)
* The presence of out-of-country bank accounts for businesses with no-out-of-country business

The investigation of white collar crime calls for the application of analytical techniques. This chapter provides a sampling of how those techniques can be applied to specific types of investigations.

INSURANCE FRAUD

Insurance fraud occurs when an individual or group of people are successful in getting an insurance company to reimburse them for an invalid claim. This covers a range of techniques from having the company pay for repairs to a car that were not necessary to having a company pay replacement costs for a building which was deliberately burned down for the insurance money.

While insurance fraud can involve only one individual as a perpetrator, it often involves several. A car repair fraud case, for example, would include the owner of the car along with repair shop personnel, the insurance company employee who verified the damage to the car, and possibly a patrolman who completed the official police report on the fictitious accident. In one state, a thorough investigation uncovered a group of car repair locations working in concert with insurance adjusters and police to defraud insurance companies of hundreds of thousands of dollars.

In a single perpetrator case, an individual reported his luxury car as stolen while secreting it in a self-storage facility. A review of his personal records and checks by an analyst brought the leasing of storage space to the attention of enforcement officials who then found the automobile hidden in the self-storage facility.

Insurance companies, state insurance departments, and criminal justice agencies employ fraud investigators whose job it is to uncover fraudulent claims. In the majority of instances, these investigators use analytical skills both to "flag" potential frauds and to investigate uncovered frauds.

Insurance companies have become aggressive in their pursuit of fraud and work closely with government regulatory and investigative agencies. Some companies provide training to investigators on fraud indicators that have been derived from a thorough analysis of numerous cases of a particular fraud type. An example of insurance fraud indicators uncovered through the analytical process can be seen in Figure 7.1.

Other types of insurance fraud investigated include Medicaid fraud and property insurance fraud. In one example of property insurance fraud, four arsons in one jurisdiction were considered suspicious but investigation did not point to definitive suspects and its leads were exhausted. The case was set aside for over a year until it was given to an analyst in a larger, cooperating agency. By reviewing the investigative reports and crime scene data, the analyst was able to uncover commonalities and patterns among the arsons. The investigating agency was provided with this "fresh look" at their material along with investigative recommendations which yielded leads to be followed. The case was reopened and arrests were made within several months.

Insurance-/inheritance-related death is included in the *Crime Classification Manual* and the companion *Pocket Guide*. An analysis of this type of insurance fraud includes checking the insurance policy to determine whether recent changes in beneficiary have been made or new policies or higher benefits have recently been added and checking the authenticity of "all signatures relating to beneficial matters" (Douglas et al., *Pocket Guide,* 1992, p. 18).

BUSINESS RELATED CRIME

Business related crime has become the venue not only of traditional organized criminals, but of entrepreneurial and enterprising criminals. There are a number of business related crimes, including tax evasion, skimming, embezzlement, and bankruptcy fraud. The ongoing popularity of business related crime has indicated common factors in businesses which are involved in criminal activities:

- Maintaining two sets of books and records.
- Destruction of books and records.
- Payments to fictitious companies or persons.
- False invoices or billings.

Figure 7.1
Auto Theft Fraud Indicators

1. The vehicle is a late model vehicle that has high mileage or an older vehicle that has very low mileage.
2. The Vehicle Identification Number (VIN) does not match vehicle type insured, vehicle inspection, or vehicle titling documents.
3. The steering lock mechanism has not been defeated.
4. The ignition has not been damaged.
5. Excessive vandal-style damage which ensures a total loss is present.
6. The vehicle was completely burned after the theft.
7. The stolen vehicle is recovered within a short period of time after loss is reported, but has been stripped or has severe collision damage.
8. The stolen vehicle has old or recent damage on it, especially if it has no collision coverage or a high deductible.
9. The vehicle allegedly had numerous repairs completed on it prior to the theft.
10. It is an older or inexpensive vehicle which the insured indicates was equipped with expensive accessories.
11. The inspection sticker on the vehicle is altered or missing.
12. The stolen vehicle is leased and has excessive mileage on it for which the insured would have incurred penalties imposed by the leasing company.
13. The vehicle has previously been stolen, involved in a major collision, or salvaged.
14. The engine appears to be blown, abused, or tampered with.
15. The recovered vehicle was neatly stripped of its parts.
16. The vehicle purchase price was exceptionally high or low.
17. The odometer has been smashed to conceal the high mileage on the vehicle.

Source: Aetna Insurance Company.

• Large company loans to employees or other persons.

• Large or frequent currency transactions.

• Excessive spoiling or defects.

• Use of photocopies of invoices or receipts instead of original documents.

• Presence of second or third party endorsements on corporate checks.
• Double payments on billings.

Particular types of business related fraud and analytical applications follow.

Bankruptcy Fraud

In bankruptcy fraud a company declares bankruptcy when it owes its suppliers and/or customers money. At their most volatile, these frauds are called "bust-out schemes." In other cases, they may appear to be inadvertent bankruptcies. The direct victims of the schemes are the business' suppliers, but the indirect victims are the consumers to whom higher item prices are passed on.

In "bust-out schemes," the company buys large amounts of products for resale from other companies and sells these to the public (or to other companies) at lower than average prices, thus assuring large numbers of customers. Customers may assume that these "good" prices are the result of large quantity buying. Money brought in from these quick sales can be dispersed into off-shore bank accounts or hidden interest deals. There is often no intention of paying the original supplier for the goods. Once the indebtedness to suppliers reaches an unacceptable amount (to the suppliers), the company contends that it cannot pay it and thus must declare bankruptcy. In some instances, bankruptcy proceedings and officials, including judges, trustees, receivers, and attorneys, are corrupted (U.S. Attorney General, 1980, p. 31). Profits from a bankruptcy fraud can be in the millions. One eastern United States scheme involved ten different companies in a number of states and defrauded suppliers of over $5 million. Organized crime figures are known to participate in bankruptcy fraud violations frequently (U.S. Attorney General, 1980).

A smaller example of bankruptcy fraud involved a furniture store which defrauded customers by accepting deposits for goods, by not delivering the goods, by not refunding the deposits, and by finally declaring bankruptcy. Ancillary to the thefts were checks returned for nonsufficient funds which the owners had given to customers who had demanded the return of their deposits.

Since the extent of the fraud was not immediately obvious to investigators in this case, an analyst was brought in to review two years worth of business records which had been seized by the investigating agency. These records reflected the orders taken, payments received, and furniture delivered.

The analyst developed a data base of key information which included the following:

• order number,
• customer name (last name, first name),
• date order,
• deposit amount,

- date promised delivery,
- date delivery,
- date cancellation of order,
- date refund,
- amount refund, and
- comments. (Peterson, 1986)

The information from several hundred orders was entered into the computerized data base. These were viewed chronologically, by delivery date, and by date of refund. Special attention was given to those instances in which the comments field showed that refund checks from the furniture store were returned for insufficient funds.

Sorting these records by cancellation date and amount of refund received, the analyst was able to give investigators a listing of all those persons possibly defrauded, thus providing significant leads in the case. Analyzing the financial data chronologically, the analyst found an ongoing pattern of not refunding deposits over the period covered. This refuted the defense attorney's claim that the business ran into financial difficulty toward the end of the period and thus went bankrupt.

As a result of the analysis, the prosecuting agency was able to expand its charges beyond the scope of the passing of a few bad checks to include theft by deception resulting from an ongoing pattern of fraud which culminated in bankruptcy fraud.

This method can be applied in a number of bankruptcy fraud scenarios. It requires the careful review of the company's records to show potential illegal activity over time.

Embezzlement

Embezzlement, or misappropriation of funds, can occur in any setting where monies are entrusted by a company or individual to another individual or group of individuals. In effect, it is the theft of funds which were placed in a person's hands for processing or safekeeping. The primary way of uncovering the extent of an embezzlement is through an audit of the company's financial records, usually by a certified public accountant or a certified fraud examiner. Using financial analytical techniques, an analyst can also uncover monetary discrepancies.

In one example of alleged embezzlement, a complaint was lodged in a prosecutor's office claiming that a former manager of an apartment complex had stolen rent monies that had been collected by him on behalf of the apartments' owners. The apartment complex included some subsidized units, so theft from a government agency (e.g., Housing and Urban Development) might also be present.

The prosecutor's office obtained copies of the manager's rent books and the owner's rent books, along with some receipts for cash from the owner, and copies of slips from the deposit of the rent monies into company bank accounts. These disparate sources of data were delivered to an analyst who created a computerized data base and entered the records to aid in their comparison.

The accounting which emerged was somewhat confused by the fact that some tenants paid in cash and copies of receipt slips were not always available. Moreover, it was seen that the rent book recordings of rents paid did not always match the amounts on the receipt copies, nor did the manager's rent books match the owner's in their tallies of rents paid.

The conclusions drawn as a result of that analysis were that the manager's and the owner's records were incomplete and inaccurate and it was impossible to tell whether any misappropriation had occurred or poor bookkeeping was the problem. The analysis showed the prosecutor the potential problems in using the records to show the alleged theft. On the basis of the analysis, the prosecutor declined to prosecute the manager, thus saving the prosecutor and the courts the cost of a trial which would have most likely been lost. This type of analytical process supports decision making and priority setting in a prosecutorial setting.

"Skimming" Business Income

Monies are "skimmed" off a business by taking income, usually generated in cash, and setting it aside rather than reporting it. This is done to avoid the payment of income or sales taxes on the larger amount. Cash businesses, such as bars, restaurants, small retail establishments, vending operations, car washes, and other cash-based service operations, are common locations of skimming operations. Organized crime–run businesses, including pizza parlors, have been known to engage in skimming activities (Pennsylvania Crime Commission, 1980; Sterling, 1991).

While police may suspect that skimming is occurring, gathering information and proving the charge require diligence and analysis. Obviously, it would be difficult for a police officer to sit in a shop and watch every transaction made and then check to see that the amounts were accurately reported and taxes were paid. Instead, records must be relied upon to show, during analysis, inconsistencies which indicate the presence of unreported income. An analysis of the ledgers of the business showing income and expenditures can be compared to figures reported for sales taxes, wage taxes, or other income reports. These may show discrepancies which indicate skimming of profits.

Business record analysis was used in a multiagency Maryland case which targeted eleven gambling machine distributors in Maryland. The case began after several agencies shared intelligence information relating to widespread video gambling activity within their jurisdictions. Although gambling has been given a low priority in enforcement during the past decade, the profusion of the video gambling machines caused concern among enforcement personnel. In initiating the investigation, the agencies tried to determine its scope and potential outcome through a preliminary assessment of the problem by answering the following questions:

- Is the distributor linked to any other distributors through common employees, corporate structure, ownership, etc.?
- How many machines does the distributor have licensed and what are their retail locations?
- Are there determined "territories" for the various distributors?
- How much money does the distributor claim to have made off the machines?
- Does the distributor or any of the corporate officers or employees have criminal records?
- Are there any known links between any distributor, corporate officer or employee and traditional (La Cosa Nostra) or non-traditional organized crime?
- Is there official corruption occurring? (Cook and Sommers, 1987, p. 34)

The agencies involved almost immediately recognized the need for analytical support which was, at that time, beyond their internal capabilities. Accordingly, the Middle Atlantic–Great Lakes Organized Crime Law Enforcement Network (MAGLOCLEN) was contacted. Virtually from the onset of the investigation, analytical support was relied upon.

The first analytical task of the investigation was reviewing corporate records and employee wage records to determine the personnel involved in thirty video machine distributors in central Maryland and see whether the companies were interconnected. In addition, video machine licenses, Division of Motor Vehicles data, and criminal history files were reviewed. An association analysis completed on these records showed that several individuals were involved in more than one company, thus linking the companies, while others showed no linkages. As a result, the number of targets was reduced to eleven.

The second analytical task was to review corporate filings, sales tax records, employee wage reports, and other state reports to provide a financial view of these targeted companies. In doing this a number of discrepancies were found. Income reported on sales tax records, for example, did not always match the income on annual corporate filings. The wages paid to employees were sometimes nearly equal to the income declared for the quarter. The number of video machines in use by the company, when compared to earnings, was inconsistent. These findings led the analyst to conclude that a potentially significant amount of earnings were being shielded from view.

In preparation for the execution of search warrants, MAGLOCLEN prepared a computerized listing of all licensed gambling machines, their serial numbers, and their locations. On March 7, 1985, seventy-three bars and eleven warehouse/office sites were raided. In one county, over $100,000 in cash and 141 video gambling machines were seized, in addition to truckloads of records.

During the prosecutive phase, four accounting students and two computer experts audited the volumes of records seized in the raids. The audit resulted in the uncovering of $34 million in income brought in by eight vendors over three years in comparison to their reported income of $13 million. The state determined the taxes, penalties, and interest owed to it from these companies to total $2.224 million. The eight vendors pled guilty to gambling charges and received $428,000 in fines. Additional taxes, penalties, and interest were to be imposed later by the U.S. Internal Revenue Service (Cook and Sommers, 1987).

The analysis of bank records for both business and personal accounts may also be conducive to uncovering profit skimming. Through that analysis, the presence of nonbusiness payments from business items can be seen, as can the transfer of funds between accounts. An example of a partial bank record analysis of a business skimming profits is seen in Figure 7.2.

INVESTMENT FRAUD

Investment fraud can involve securities fraud, commodities fraud, real estate fraud, tax shelter fraud, and Ponzi schemes.

Securities fraud is a highly complex type of fraud which includes violations of security regulations, misrepresentation, stock manipulation, and theft by deception and may often be accompanied by tax violations.

Commodities fraud involves schemes to sell investors commodities (gold, silver, oil, crops, etc.) which the sellers do not have and cannot deliver. This type of fraud is usually conducted on a multistate basis, using ''boiler room'' operations, direct mail, and other techniques (U.S. Attorney General, 1980).

In Ponzi schemes victims are promised large returns on investments which never materialize. Some investors are paid from monies collected from additional investors and the schemes may continue for years until they collapse from the weight of fewer new investors and larger numbers of older investors demanding return.

Securities fraud may be perpetrated by companies involved in the sale of stocks or commodities or by persons who begin a company and issue stock in it without complying with various securities registrations and regulations.

In its simple form, a stock manipulation may involve an individual or group which gains control of a significant amount of a particular stock which is for sale, artificially raises the price of the stock by trading among themselves, and then convinces members of the public to buy it for considerably more than it is worth on the basis of incomplete or inaccurate financial statements and other data. An activity flow chart which shows the general steps of stock fraud is seen in Figure 7.3

In order to ascertain a manipulation, the sales and prices of the stock must be analyzed to determine what occurred. Further, the financial statements must be analyzed and compared to the actual state of the finances to determine whether misrepresentations were made. Also, an analysis of bank records is done

Figure 7.2
Bank Record Analysis (Partial): Potentially Profit-Skimming Company

Bank of Louisville

Account # 32-58301

ABC Corporation
733 Gordon Avenue
Louisville, NJ

Opening Balance 1/15/94	$ 3,784.50
Checks: 42; 1/15-2/14/94	$12,732.26
Deposits: 8; 1/16-2/12/94	$19,071.78
Closing balance 2/14/94	$10,070.02

Expenditures:

Main Line Realty (rent)	$1,500.00
Public Service Electric	267.50
New Jersey Bell	427.80
Payroll (salaries, taxes, etc.)	6,475.20
Office Serv (supplies)	74.30
Coffee-tron	48.00
Compu-Connect	439.66
Louisville Business Assn.	500.00
Cash	3,000.00
	$12,732.26

By identifying expenditures and categorizing them, the analyst can see what expenditures have the potential to indicate skimming. In the above example, the cash withdrawals may indicate skimming. In other examples, payments for personal items—food, personal rent, clothing, etc.—may also indicate skimming.

to see where the profits from the sale of the stock went, that is, who benefited from the crime. The perpetrators of investments fraud are often persons with sophistication in finance and business. Some may have experience in other forms of fraudulent activity (U.S. Attorney General, 1980).

These unscrupulous operators hide behind securities laws designed to help young companies raise capital without excessive red tape. If caught, fraudulent

Figure 7.3
Activity Flow Chart—Stock Manipulation

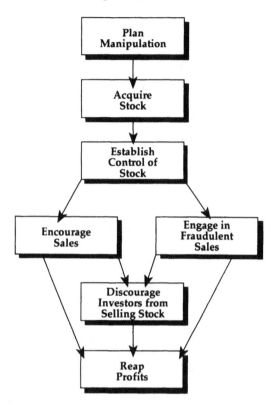

securities salespeople are fined or temporarily suspended from the business. Proving that the individual acts of wrongdoing are part of a larger conspiracy can be very difficult.

Because of their complexity and the preponderance of records which must be reviewed and compared, securities fraud cases are virtually impossible to complete successfully without the assistance of someone with financial analysis skills. Financial analysts or accountants are used to testify in court as "expert" witnesses to lead the judge and jury through the financial activities in the simplest way possible.

Other types of analytical products may be of use in explaining a complex securities case. An event flow chart may be made to show the series of activities which occurred during the manipulation. A commodity flow chart can be used to show the close control the suspects had over the stock and how they sold it among trusted individuals to inflate the price artificially. A bar or line graph may depict a time series analysis to show the rise (or fall) in the price of the stock in response to the release of false or misleading information on the com-

Figure 7.4
Magic Marker Stock Prices 11/10/71–12/27/72

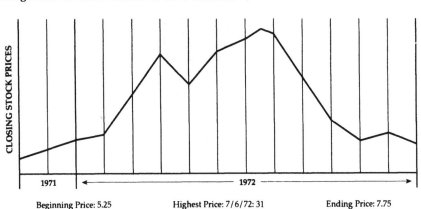

<table>
<tr><td>Beginning Price: 5.25</td><td>Highest Price: 7/6/72: 31</td><td>Ending Price: 7.75</td></tr>
</table>

Source: Pennsylvania Crime Commission, *A Decade of Organized Crime: 1980 Report* (1980): p. 145.

pany's financial health. An example of a line graph is seen in Figure 7.4. Stock price manipulators drove the price of Magic Marker Corporation Stock from $6.50 a share to a high of $30 a share. At the end of the manipulation, the stock dropped to $7.75 per share (Pennsylvania Crime Commission, 1980, pp. 195–96).

A combination of stock manipulation, corporate fraud, and bankruptcy fraud was seen in the case of Eddie Antar, of the ''Crazy Eddie'' chain of forty-three electronics stores on the East Coast of the United States, in which the Antar family was accused of bilking stockholders in the chain of $80 million by inflating the value of the stock. Sales in the stores reached $350 million in the mid-1980s.

According to a key witness in the 1993 trial, inventory figures were bloated through borrowed goods and doctored figures, and invoices for goods were dated a month after a shipment was received. ''Debit memos'' showing that manufacturers owed the chain millions in rebates and promotions were fabricated, and money previously skimmed by the family was used to maintain the appearance that profits were high. In 1987, the store had lost $25 million but had reported a profit of about $20.7 million. When stockholders became concerned and led a fight to take over the company, the losses were uncovered. The chain filed for Chapter 11 bankruptcy soon after.

Antar fled the country in 1990 after the Securities Exchange Commission (SEC) got an order to secure $52 million of his assets, much of which had been sent to Israel or had been placed in the hands of relatives (Associated Press, July 25, 1993). He was found guilty on seventeen counts of stock fraud, mail fraud, racketeering, conspiracy, and related charges on July 20, 1993, and could face imprisonment up to eleven years combined with up to $160 million in fines. His brother, Mitchell Antar, was also convicted (Gold, July 21, 1993).

Tax shelter fraud occurs when promoters entice investors to participate in ventures on the basis of tax incentives designed to allow the investor to deduct the cost of the investment from his or her income for that year. These investments are attractive as a result of their tax effect, but the investors also expect a return for the funds invested; unscrupulous promoters can pocket the investment and walked away from the venture.

Several examples of this activity were seen by the Pennsylvania Crime Commission in an investigation in the early 1980s. In one, involving Churchill Coal, investment revenues of over $10 million were received but not one shovelful of coal was produced (Pennsylvania Crime Commission, 1984). The scheme included several "paper corporations" which were designed to let the operators of the scam circumvent regulators and investors. Complex leasing arrangements were made; they are shown in a flow chart in Figure 7.5.

ANTITRUST ACTIVITIES

Antitrust activities, including monopolies, bid rigging, and unfair competitive practices, constitute another area of white collar crime. Antitrust violations affect industries in a way that limits competition through price fixing and other means. These violations are generally considered crimes against consumers (U.S. Attorney General, 1980).

The investigation and prosecution of antitrust matters require the diligent review and comparison of business and financial records to uncover the illegal activities. As in the area of securities fraud, an experienced financial analyst or an accountant can produce numerous products which will support the success of an investigation.

Antitrust investigations also include associations among companies apparently in competition with one another but covertly in league. These connections can be uncovered through a review of corporate records and other data which will bring these associations to light; they can then be easily illustrated and explained through the use of an association or link chart and a summary of the links which lead to the conclusion that collusion is occurring. Activities of this nature can be far-reaching and long-standing. In one New Jersey case, a civil complaint charged thirty-eight solid waste companies, sixty-three individuals, Teamsters Local 945, and the New Jersey Municipal Contractors' Association with horizontal market and customer allocation of solid waste collection contracts in twelve counties for over twenty years.

In another case, a major electronics manufacturer was sued for price fixing by forty-nine states and the District of Columbia. The settlement agreement called for the manufacturer to pay up to $16 million in rebates.

An investigation into the Trade Waste Association in New Jersey in 1980 resulted in the conviction of thirty-one individuals, twenty-four businesses, and

Figure 7.5
Churchill Coal Corporation—Cambria County Land Transactions

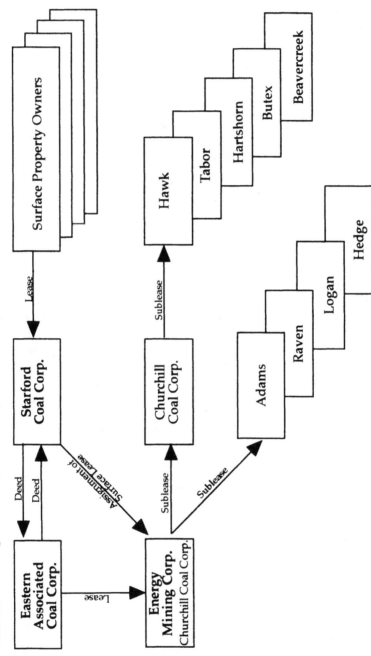

Source: Pennsylvania Crime Commission, *Coal Fraud: Undermining a Vital Resource* (February 1985): p. 38.

two associations for antitrust activities. Forty-four defendants were convicted and received penalties of $767,500.

Some states have units which employ analytical, legal, and contracting personnel to monitor bidding for road contracts through a Bid Analysis Management System (BAMS) originally devised by Infotech of Gainesville, Florida. This computerized system allows an experienced user to construct market analyses, geographic distributions, and other analytical products to determine whether bid rigging, collusion, or other antitrust violations are occurring. It includes vendor competition models which show how major contractors have bid against each other, market share models to show how the market is divided among various vendors, and pricing analysis models to show what the prices should have been rather than what they really were.

Antitrust investigations are paper-intensive undertakings that can benefit significantly from analytical expertise.

RACKETEERING

There are two forms of racketeering: labor racketeering and racketeer involvement in legitimate industries. Labor racketeering includes the use of union funds or capabilities for fraudulent or extorsive purposes. It comprises pension fund manipulation, electioneering, infiltration by organized crime, extortion, and related crimes. Organized crime is attracted to union treasuries and welfare funds "because they represent large aggregations of capital, 'cash cows' that can be milked with relative impunity" (Edelhertz, 1992, p. 3).

In racketeering in legitimate businesses individuals use coercive threats to monopolize business dealings and thereby increase profits to those who are involved in the racketeering. The latter type of racketeering may, in fact, be a spin-off of the former, as the entry of many racketeers into legitimate business has been through the invitation of industry leaders in an attempt to forestall union problems (Reuter, Rubinstein, and Wynn, 1983).

One example of labor racketeering was shown by the Pennsylvania Crime Commission in a 1981 publication on health care fraud. It showed that some union officials or trust fund trustees made decisions on who would provide the membership with benefits including health care services after receiving financial remuneration for agreeing to certain contracts.

In 1981, for example, the Pennsylvania Crime Commission investigated and reported on union health care plans in the Philadelphia area and the illegal involvement of La Cosa Nostra members and associates in these enterprises. The public report documented nine La Cosa Nostra family members and eight associates who were connected to the International Brotherhood of Teamsters in five locations. The report also included excerpts from testimony given by Jimmy "The Weasel" Fratianno, former boss of the Los Angeles family, who testified that he was promised $10,000 per month if he used his influence to induce the Teamsters to sign a contract with a Chicago health plan firm. Several analytical charts were included in the report to depict the associations of organized crime members and associates involved in health care fraud schemes. One of those charts is reproduced as Figure 7.6.

One Philadelphia area health care firm was shown in the report to have profits over five times greater than reported. Another firm reported over $2 million in services rendered to union members which they never received. The Commission also pointed to several methods used by organized crime to defraud health funds and pension funds:

1. kickbacks to union or trust fund officials,
2. multiple billings to the trust fund by health care providers,
3. false or fraudulent loans from the trust fund to outside parties,
4. inflated service contracts,
5. unnecessary or inflated commissions,
6. questionable investments. (Pennsylvania Crime Commission, December 1981)

Union funds have also been used illegally as collateral for personal loans for union officials and as payments to "ghost" employees, and they have been embezzled by union officials (U.S. Attorney General, 1980).

Two examples of racketeer involvement in legitimate business were shown by Reuter, Rubinstein, and Wynn in their analysis of solid waste collection and vending industries (1983). The solid waste industry was estimated to generate $1.5 billion in revenues per year, most of it by small firms at that time. The group concluded that in the 1960s the association of carting companies had formal customer-allocation agreements which, in effect, created monopolies by territory.

The vending industry, with its potential for cash skimming, was also seen to encourage territorial monopolies. In some areas, organized crime members were partners or employees of vending companies (Angelo Bruno, the Philadelphia Mafia chieftain who was killed in 1980, was paid as a cigarette salesman for a vending company). Reuter et al. concluded that "a major incentive to entry for outsiders appears to be its potential for tax evasion" (1983, p. 31).

The Reuter studies analyzed the waste carting and vending industries to bring better and more in-depth information to law enforcement about how these industries, both of which have been branded as organized-crime-connected, run. Without analysis, enforcement officials might continue to investigate incidents in a case by case manner and on a reactive and superficial level, rather than seeing the impact of criminal activity on entire industries.

ENVIRONMENTAL CRIME

Environmental crime has long been viewed as a regulatory problem but has also received criminal enforcement attention during the last two decades. Crim-

Figure 7.6
Organized Crime Association with Union Health Plans

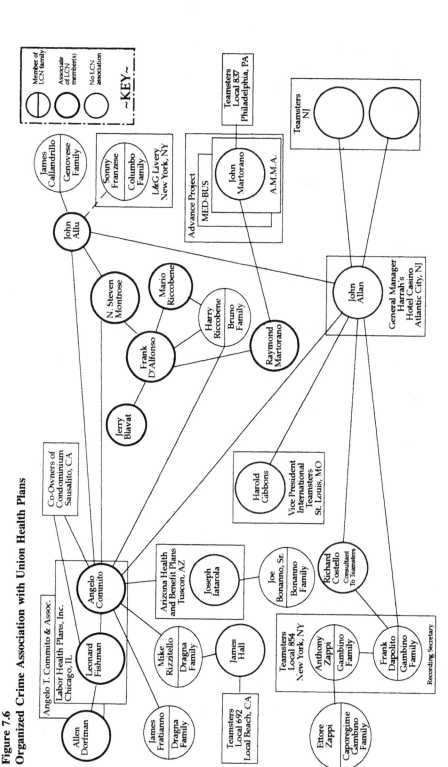

Source: Pennsylvania Crime Commission, *Health Care Fraud: A Rising Threat* (1981): p. 17.

inal fines imposed in U.S. federal courts rose from less than $1 million to about
$11 million between 1983 and 1989 (Stipp, 1990). In 1990, a bill was passed
that would triple the number of federal investigators going after polluters to at
least two hundred by 1996.

Environmental crimes range from the emission from industries of toxic substances to the unsafe disposal of hazardous waste. The toxic substances can be
allowed to foul air, water, or building materials.

In the 1970s, midnight dumping was a typical environmental crime. Haulers
would drive to remote sites and unload a hazardous cargo or drive down a
highway with a release valve open, allowing toxic liquids to spill out along the
road as they went. These crimes were usually uncovered by patrol officers who
came upon fifty-gallon barrels or noticed a truck "leaking." A typical response
to abandoned barrels would be to examine them for markings which might
indicate their source and provide leads to be followed. If the exterior of the
barrels yielded no clues, a sample of their contents would be chemically analyzed. Depending upon the chemical's common use or manufacture, it might be
traced to a perpetrator.

The 1980s brought more force to bear on environmental crime investigation
and prosecution. This additional effort was necessitated by the increasing sophistication of the lawbreakers. To combat this growing sophistication, teams
of investigators, attorneys, scientists, and analysts have been formed not simply
to collect physical evidence and arrest the immediate perpetrator, but to investigate the corporation and prosecute its management.

One example of this is the A-901 Disclosure Law passed in New Jersey,
which created more in-depth regulation of those involved in the solid waste
industry. Haulers' licensing fees fund an office which makes background investigations on those applying for licenses and monitors violations for potential
civil and criminal investigation. An analyst compiles and presents data collected,
evaluated, and compiled on a variety of areas, including possible organized
crime ties to those attempting to receive licenses, possible antitrust violations,
and connections to companies with past environmental violations.

Stringent environmental laws which have been passed during the last decade
provide stronger sentences and higher fines for those convicted. In one instance,
a Virginia corporation pleaded no contest to 940 counts of criminal pollution,
agreed to a $5 million fine, and established an $8 million endowment to improve
the environment. An additional $3 million was awarded to former employees.
It was considered a landmark case because it altered the corporation's behavior.

Environmental crime cases can involve a multiplicity of violations including
bribery and tax evasion as well as environmental law charges. Detecting paper
trails which lead from disposal site to hauler to generator of toxic waste can be
laborious. Analysis is an integral part of the environmental crime investigation
process.

An analysis of the characteristics of environmental violators can offer significant clues to the methods used to commit crimes, the patterns of criminal as-

sociations, and the degree to which organized crime has been involved. One study, which involved four states, looked at the types of firms most commonly charged with hazardous waste crimes, the criminal backgrounds of convicted perpetrators (and the degree to which they were "career criminals"), common methods used to dispose of hazardous waste, and the degree of interconnection among violators operating in different geographic areas (Rebovich, 1987).

Also of interest to the investigator and analyst is the possibility that persons involved in a solid waste hauling company might be involved in antitrust or racketeering activity. Trade associations may set hauling routes. The "aura" of organized crime may be found in the solid waste industry (State of New Jersey Commission of Investigation, 1989, p. 4).

Strategic assessments and plans are also becoming more widely used in the environmental regulation area. These plans require a thorough analysis of the following:

- current and projected needs;
- environmental, health, safety, and financial impacts of environmental policies;
- estimates of future production of wastes and strategies which could be used to deal with future production. (Emergency Solid Waste Task Force, 1990)

The use of analysis within environmental regulation agencies has been proposed and supported by Harvard Professor Malcolm K. Sparrow in particular. He comments that certain environmental agencies appear to be using a problem-solving, almost community policing, approach to environmental issues (Sparrow, 1993). He concludes that strategic selection of enforcement targets, based on a strategic analysis, is key to the effective functioning of police and regulatory agencies.

MONEY LAUNDERING

Money laundering is the movement of currency, which has often been generated illegally, through accounts and businesses in an effort to disguise its source and make it available for expenditures by those who generated it.

Professional money laundering was estimated as an $80 billion business in 1983, before the drug trafficking explosion of the mid-1980s. That figure may well have tripled since.

Several methods are used to launder funds:

- making large purchases (houses, cars, furs, jewelry) with cash,
- moving funds to off-shore bank accounts,
- storing cash in safe deposit boxes,
- taking cash to a casino and buying a large volume of chips which are later turned in for "clean" money,

- moving cash through various bank accounts,
- moving cash through paper corporations,
- transporting cash to other countries,
- providing cash to relatives and friends for investments which hide true ownership.

In one example of money laundering, an accused heroin smuggler played baccarat at an Atlantic City casino, losing $20,000 every forty seconds for a total loss of $360,000. He had, however, entered the casino with $1.2 million in small bills and left with $800,000 in $100 bills which authorities claimed were "laundered" funds. The man, along with others, was later charged with laundering $3.6 million in drug profits through four Atlantic City casinos.

In another example of money laundering, the head of a pornography empire used fictitious names, nominees, sham financial transactions, paper foreign corporations, foreign bank accounts in countries with bank secrecy laws, and unreported domestic and foreign transfers of funds to allow him to evade $1.6 million in personal income taxes over a four-year period. Through tracking the activities of him and his associates, as well as his financial actions, the federal government was able to gather a picture of those activities and determine that he was using the foreign companies and bank accounts to obscure the source of the funds. An analysis of indictments and other data provided to MAGLOCLEN supported the development of a commodity flow analysis which became part of testimony given before the Attorney General's Commission on Pornography in 1986.

One of the more widely publicized cases of money laundering involved Don Michele Sindona, an Italian lawyer who began several banks and a currency brokerage firm. He was alleged to have been a principal money launderer for the Sicilian Mafia, moving $1 billion per year from heroin sales in the United States through banks in several countries and back to Sicily. In 1979, Sindona was indicted on ninety-nine counts of fraud, perjury, and misappropriation of bank funds. He received a twenty-five year sentence in the United States and a life term in Italy and died of strychnine poisoning the day after his trial (Sterling, 1990).

One key analytical component in the investigation of money laundering is the U.S. Treasury Department data base on persons filing Currency Transaction Reports (CTRs; Form 4789) and Reports of International Transportation of Currency or Monetary Instruments (CMIRS; Form 4790). CTRs are filed by financial institutions for each deposit, withdrawal, exchange of currency, money order purchase, wire transfer, or other payment or transfer involving that institution which involves a transaction in currency more than $10,000 or multiple transactions in one day which exceed that limit (*31 CFR* 103). Financial institutions include banks, securities or commodities brokers, foreign banks, common carriers, money exchangers, telegraph companies, the postal service, a maker of financial instruments (money orders, traveler's checks, etc.), a licensed transmitter of funds, and gaming casinos.

The information is gathered into a computerized data base by the Department of the Treasury and reviewed by analysts to determine whether there are patterns which might indicate illegal activities. One indicator, for example, would be multiple transactions involving the same individual that included funds being sent to narcotics source countries. This has been done since 1982 when T-Flec (the Treasury Financial Enforcement Center) was instituted. T-Flec analyzed reported data to trace currency flow, reveal companies involved in possible organized criminal activity, and identify the individuals making suspicious transactions (President's Commission on Organized Crime, March 1984, p. 155).

One analytic stronghold in the financial crimes arena is FinCEN—the Financial Crimes Enforcement Network—operated by the U.S. Department of the Treasury. One of the missions of FinCEN is to identify suspected offenders and report on trends and patterns in money laundering. FinCEN reports that 35 percent of its contacts involve potential money laundering violations (General Accounting Office, March 1991).

FinCEN had an authorized staffing level of 196 in 1990, 84 positions of which were analysts. It is the only agency in the United States where analysts greatly outnumber investigators. One example of FinCEN's analytical work was an analysis of money flow at a federal depository that uncovered six businesses in a Southwest U.S. city which had discrepancies in CTR reporting. One of the business owners was found to be a suspected narcotics smuggler (General Accounting Office, March 1991).

In spite of efforts in the last decade to prevent money laundering, a number of avenues are still open to those who wish to launder funds. These include investing in "paper" corporations, placing the monies in banks in countries that retain bank secrecy laws, using others to purchase property and business for the generator of the funds, declaring the monies as investment returns or loans that have come due, or creating bogus business transactions in which a commodity is bought from an associated company using illegal assets.

The net worth or source and applications of funds method is a valuable analytical tool in money laundering investigations. These financial formats depict the expenditures of an individual over a period of time and show the assets the person has amassed. The cost of these assets and the cost of living expenses are compared to the amount of income reported to taxing authorities, and the difference between them is the potentially illegal income.

Another analytical technique used in detecting money laundering is commodity flow analysis. This traces the movement of the funds through businesses, bank accounts, and individuals to show the attempt by the launderer to hide the source of the funds. The analysis of bank records may provide leads to other assets owned by the suspect. A commodity chart depicting a money laundering scenario is seen in Figure 7.7.

Figure 7.7
Commodity Flow Chart—Money Laundering

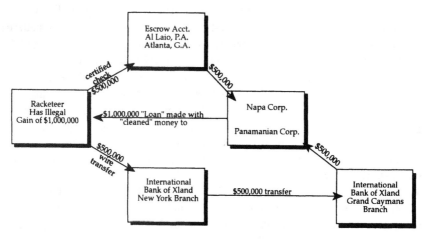

COMPUTER CRIME

Computer crime is a rapidly growing area of white collar crime. It includes unauthorized access to confidential computer systems, software piracy, and use of a computer to help commit a crime.

A recent innovation in credit card fraud, for example, uses computer software to generate strings of valid credit card numbers which are then used to place illegal telephone and mail orders for goods and services. The cards themselves are not stolen; thus the cardholder is not alerted to the potential fraud until a bill for unauthorized purchases arrives.

This type of crime can be reconstructed with the intent of finding leads to the perpetrators through a careful analysis of the types of goods purchased and the addressed to which the purchased goods were shipped. This, combined with a thorough investigation of the locations, should uncover the perpetrators.

A more traditional use of computers to support illegal activity is the embezzling of monies from bank accounts. This is most often done by bank employees who have access to computer subprograms which allow them to manipulate certain types of payments. In one example of this activity, a bank clerk had interest payments to accounts rounded to the lower penny and had the overages (tenths of cents) transferred to an account under his control. He amassed hundreds of thousands of dollars before he was discovered.

Computer ''hackers'' are one potential target of computer crime investigators. In the last decade, they have been accused of gaining unauthorized entry into computer networks, of defrauding telephone companies, of transmitting stolen software, and of publishing confidential phone company information.

One difficulty noted in prosecuting this type of computer crime is that enforcement officers have generally not been computer-literate. Accessing a computer, its programs, and its files is not taught in basic investigative training. Another difficulty is that computer crimes require the review of vast numbers of records with which investigators are not accustomed to dealing. In one 1990 case, Operation Sundevil, raids on the group Legion of Doom netted 23,000 disks which overwhelmed the U.S. Secret Service team assigned to the case (Lewyn and Schwartz, 1991).

Because many agencies require beginning analysts to be computer literate and a significant amount of analysis is done via computer, analysts could play a key role in the targeting of computer crime. Their familiarity with data bases and financial programs, in particular, could greatly assist in the recovery and analysis of records which could provide evidence of the crimes being committed.

The alternate side to computer crime, that of using computers to support criminal activity, requires computer-literate personnel in the investigation. People involved in various criminal activities have been shown to use their computers to log in their activities, to keep illegal business records, or to access fellow criminals through bulletin boards.

The uncovering of these records requires knowledge of the types of records that may have been retained and technical access knowledge. Once the records have been accessed, they may be analyzed to provide corroborating evidence of crime. Certain rules of evidence allow for the admission of computerized records in a court of law, but these records must be shown to be genuine and trustworthy (Sauls, 1985).

RICO AND FRAUD

The federal Racketeer Influenced and Corrupt Organizations (RICO) statute (Pub. L. No. 91-452, 84 Stat. 941 1970) defines racketeering activity to include mail fraud and securities fraud. It provides substantial civil and criminal penalties for those who engage in a "pattern" (two or more activities within ten years) of racketeering activity that is related to an enterprise (group, partnership, or legal entity) which affects interstate commerce.

While the RICO statute has been used successfully against major traditional and nontraditional organized crime members and groups, it has seldom been used in cases of stock manipulation and fraud. It has, however, been used in bribery, mail fraud, and wire fraud cases. There are those who argue that the intent of RICO was to be used against organized crime and not fraud violators in spite of its language to the contrary.

One significant feature of the use of RICO is that it allows for the forfeiture of assets used in the commission of a crime or purchased as a result of profits made from a crime. In an oil fraud case, an office building was forfeited; in a bribery case, interests in two businesses were forfeited (White et al., 1985).

Analysis can be used to support RICO cases as it is designed to uncover patterns of activities as well as participation of groups or organizations. Event flow charts, association diagrams, telephone record analyses, and other analytical products are used in RICO cases. Analysis can also be used to construct indicator listings to use to evaluate groups or cases for their RICO potential.

GOVERNMENT FRAUD

Government fraud at the federal level includes the following:

- procurement fraud,
- health and welfare program fraud (Medicare, Social Security, food stamps, welfare aid),
- bribery or kickbacks involving federal officials,
- overbilling,
- tax fraud,
- loan fraud,
- labor fraud (Department of Labor program fraud),
- housing fraud (Housing and Urban Development program fraud). (U.S. Attorney General, 1980, pp. 11–12)

Similar programs and areas of fraud can be seen at the state and local levels of government.

Government fraud is usually viewed as criminal activity which threatens the integrity of government institutions (U.S. Attorney General, 1980). Program-related fraud includes schemes used to divert federal grants, loans, subsidies, and other benefits from their intended use to the perpetrators.

Defense procurement fraud is one area of governmental fraud which seems to require eternal vigilance. In one fiscal year in the early 1980s, the total spent on defense procurement was $28 billion. During the nine month period from October 1991 to June 1992, ninety-two civil fraud settlements and thirty-eight criminal fraud convictions were obtained against thirty-eight of the top hundred U.S. defense contractors (General Accounting Office, September 1992). Criminal fines ordered were in excess of $167 million and restitution ordered totaled over $64 million. Civil penalties awarded to the government in the ninety-two defense fraud settlements amounted to over $631 million (General Accounting Office, September 1992).

A few years earlier, in 1986, Litton Industries, one of the top ten defense contractors, was suspended from doing business with the Pentagon after the firm agreed to plead guilty to overcharging the government by $6.3 million and agreed to pay $15 million in penalties (*Organized Crime Digest,* July 1986, p. 5).

Government fraud can be uncovered by fraud examiners, auditors, or analysts. Records review, analysis, and pattern extraction are critical to the identification of fraudulent activities. Every federal department has an office of the Inspector General (OIG) with the responsibility for investigating these crimes. During recent years, more investigators from these offices have been given analytical training to bolster their investigative skills.

BUNCO SCHEMES

The final component of fraud to be discussed is "bunco" schemes—instances in which an unknown person ("con artist") gains the trust of another and thereby parts the individual from his funds. These have also been called "stings" or "flim flams."

There are a number of types of schemes involved. Some of the better known include the pigeon drop, the Jamaican switch, badge games, and home improvement scams. The latter often prey on elderly victims, promising low-cost repairs which result in the use of inferior materials and the need to have the work redone.

Bunco crimes are often crimes of opportunity accomplished through the guile and deceit of the perpetrator. "The key elements of bunco crime appear to be trust and greed . . . the suspect looks and acts trustworthy and the victim succumbs to the lure of easy money" (MAGLOCLEN, 1986b). Bunco crimes are some of the least reported and prosecuted crimes in the United States. Its victims often blame themselves for being duped, and its suspects are often far away before the crime is ever discovered.

One example of a bunco crime is the badge game (or bank examiner game). It is primarily perpetrated by well-dressed and well-spoken white males who identify themselves as officials of law enforcement or banking institutions who need the assistance of a citizen (often elderly) to prevent a crime or catch a criminal. In one variation of this game, the male shows the victim some currency, claiming it is counterfeit, and expresses concern that the victim may have received some of this counterfeit money. He then asks to see the victim's money, to check it for counterfeit characteristics. The examination must occur at a different site; the victim allows the male to take the funds for examination and the male never returns.

One common feature of bunco crimes is that they are perpetrated over large geographic areas on an uninformed public. Bunco crime can be prevented through public education and police information sharing. The modus operandi of con artists can be gathered and placed into crime bulletins by analysts who become familiar with the games being played. An analysis of the locations and times the crimes occurred may also help police to catch a perpetrator on site. An extension of the information gathering, analysis, and dissemination process was the initiation, in 1984, of the National Association of Bunco Investigators. This group provides biweekly newsletters and training to its members.

CONCLUSIONS

The range of white collar crime cases involves complex criminal activities which require a thorough investigation and analysis of countless records and other data. The incidence of white collar crime appears to be growing in spite of the increased severity of punishment.

Investigators (including fraud examiners and accountant/investigators) should work together with analysts for maximum efficiency and success in the investigation and prosecution of white collar crime cases.

CHAPTER VIII

Street Crime
Applications

For the purpose of this chapter, "street crime" is used to refer to the types of crimes which occur against persons or property. They include muggings, burglaries, larceny/theft, motor vehicle theft, street gang activity, and those incidental crimes which are covered by the phrase "incivilities" (including graffiti and vandalism) and are reflected in "fear of crime" surveys. Crime analysis and certain types of investigative analysis are used in cases involving street crime; those applications are shown here. The chapter also shows how analysis is used to support varied law enforcement strategies against street crime including community policing, problem oriented policing, repeat offender programs, and the federal Weed and Seed initiative.

This chapter focuses on the most common crimes in the United States. Burglaries, larceny/thefts, and motor vehicle thefts accounted for 87 percent of all crimes reported during 1992 in the United States. Because of the large number of these crimes, demographic and geographic patterns emerge which can give insight into the perpetrators. The uncovering of these patterns will also be reviewed in this chapter.

BACKGROUND

Street crimes have been the focus of analysis for decades. Just as the organized crime unit has been the home of "intelligence" analysis or "investigative" analysis, the unit responsible for investigating street crimes—usually a detective unit which may be broken down by precinct or other geographic demarcation—has been the primary user of "crime" analysis. The traditional "crime analysis" units of municipal police departments have been involved in uncovering crime patterns that impact on the deployment of patrol personnel. Originally this type of analysis focused on departmental, administrative, and resource allocation matters rather than on uncovering offense patterns with an eye toward preventing crime (Maltz, Gordon, and Friedman, 1990). Its role has since expanded to include the development of suspect composites, crime bulletins, crime indicators, crime patterns, and deterrence information. Within the current policing environment, crime analysis techniques play a major role in national strategies of community policing and street gang interdiction.

Crime analysis is defined as "a system of identifying patterns or trends where they may exist" (Buck et al., 1973, p. 2) or as "the compilation, review, and articulation of conclusions drawn from criminal incident data for the purpose of optimally deploying police personnel to prevent crime and arrest offenders" (Sommers, 1986, p. 26). The dual purpose of crime analysis—to prevent crime and to arrest offenders—makes it unique. While investigative analysis supports solving crimes and prosecuting criminals, crime analysis supports deterring crime through preventive patrol or other activities and supports solving crime and arresting violators.

Crime analysis can save police departments money. The Los Angeles Police Department reported in 1972 that its PATRIC system (Pattern, Recognition and Information Correlation) yielded over $6 million in savings on the basis of saving 4.5 hours of investigative time per case (Buck et al., 1973, p. 2).

The steps of crime analysis are virtually identical to those of investigative analysis: collection, collation, analysis, dissemination, and feedback/evaluation. The dissemination stage includes the development of conclusions or hypotheses and the qualitative arriving at a measure of reliability attached to the hypotheses (Buck et al., 1973, p. 8).

The output from a crime analysis can include crime summaries, known offender information, crime pattern information, crime correlation information, and special deployment plans. These can be used by patrol units, investigation units, specialized units, police administration, and outside agencies (Buck et al., 1973, p. 10). Products included in this output could be tables, charts, frequency distributions, statistical analyses, geographic distributions, suspect composite descriptions, time series analyses, crime composite tables, crime bulletins, modus operandi charts, and summaries.

Crime analysis units receive data from a variety of police sources including dispatches, crime reports, field interrogation reports, arrest reports, intelligence reports, warrant data, and crime statistics (Buck et al., 1973, p.17). In today's police environment, these data are computerized, allowing the analyst to arrange the information so that the patterns of activity are more readily discernible.

Crime mapping, including use of "pin maps" in which varied colored pins are placed on maps to show locations of crimes committed during a particular time frame, has been a traditional part of crime analysis. The colors of the pinheads refer to different types of crime—burglaries, vehicle thefts, and so on.

Today, computerized mapping systems, called geographic information systems (GISs), allow police analysts to collect many more types of information than reported crimes and allow them to draw temporal comparisons which may alert the department to emerging crime problems. These are available for all sizes of computers and can be tailored to the police jurisdiction. Geographic information systems combine computer graphics capabilities with information stored in relational data bases to produce clear and compact presentation of data (Garson and Biggs, 1992, pp. 2–3). Two such systems have been MAPADS, used by the Chicago Police Department, and MapInfo, used by the Jersey City, New Jersey, Police Department. (See Appendix 2 for information on computer software.)

There are certain universal factors in crime analysis, which are shown in Figure 8.1. These factors become the basis for developing trends, patterns, and modus operandi information. In addition, there are crime-specific factors to be analyzed for street crimes; a listing of those is found in Figure 8.2.

On the basis of reported activities, the crime analysis unit predicts the future occurrence of crime. Thus, if a series of muggings occurred, the first analytical response to the muggings could be to analyze their locations and increase the deployment of patrol officers to those locations. Along with location, the times of the muggings and the days of the week they were perpetrated could be compared to determine patterns. Armed with locations and times, patrol officers could saturate the location for brief periods in the hope of deterring a further mugging or catching the mugger in the act. However, the mugger might be deterred from attempting another incident in the previous area or time of day because of the police presence in the area and might begin a new series of muggings in a different location or area ("displacement").

But more facts than time and location are provided by the incidents which have occurred. At least partial descriptions of the attackers are known. Their use of weapons, their tendency toward violence, the property they take, their spoken demands, their methods of fleeing are all known. Information on victims—age, race, sex, habits—is known. It is all of this information, compiled and analyzed, which allows the analyst or investigator to prepare the crime alerts for which these units are known.

These crime alert flyers, brochures, or bulletins provide composite descriptions, modus operandi, and other data which will aid in the apprehension of the violator. Their dissemination to patrol officers, the media, community groups, or victim-specific groups may generate public assistance in the violator's apprehension as well as caution potential victims about the perpetrator's methods.

The new crime analysis uses the traditional methods as a basis but expands the data to be analyzed to receive a fuller picture of the criminal incident. As Maltz comments, "The geographical and social contexts of the incident—such as the community's perception of dangerousness of the incident's location, what might have brought the victim and/or offender to that location (e.g., open stores, public transit), and other environmental factors (e.g., the type of street lighting; the amount of traffic on the street; the locations of bars, parks, abandoned buildings, etc.)"—are usually not taken into consideration but affect when and where

Figure 8.1
Universal Factors for Crime Analysis

<u>Crime Type</u> - burglary, robbery, auto theft,
     larceny, fraud, rape, sex crimes,
     aggravated assault, homicide

<u>Geographic</u> - location, street address, block,
     census tract, patrol area or beat, zone or
     precinct.

<u>Chronologic</u> - specific time or time span, day of
     week, week of year, month of year.

<u>Victim Target</u> - person's sex, age, race;
     building's type (residence, apartment),
     premise type (commercial, industrial, etc.),
     type of business, victim knowledge of
     suspect.

<u>Suspect</u> - name, age, race, sex, height, weight,
     clothing, unusual characteristics.

<u>Suspect Vehicle</u> - license number, vehicle make,
     model, year, color; marks or damage to
     vehicle.

<u>Property Loss Descriptive</u> - serial number of
     property, make and model number of property,
     type of property.

Source: George A. Buck, R. Austin, G. Cooper, D. Gagnon, J. Hodges, K. Martensen, and M.
     O'Neal, *Police Crime Analysis Unit Handbook* (1973): p. 33.

crimes are committed (Maltz, Gordon, and Friedman, 1990, p. 21). There is,
therefore, a good argument for the use of community data to augment incident
data in analyzing street crime violations.

In particular, Maltz, Gordon, and Friedman refer to information about "incivilities, which are acts or situations that may not be criminal, but have an
adverse effect on a community" (1990, p. 35). These can include graffiti, loitering, trash can dumping, physical conditions including boarded-up buildings
and littered alleys (Maltz, 1990, p. 38), and other actions people perceive as
threatening or dangerous. When this type of information is captured and added
to traditional crime report information, a more accurate picture of the level of
crime (or perception of crime) in a particular area emerges.

Figure 8.2
Crime Specific Factors for Crime Analysis

<u>Residential Burglary Specific</u>
      Type premise attacked
      Occupied vs. unoccupied
      Point of entry - Method of entry
      Presence of physical evidence

<u>Commercial Burglary Specific</u>
      Type of business attacked
      Alarm information
      Point of entry - Method of entry
      Safe attack method

<u>Robbery Specific</u>
      Type of business victim
      Victim person descriptors
      Type weapon used - Suspect mask
      Suspect statement or note
      Modus operandi

<u>Theft From Person Specific</u>
      Exact location/description of victim
      Victim condition after attack
      Modus operandi - Object of theft

<u>Auto Theft Specific</u>
      Area stolen from vs. area recovered in
      Exact last location of auto
      Make, year and model number
      Degree of strippage and parts taken
      Presence or absence of physical evidence

<u>Larceny Specific</u>
      Type victim property
      Location and specifics of property
      Suspect particular modus operandi
      Presence or absence of physical evidence

Source: George A. Buck, R. Austin, G. Cooper, D. Gagnon, J. Hodges, K. Martensen, and M. O'Neal, *Police Crime Analysis Unit Handbook* (1973): p. 35.

Street crime is the most omnipresent criminal activity in the United States. The analysis of street crime data supports not only safe streets, but also various police-community programs.

BURGLARY

Burglary is breaking and entering with the intent to commit a crime. During 1992, an estimated 2,979,884 burglaries occurred in the United States, 21 percent of all crimes committed in the country. This figure was down 7 percent from 1988 levels (Federal Bureau of Investigation, 1993).

Burglary victims suffered losses estimated at $3.8 billion in 1992. Two-thirds of all burglaries were residential. July and August were peak months for burglaries, which occurred equally during the day and night. A 13 percent clearance rate (cases in which an arrest occurred) was seen in 1992 burglaries. The "typical burglar" was an adult (80 percent) white (64 percent) male (91 percent) (Federal Bureau of Investigation, 1993).

There are several different types of burglars. The novice burglar is often a juvenile who is burglarizing houses in his neighborhood to support a drug habit. Items stolen by the novice are often routine and obvious (cameras, televisions, liquor, cash). A more experienced burglar, usually an adult, methodically searches the premises for the most expensive materials which can be taken away in the least amount of space. An experienced burglar might steal a coin collection, jewelry, or other valued items. Burglary rings may include the most experienced burglars. They will search for valuables and may even be looking for particular merchandise to "fill an order."

A burglar's modus operandi (MO) includes the following:

- the type of structure entered (residence, business, apartment building, commercial building),
- the type of goods stolen (cash, silver, electronic goods, jewelry),
- the time of day or night the burglary occurs,
- the place of entry to the building (basement, back door, front door, window, and so on),
- the method of entry (tools, and so forth),
- the method or thoroughness of the search for goods,
- the number of offenders,
- the geographic location,
- the type of victim (socioeconomic level, age, sex, and so on).

Just as there are "signatures" to violent crimes, there can be signatures to burglaries, which were previously considered part of the modus operandi. However, as discussed in Chapter 4, the modus operandi relates to factors of the crime needed to commit the crime, whereas "signatures" are often extraneous.

Signatures found in burglaries may include the burglar's drinking liquor or eating food found in a residence, stopping to watch television, using bathroom facilities, using the telephone, stealing relatively worthless mementos, or vandalizing the property. An example of a recent burglary signature in Dover Township, New Jersey, was the theft of women's underwear. The burglar's targeted residences were the homes of recently-widowed women whom he identified through obituary notices in the local newspaper. In addition to valuables, he stole pieces of the women's underwear; an extensive collection of them was found both in his automobile and in his apartment. These activities often provide evidence helpful in connecting the perpetrator to several occurrences.

Burglaries are crimes which are repetitive. They continue until the burglar is caught or moves on to another crime specialty. Seventy-three percent of burglars caught once are rearrested, while 63 percent are convicted again (Ward and Osterburg, 1992, p. 668). As a result, they provide information over an extended period which can be categorized and compared by the police to lead to an eventual arrest. The components of the modus operandi form the basis of the "criminal profile" of the burglar which emerges over several incidents.

In many police departments, the job of comparing the known burglars or MOs to the new set of facts is given to the crime analyst. This person devises various reports which summarize the data from the burglaries and allow it to be compared.

The Tucson Police Department Crime Analysis Unit participated in a crime prevention effort funded by the Bureau of Justice Assistance. The final report of the "Team Tucson" grant showed some of the techniques used in the unit. One statistical report showed burglaries by standard component factors:

- Entry Type (window, door, wall, pet door, roof, sky light, vent, unknown)

- Entry Location (front, rear, side, top, unknown)

- Entry Means (breaking, cutting, gripping, key, kicking, no force, force, picking, prying, other, unknown)

- Time of Day (day, night, unknown, 0000–0559, 0600–1159, 1200–1759, 1800–2359, unknown)

- Day of Week (Sunday, Monday, Tuesday, Wednesday, Thursday, Friday, Saturday, Unknown)

- Beats (Beat 1, Beat 2, Beat 3, Beat 4, Beat 5, Unknown)

- Property Taken (TV/Stereo, Office Equip., Home Computers, Silverware, Antiques, Jewelry, Clothing, Currency, Firearms, Photo Equip., VCR, Other, Unknown)

- Premises (Single-Family, Duplex, Apartment, Townhouse, Other Residential, Church, School, Business, Non-Structure, Unknown)

Another product of the Crime Analysis Unit was a summary of those persons who pawned several items in area pawn shops during a period comparable to that of the burglaries being studied. Thus, a comparison could be made of goods stolen and goods pawned during the period to provide leads to perpetrators.

The Tucson Police Department Crime Analysis Unit has data bases which include a burglary event table, a suspect table, a known offender table, an arrest table, a pawn table, a drug arrest table, and a field interview table. It also uses a mapping system to look at geographic relationships among the burglaries. A sample map is seen in Figure 8.3.

The components of a burglary event data base include information on each incident under categories shown in Figure 8.4. The information in this file is related to data in the other files to provide a complete picture of a single event while allowing the event factors to be compared within this particular data base to see whether patterns or similarities emerge.

Computer-aided analysis is used in a number of jurisdictions to support burglary investigations. In Baltimore County, Maryland, the police have used a computer "expert system" which has a data base of information on burglars, their MOs, and the burglaries they committed. Facts from a current burglary are put into the computer and compared to previous known information in those categories. Police Department personnel are then given a list of possible suspects, based on data matching, in return (Reboussin and Cameron, 1989).

While crime analysis is the primary analytical method used in burglary investigation, other forms of analysis beyond the traditional time series/geography can be of assistance. Similarity in modus operandi but differences in actor description, for example, could indicate the work of a burglary ring. An association analysis could be done to identify members of the ring and uncover the extent of the burglary conspiracy.

Another type of analysis used is commodity flow analysis. This shows the theft of goods and the flow of those goods through a pawn shop, or "fence" (reseller of stolen goods). A commodity flow analysis is an appropriate graphic to show in court.

An event flow chart is used to depict the MO of the criminal or to show a series of burglaries committed by him. A cycle of burglary/pawn shop or fence visits could be detailed via event flow chart.

One strategy for interdicting burglars which has been shown to be effective is to work through the local fence or pawn shop to get the cooperation of individuals running those shops. Also, jurisdictions have participated in "sting" operations in which police established their own "fencing" operation to identify thieves and recover stolen property. These begin as intelligence-gathering operations and continue until the major sources of stolen property (usually organized burglary rings) are identified and have participated in the fencing process. In this way, entire burglary groups can be arrested and prosecuted. As a program of this nature is in progress, analysis is used to capture and analyze information

Figure 8.3
Midtown/1800–2400 Burglaries Jan. 27–Feb. 17, 1989

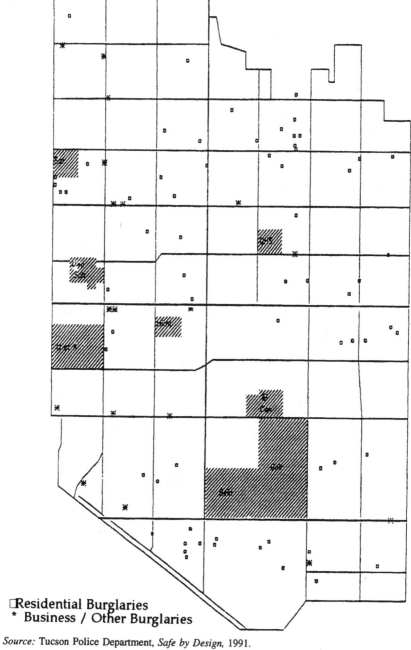

☐Residential Burglaries
* Business / Other Burglaries

Source: Tucson Police Department, *Safe by Design*, 1991.

Figure 8.4
Burglary Crime Analysis Data Base Components

Case number	Material entered through
Victim number	Entry means
Victim name	Alarm functioning?
UCR crime class	Alarm activated?
Location street number	Alarm defeated?
Location street direction	Room of entry
Location street name	Open yard?
Location street type	Fenced yard?
Team	Park?
Beat	Bushes?
Location cross reference	Trees?
Location cross direction	Property taken #1
Beginning date	Serial number #1
Beginning time	Brand #1
Ending date	Property taken #2
Ending time	Serial number #2
Day of week	Brand #2
Day or evening	Vandalism (painted,
Instrument used	ransacked)
Drugs	Vandalism means
Damage amount	Wrought iron?
Link up case #1	Alarm (audible)?
Link up case #2	Alarm (silent)?
Grid number	Neighborhood watch?
Premises type	Dead bolts?
Business or residential	Secured windows?
Inhabitants (Y/N)	Other security measures?
Entry type	No security
Entry location	Remarks

Source: Tucson Police Department, *Safe by Design,* 1991.

on the various burglars with the goal of obtaining sufficient evidence to prosecute.

A new type of burglary occurring on the West Coast in the 1990s are "home invasions." According to the California Department of Justice, these are perpetrated by Southeast Asian gangs, usually against victims of the same ethnic background. The perpetrators are confrontational and enter a home as a group, tie and gag the residents, and remove the valuables. The solution to these types of crimes begins with the victimology, that is, the ethnic background of the victims, and continues in identifying the known Southeast Asian gangs in a geographic area.

LARCENY/THEFT/SHOPLIFTING

Larceny is the unlawful taking of property, which includes shoplifting, purse snatching, theft of motor vehicle parts, baggage theft, bicycle theft, and other types in which no use of force, violence, or fraud occurs.

In 1992, there were 7,915,199 acts of larceny committed in the Untied States, down by almost 3 percent from the previous year, but still up 3 percent from the 1988 rate. Larceny comprised 55 percent of the total number of crimes committed in the country during 1992. The total property lost to larceny/thefts during 1992 was estimated at $3.8 billion (Federal Bureau of Investigation, 1993).

July and August were the highest months for larceny/theft in 1992. Forty-four percent of those arrested for larceny/theft were under twenty-one. Males comprised 68 percent of all arrestees and whites accounted for 66 percent. This category totals more than 100 percent because it includes the highest number and percentage of females arrested (Federal Bureau of Investigation, 1993).

There was a 21 percent clearance rate for larceny/theft in the United States during 1992. Clearances were highest in cities.

Larceny/theft is another area in which traditional crime analysis has been used. Crime analysts take the police reports and interviews of the victims and witnesses to compile a physical description and MO of the perpetrator. These are put into a crime bulletin format and disseminated to patrol officers and the public.

Geographic mapping can also be used to support larceny/theft investigations. The locations in which the crimes were committed may form a pattern which could indicate that the perpetrator lives or works nearby or favors particular areas or locations in which to commit the crimes.

Shoplifting is a multibillion-dollar business in the United States. Shoplifters include teenagers, kleptomaniacs, and professionals. As with burglars, it is expected that the bulk of expensive items shoplifted from stores are taken by professional shoplifters, who are often organized into rings. These people are sometimes called "boosters."

The first line of deterrence to shoplifting is the use of physical surveillance in the stores, such as two-way mirrors, surveillance cameras, security personnel dressed as shoppers, and use of security tags on items which emit a sound when a person attempts to leave the store with the goods. These systems are most likely to catch the nonprofessional shoplifter.

Professional shoplifters have the know-how to defeat security personnel and security tag systems. They may work individually or in rings. While amateur shoplifters steal goods for the "thrill," for their own use, or for friends, professional shoplifters steal a greater number and dollar value of goods which must be resold for profit. As a consequence, they must have contacts with fences or other means to resell goods.

In one professional ring of shoplifters, a multistate agency worked with a major discount department store chain in the early 1980s in an attempt to stem the flow of records and tapes from several chain locations in a hundred-mile radius of a midwestern city. Using information supplied by the store chain's security department, the agency analyzed the data to develop crime bulletins on the known offenders and their modus operandi. Those bulletins were then provided to all police agencies throughout the affected area. As a result, the store chain experienced a reduction in losses of over $2 million for the year in that geographic area. Further, it was seen that the ring consistently used a retail outlet in a major eastern city to repackage and resell the stolen materials; it was also prosecuted for receiving stolen property.

If the existence of a shoplifting ring or group is suspected, the activities of all shoplifters interdicted should be analyzed to determine similarities and patterns among the incidents. Know data (time, day, goods stolen, etc.) about incidents in which no recovery was made can also be used to piece together an overview of the realm of shoplifting activity. Together, these can give an indication of what individuals may be involved in the ring and its potential size and illegal income. Association analysis can then be used to uncover and depict the hierarchy and other connections (e.g., to resellers) the group has.

MOTOR VEHICLE THEFT

Motor vehicle theft is the theft or attempted theft of a motor vehicle, including autos, trucks, buses, motorcycles, and mobile homes. There were 1,610,834 motor vehicle thefts in the United States during 1992, down 3 percent from 1991 but up 12 percent from the 1988 level. Motor vehicle thefts account for 13 percent of all crimes committed in the country. The estimated value of motor vehicles stolen is $7.6 billion (Federal Bureau of Investigation, 1993).

January, July, and August were the top months for motor vehicle theft in 1992. Eighty percent of all vehicles stolen were automobiles. Motor vehicle theft is predominantly a metropolitan problem, with higher crime rates in large cities than in smaller cities or rural areas. The highest rates of vehicle theft are found in the Northeast section of the country, but only the West experienced an increase in vehicle thefts between 1991 and 1992 (Federal Bureau of Investigation, 1993).

The "typical" motor vehicle thief is under 21 (62 percent)—those under 18 composed 44 percent—male (89 percent), and white (58 percent). There was a 14 percent clearance rate for motor vehicle thefts in 1992.

Motor vehicle theft can be a function of a number of factors. Among these are the location in which the vehicle is parked and the length of time for which it is parked. The more anonymous the parking location and the longer the time parked, the more likely the vehicle is to be stolen. For example, large parking lots at shopping centers and railroad stations in the United States are common locations from which cars are stolen. Likewise, vehicles are stolen from city streets on the presumption that the owner is several blocks away for several hours (at work or at home).

Other major factors relating to vehicle theft appear to be the make, model, and year of the vehicle. Although the prime targets change from year to year, they are usually late model luxury or sports cars. According to the Highway Loss Data Institute in Arlington, Virginia, theft losses for automobiles for 1990-1992 models were highest for Mercedes SL convertibles, Volkswagen Cabriolets, and Chevrolet Corvette convertibles. Among utility vehicles, the Toyota Land Cruiser and Nissan Pathfinder had the highest theft losses.

The final major factor relating to vehicle theft is the motivation of the thieves. There are several purposes for stealing vehicles: joyriding, assistance in the commission of a crime, resale, and stripping for parts. The motivation of the crime may determine the likelihood of recovery of the vehicle. In the first category, joyriding, vehicles (generally cars) are stolen by young offenders (often under legal driving age) for a lark or as some gang-related ritual. These cars are often abandoned after running out of gas or running into another vehicle or a stationary item. Joyriders are sometimes intercepted by police, are seen by witnesses, are injured in accidents, or leave behind evidence (including fingerprints) which can assist in their apprehension.

A rapidly rising rate of car thefts in Union and Essex counties, New Jersey, resulted in the creation of an Auto Theft Task Force composed of investigators from thirteen law enforcement agencies. The Task Force is led by the Essex County Prosecutor's Office and the Union County Prosecutor's Office. An analysis of the data on vehicles stolen indicated that 95 percent were being abandoned in a particular area. The tactical response was to increase surveillance and patrol of that area. This resulted in the apprehension of numerous car thieves and the recovery of nearly 1,000 vehicles.

In the second motivation, the vehicle is used as transportation to or from a crime scene. This is often abandoned after the crime to make apprehension of the criminals more difficult; thus the vehicle is likely to be recovered.

The third motivation, resale, is such that the vehicle may not be recovered. Vehicles stolen for resale are usually quickly transported to another state. These vehicles can be stolen on demand: that is, a buyer wants a particular type of car and the thief supplies that car. In some instances, cars are stolen for shipment to other countries with a limited supply of automobiles; there the cars can bring two to three times the price they would in the United States.

The final motivation, stripping a vehicle, also means that recovery is unlikely. These thieves generally work in tandem with an auto body or "chop shop" which specializes in breaking the vehicle down into its parts. This may earn a thief (or the resale business) a greater profit than selling the car whole as the market for "genuine" parts is high.

Indicators of a Stolen Vehicle

Following are some indicators which, when present, may show that the vehicle in question has been stolen:

New tags shown on a used auto

New bolts used with old tags showing recent replacement of tags

Recent registration of a used car

A notarized bill of sale (this is unnecessary and therefore suspicious)

Use of duplicate (not original) keys

Vent glass which has been replaced (the vent is a common entry method to cars for purposes of theft)

The ignition has been previously tampered with (O'Hara and O'Hara, 1980, p. 350)

Auto theft investigation uses several analytical techniques, including crime analysis, association analysis, event flow analysis, activity flow analysis, commodity flow analysis, telephone record analysis, business record analysis, and geographic analysis.

As auto thefts occur, crime analysis techniques and geographic analysis should routinely be applied. Factors in the theft to be viewed for patterns and modus operandi are as follows:

- make, model year, and color of car;
- "extra" equipment in car (tape decks, disc players);
- location of vehicle when stolen (including address and type of location—mall parking lot, residential driveway, street near train station, industrial area);
- date stolen (including day of week);
- time of day vehicle stolen (usually a time span);
- known or possible method of entry to car (e.g., glass left at the scene indicating entry through window);
- presence of security system;
- approximate value of car;
- any physical evidence left at the scene;
- any testimony provided by persons who work or live near the site of the theft;
- possible motive for stealing the car.

The final factor—motive—may not be known until the car is recovered or not recovered. If the car is recovered, it may be an indication that it was stolen for a "joyride" or transportation in a crime. Cars so used may be found abandoned along the road with minimum to major damage. Stereo systems and speakers may be missing. If it is believed that the theft may have been accomplished by a ring of thieves or used in the commission, then information should be gathered from the car and analyzed to assist in the broader investigation.

Investigative analysis techniques can be used to support investigations of car theft rings. An association analysis could show the relationships and hierarchy of the theft ring. Event flow analysis could depict the series of thefts which have occurred. An activity chart could be made to show the modus operandi of the group in terms of favored locations, methods of entry, and so forth. A commodity flow chart could show the removal of the vehicles and their delivery for resale or disassembly.

The analysis of telephone records from suspects' homes or records could indicate contacts in other states or countries that might prove to be the destinations of the stolen vehicles or the locations of resellers. Business record analysis could be used on records subpoenaed from the owners of vehicle repair shops which are suspected of being involved in resale or disassembly of stolen cars. This could show the presence of parts or cars with no source documentation and would uncover the profits made from the thefts. An investigation of this type of information could result in additional tax evasion charges for the shop owner.

Auto theft task forces have developed in many metropolitan areas because of the high numbers of thefts. These bodies, often composed of multijurisdictional enforcement officers, can use the assistance of an analyst to collate and analyze data from all sources gathered by the investigators. Some agencies also work with insurance companies and the National Auto Theft Bureau (NATB) to develop warnings and overviews regarding auto theft. Analysis is used to organize data and provide threat assessments to local police as well.

INCIVILITIES AND FEAR SURVEYS

"Incivilities," as earlier mentioned, are noncriminal or misdemeanor acts which may appear threatening to nonparticipants. These can include graffiti, noise disturbances, street corner loitering, trash dumping, vandalism (or appropriation) of abandoned buildings, parks filled with refuse, and other misdemeanor behavior. Research in 1968 by Wilson found that communities' failure to control the conduct of residents was a major cause of "urban unease." Incivilities are considered "signs of crime" and may form the basis for the residents' perceptions of danger. These perceptions of danger are most often measured by what have been called "fear surveys."

Incivilities have, in the past, not been catalogued by police departments because of their extensiveness and a limit on the time police have to deal with minor crimes. Maltz, Gordon, and Friedman (1990) argue that incivilities should be captured and blended into crime incident report data to get a more accurate picture of what is going on in a community. They quote Merry (1981) as saying that "dangerous experiences include far more than crime. Insults, mockery, racial slurs, harassment . . . awaken feelings of danger . . . trash, broken fences, graffiti, rusting cars, and general appearance of neglect suggest that no one cares about the neighborhood" (p. 36). Citizen calls to police ("calls for service") often are the result of incivilities or misdemeanors.

Recent work in law enforcement has shown that the perceptions of fear are often separate from traditional measures of crime such as crimes reported; thus means of capturing other activities such as incivilities have evolved. One collection method is a fear survey which looks at several factors in the community:

1. Perceived area social disorder and physical deterioration problems,

2. Fear of personal and property crime victimization in the area,

3. Perceived area crime problems,

4. Victimization experiences,

5. Recorded crime,

6. Crime prevention activity,

7. Attitudes toward the police, and

8. Satisfaction with area. (Pate and Skogan, 1985, pp. 17–19)

Evaluations of police service and aggressiveness as well as defensive actions taken to avoid personal crime were also evaluated (Police Foundation, 1985, pp. 79–80). These surveys are often designed by on-staff analysts or by outside academic consultants.

In Lawrence, Massachusetts, a survey of residents about fear of crime did not ask about victimization of the respondents or their relatives, but rather about how unsafe they felt. The questions asked included the following:

1. Within the past year, has crime in your neighborhood increased, decreased or remained the same?

2. Have you limited or changed your activities in the past year due to your fear of crime?

3. Is your neighborhood dangerous enough that you have considered moving?

4. How worried are you about:

    a. having your home broken into while you are away during the day?

    b. walking through your neighborhood during the day?

    c. driving through your neighborhood during the day?

    d. your children being exposed to danger during the day?

    e. your children being exposed to drugs during the day?

    f. strangers loitering near your home during the day?

    g. having your home broken into while you are away during the night?

    h. walking through your neighborhood during the night?

    i. driving through your neighborhood during the night?

    j. your children being exposed to danger during the night?

    k. your children being exposed to drugs during the night?

    l. strangers loitering near your home during the night? (Cole and Kelley, 1992, p. 99)

The Tucson Police Department used a survey as part of its Team Tucson, which had the goal of integrating crime prevention activities into daily routine operations throughout the department. It asked residents to respond to the following questions:

1. In the past year, this neighborhood has gotten to be: (A better place to live, A worse place to live, Stayed the same)

2. In this neighborhood, do people generally: (Help each other, Go own way)

3. How much do you trust your neighbors? (Trust many, Trust one or two, Do not trust any)

4. How easy is it to identify strangers? (Easy, Hard)

5. Has crime over the past year: (Gone up, Gone down, Stayed the same)

6. Have troublesome problems over the past year: (Gone up, Gone down, Stayed the same)

7. Has drug use over the past year: (Gone up, Gone down, Stayed the same)

8. During the day, how safe do you feel being out alone in your neighborhood? (Very safe, Reasonably safe, Somewhat unsafe, Very unsafe)

9. After dark, how safe do you feel being out alone in your neighborhood? (Very safe, Reasonably safe, Somewhat unsafe, Very unsafe)

10. How safe do you feel at home? (Very safe, Reasonably safe, Somewhat unsafe, Very unsafe)

11. How worried are you about your home being broken into when you are at home? (Very worried, Somewhat worried, Just a little worried, Not at all worried)

12. Particular concerns mentioned (types of crime: top five were burglaries, drug use, traffic, lighting, and high crime rate) (Tucson Police Department, 1991, pp. 30–31)

In October 1993, the Bureau of Justice Assistance released *A Police Guide to Surveying Citizens and Their Environment.* It included survey samples such as one which focused on problem-solving in convenience stores around Austin, Texas. Among other questions, it asked about robbery, shoplifting, loitering, burglaries, drug dealing and other incidents in or near the store. It also surveyed personnel practices, location, street lighting, parking, and similar environmental factors. Based on the results of the survey, an analyst could then draw conclusions about factors that may impact criminal behavior and ways to prevent or deter that behavior. The result of an analysis of convenience store robberies in another area which indicated that most robberies occurred when only one clerk was on duty, led to a regulation requiring that at least two clerks be on duty in stores at all times.

The compilation and analysis of information attained through fear surveys can be analyzed for geographic and temporal trends. Locations of calls for service and areas which residents categorize as dangerous can be mapped and compared to crime locations. "Hot spots"—areas with much heavier than average criminal/dangerous activity—can be identified for enforcement action. Shifts in criminal activities from location to location can be charted. Fear surveys can also form a part of community-/ or problem-oriented policing programs. As Trojanowicz notes, "Surveys provide a good baseline against which community policing can be evaluated and also allow for continued monitoring to prevent the momentum from becoming stalled'' (1992, p. 9).

GANGS

Interest in gangs grew rapidly in the early 1990s. Street gangs were first given serious attention in the Los Angeles metropolitan area when the "Crips and Bloods" were discovered. That group, spin-offs, and emulator groups were soon seen in every region of the country. The definition of a gang, as developed by an Arizona gang task force, is "a cohesive group of youths, usually between the ages of 11 and 23 years, who have recognizable leadership, a purpose, and various levels of membership. Factors that distinguish a gang from other youth groups include: consistent use of violence, involvement in multiple criminal activities, a designated turf, and a pathological need for recognition" (Pavlock, 1993, p. 51).

A Palm Springs, California, task force defined gangs as "an ongoing organization, association or group, whether formal or informal, of three or more people which has a common name or identifying sign or symbol, and, as one of its primary activities, engages in a pattern of criminal activity" (Slahor, 1993, p. 55).

Gangs appear to be most prevalent in metropolitan areas in the United States. California, which has taken the lead in gang investigation, had an estimated 175,000 to 200,000 gang members in 1993. Gangs there are active in drug trafficking, robberies, burglaries, auto theft, extortion, assault, drive-by shootings, and murders (California Department of Justice). Gangs can range from major importers of heroin who routinely engage in violent crime to street "sets" that specialize in graffiti and loitering. Gangs may organize along neighborhood or ethnic lines and their criminal specialties may be a function of their background; for example, extortion is the most prevalent form of crime committed by Chinese gang members (Kelly, Chin and Fagan, 1993, p. 22).

Gangs moved from California to various cities around the country including midwestern cities such as Kansas City, Missouri, and Wichita, Kansas. In 1992, Wichita was rated seventh in the nation for known gang members (twelve hundred members, with three hundred hard-core members) (Bloom, 1993, p. 45). Gang colors and graffiti were two early indications that gangs had come to Wichita. Using intelligence and investigative data, the Wichita Police Department developed profiles of "typical" gang members. When a child meets the criteria for potential gang involvement, a letter is sent to the parents warning them of that likelihood (Bloom, 1993, p. 46).

A Palm Springs, California, task force found common factors among gang members: "family setting, sense of hopelessness, lack of identity, protection of neighborhoods, need for power, and need for money" (Slahor, 1993, p. 55).

Gang activity, ranging from loitering to drive-by shootings, is a common cause of neighbors' complaints. As one police officer commented, "Residents in neighborhoods are intimidated by gang members'' and feel imprisoned in their homes (Bloom, 1993, p. 46).

The approach to street gangs has not been dissimilar to the strategies and programs developed under narcotics control programs, possibly because of the link some people perceive between street gangs and drugs and possibly because of the lessons learned during the multiyear effort against narcotics trafficking and consumption.

One part of that approach has been the use of analysis to identify gang indicators and thus develop effective deterrent strategies. One indicator of gang involvement has been that most gang members are school drop-outs. Accordingly, the Gang Resistance Education and Training (GREAT) was developed by the Federal Bureau of Alcohol, Tobacco and Firearms in conjunction with the Phoenix Police Department. Similar to the Drug Abuse Resistance Education (DARE) program, it focuses on elementary and middle school (sixth- to eighth-grade) students in an effort to help them overcome pressures to join gangs. The Los Angeles Police Department uses ''Jeopardy,'' which is also based on DARE (Slahor, 1993, p. 55).

Another approach, taken by the Mount Prospect, Illinois, Police Department was the Regional Action Planning Project (RAPP), which is developing an information clearinghouse to maintain current data on gang activity. RAPP has three strategic planning committees: prevention, crisis intervention, and crisis suppression, the goals of which are to develop action plans to achieve the organization's goals (Pavlock, 1993). Clearly, the analytical function is a key ingredient to the success of this project.

Yet another approach to the gang problem was the development of a computerized data base to allow the compilation of information on gangs in support of police activities in the Evansville, Indiana, Police Department. The program was begun in the belief that gangs in larger urban areas were moving to smaller urban areas to expand their ''market areas'' for narcotics. The Chief of Police in the city, Art Gone, had previously headed the department's crime analysis unit when it developed a software program called ''NARC'' for processing narcotics intelligence. This program evolved into a tool for documenting, analyzing, and predicting organized gang activities (Whitworth, 1993).

Gone comments that analysis is the key to policing: ''Police work is, and always has been, the process of collecting information about events happening in the community, times and dates and the people involved with the events'' (Whitworth, 1993, p. 53). On the larger, statewide scale, it has been reported that Indiana State Police crime analysis experts have identified 156 ''gangs'' throughout the state (Whitworth, 1993, p. 54). In Evansville, the crime analysis officer uses information from local sources and other departments as a data base. If information indicates that there is possible gang-related activity occurring, the facts are passed along to operational patrol units.

The Los Angeles County Sheriff's Department and the Los Angeles Police Department also initiated a computerized data base on gangs, called Gang Reporting, Evaluation, and Tracking (GREAT). Los Angeles County estimated it had eighty thousand gang members in 1989. The data base included information on gang members' names, "monikers," addresses, physical descriptions, tattoos, license plate numbers (and partial numbers), conditions of probation, and so forth (McBride and Jackson, 1989, p. 31).

Gathering information on gangs and gang members is beneficial, but using the gathered data is critical. Gang member information should be supplemented by locational data on gang hangouts, graffiti, residences, schools or businesses, and established "turf." This information can be compared to calls for service and crime locations to determine connections between the gang and criminal activities.

Other data in the computerized files should be reviewed and analyzed to determine gang affiliations, relationships between gangs (cooperation or "turf wars"), and newly emerging gangs. In this manner, the department can keep aware of gang activities and target the most serious gangs for enforcement efforts.

Gang enforcement efforts by the Baltimore Police Department included a look at the psychological rewards of gang membership. Investigators found that gangs there were organizations of "tightly bonded youths controlled by a single personality who uses the group as the primary vehicle to gain and maintain a position of power . . . the group leader is manipulative, has a talent for leadership and organization, and is motivated by an egotistical desire to control others" (Burns and Deakin, 1989, p. 21). The terror generated by gangs, the investigators found, is generated by the leader's thirst for power (Burns and Deakin, 1989, p. 21). Violence is done to produce a fearful reaction, rather than to further a criminal activity.

Baltimore also found that gang activities should be investigated in the context of all legal and illegal activities in the gang world. By investigating gang activity as though it is a criminal conspiracy, more charges of a more serious nature can surface and members can be prosecuted more effectively. These more complex investigations can be supported by various investigative analysis methods, as seen in Chapter 5.

The California Department of Justice (DOJ) approach has been to collect as much information on gangs and gang members as possible and to disseminate those data to law enforcement agencies throughout the state. In March 1993, the DOJ Bureau of Investigations released *Gangs 2000: A Call to Action*. It included profiles of street gangs, their impact on the criminal justice system, gang trends, and gang prevention.

Gangs 2000 is an analytical exercise prepared by the Gangs/Criminal Extremists Unit of the Bureau of Investigation. Some conclusions/trends which they uncovered were as follows:

- There could be 250,000 gang members in California by the year 2000.
- Gangs will become more violent.

- Gang members will continue to be predatory criminals.
- Gangs will remain territorial but some may become multiethnic.
- There will be more female gangs and gang members.
- More gang members will become career criminals.
- Gang members will become more organized, clandestine and sophisticated in their criminal activities. (California Department of Justice, 1993, pp. 33–37)

Gangs 2000 also relied on a "nominal group technique" (NGT) of forecasting, in which a group of experts addressed the issue of gangs and identified emerging trends and events and forecast their impact on the year 2000. It identified ten trends and eleven events which it felt could be significant if they occurred:

Trends:

1. The level of support services in schools, such as training for teachers and counselors to recognize gang activity in school.
2. The number of violent acts in schools.
3. Gangs networking at a national level.
4. The level of parental control over children.
5. The disintegration of the nuclear family.
6. The level of deepening racial divisions or ethnic group conflict.
7. The level of demographic changes.
8. The level of overall violence.
9. Immigration to the state.
10. The level of economic disparity.

Events:

1. Los Angeles–type riot.
2. Media effects on gangs.
3. Narcotics decriminalized.
4. Law enforcement, prosecution, incarceration, probation and parole, prevention, schools, and community networking.
5. Agencies networking.
6. Nonwhite population exceeding 50 percent.
7. Immigration quotas changed.
8. Proposition 13 repealed.
9. Legislation banning handguns.

Figure 8.5
Gang Indicators

Formal Membership

Required Initiation

Rules for Members

Recognized Leader(s)

Common Clothing

Group Colors

Symbols, Tattoos

Special Language

Group Name

Street, Neighborhood or
    School Commonality

Turf/Territory/Hangouts

Source: Bureau of Justice Assistance, March 1993.

10. Legislation restricting individual rights.

11. School vouchers implemented.

The events which were said to have the greatest impact were the nonwhite population's exceeding 50 percent and immigration quota changes (California Department of Justice, 1993, pp. 61–62).

As part of its ongoing work on gangs, the California Department of Justice Bureau of Investigations initiated a series of *Intelligence Operations Bulletins* in 1993 which covered topics on gangs and organized crime. These analytical products were disseminated to law enforcement agencies and included warnings of particular gang activity, modus operandi, trends, and potential for violence.

As a result of the recent emphasis on gangs, indicators of gang involvement have been developed. Figure 8.5 shows one set of gang indicators.

A profile of gang motivated murder was developed by the FBI in 1992. In it, gang crime scene indicators were as follows:

• Location critical (gang territory)

• Location often open, public place; drive by can include several cars

• Weapons are brought to the scene

- The crime scene is disarrayed
- The firearms—semi-automatic weapons most often—are concealed
- No concern is shown for the body
- Shows multiple wounds from magazine being emptied
- Head and chest are targeted
- Can be ritualistic or execution-style
- Sometimes bystanders yell gang name (but can be deceptive to focus retaliation on other gang) (Douglas, et al., 1992, p. 7)

Intelligence gathering and analysis are key to most of the model gang programs found in the United States today. In addition to the examples of analytical products given, crime analysis and investigative analysis are used to support gang investigations. Crime analysis helps to define gang territories through geographically pinpointing the gang's activities. Investigative analysis, such as association analysis, can be used to determine group relationships and hierarchy.

REPEAT OFFENDERS

Those criminals with five or more arrests are considered repeat offenders (those who have committed a series of crimes without being arrested, then, are not usually considered in this data set). Information on these offenders derived from criminal histories and prison interviews is gathered. The results of this research suggest that certain characteristics are often found in repeat or chronic offenders. Flowers, for example, notes the following:

- Early onset of criminal behavior is the strongest predictor of chronic offender.
- Chronic offenders constitute a small proportion of aggregate offenders, yet are responsible for a very high proportion of the total crime.
- The average criminal career is 5 to 10 years in length.
- Males are more likely than females to be chronic offenders.
- Minorities are disproportionately likely to be chronic offenders.
- Criminal careers peak in the late teens and decline steadily with successive age groups.
- Habitual offenders commit a disproportionately large amount of urban street crimes.
- Substance abuse is strongly related to high-frequency criminal behavior.
- Few chronic offenders are "career" offenders with crime as sole source of income.
- Career violent offenders generally begin and remain as violent offenders.
- Habitual offenders' crimes tend to vary between misdemeanors and felonies as well as violent and property crimes. (1989, pp. 142–43)

Most law enforcement repeat offender programs are focused on those individuals who commit robberies and other felonies. Their recidivist status makes them identifiable by police and therefore suitable for targeting and surveillance.

Repeat offender programs have been run in Baltimore County, Maryland; Albuquerque, New Mexico; San Diego, California; West Covina, California; Washington, D.C.; Kansas City, Missouri; New York; and St. Louis County, Missouri. Their components include developing target selection criteria, gathering and analyzing information, developing and managing informants, and using surveillances, warrant service, and postarrest case enhancement. The information gathering and analysis stage is one which can be supported by the use of intelligence analysts.

The Knoxville Police Department, along with the Knox County Sheriff's Office, developed a narcotics repeat offender program which received federal funding. It comprised four components: apprehension and prosecution, education, tenants' leadership groups, and interagency cooperation. Directed patrols (the focusing of patrol officers on areas analyzed as being "hot spots") were used to maximize the impact of limited police resources. Within the fourth component, interagency cooperation, Knoxville collected and analyzed various data relating to types of drugs seized, locations of arrests, and so on, in an effort to assist the public housing residents with drug elimination. This program seems to be a hybrid of repeat offender and community policing programs.

Another repeat offender program has targeted juveniles: the serious and habitual offender comprehensive action program (SHOCAP). This federally funded program (OJJDP) looks at juvenile career criminals: that is, those with five or more arrests including three felony arrests, three arrests of which have been in the year immediately preceding. Juveniles are certified as "SHO" by the prosecutor or district attorney. A broad range of information is gathered on the individuals and their activities are monitored. The program also includes monitoring potential "SHOs" who may be one arrest away from certification. Some departments have an analyst whose sole function is to gather and analyze information on serious and habitual offenders.

Through varied and individualized repeat offender programs like these, indicators or profiles of repeat offenders in particular jurisdictions have been developed that allow for the identification, targeting, and apprehension of the most flagrant criminals. The analytical process—collection, analysis, conclusion, dissemination—forms the basis of all these programs.

COMMUNITY AND PROBLEM ORIENTED POLICING

Community/problem oriented policing has been lauded as a means to deal with drug sales and other street crimes. Simply put, it uses police officers to deter crime and to work with the community to solve a range of enforcement and nonenforcement problems. While many equate community policing with "foot patrol," that is but one aspect of community oriented policing. Other components include town watch groups, referrals to various social service agencies, decentralization of police authority, encouragement of community organization, participation in Police Athletic League activities, and gathering of information about criminal activities and groups. As Mastrofski notes, "Community policing . . . (is a) significant departure from the ways in which issues of role, control and legitimacy are addressed. Order maintenance replaces law enforcement as the police mission; . . . and policies and actions are justified less in terms of their impact . . . on criminal victimization and more in terms of the sense of peace, order, and security they impart to the public" (Greene and Mastrofski, 1988, pp. 48–67).

The term "community policing" is sometimes used interchangeably with the term "problem oriented policing." In actuality, they have many of the same components. Their difference appears to lie in semantic emphasis: community oriented policing focuses on working with the community to combat crime, while problem oriented policing focuses on the problem identification and solution process.

The concept behind problem oriented policing is that traditional police work has focused on calls for service and incidents, which are a "superficial manifestation of a deeper problem—not the problem itself," according to Herman Goldstein, who coined the term "problem-oriented policing" (1990, p. 33).

Community/problem oriented policing has been adopted in dozens of cities around the United States and around the world. The term "community" has been interpreted to mean not only municipalities, but universities, business districts, shopping malls, and transit systems.

Analysis Within Community Policing

According to Riechers and Roberg, effective community policing requires certain skills, "including problem conceptualization, synthesis and analysis of information, action plans, program evaluation, and communication of evaluation results and policy implications" (1990, p. 111). The average police officer probably does not have these skills or training in these areas, while the average police analyst probably does.

Vaughn comments that under community policing, "activities of the police are much more directed, relying on improved, timely, and practical crime analysis information," and "when analyzing crime problems, consideration must be given to the characteristics of all the people involved, the environment in which they live and interact with one another, and the community reaction to those factors" (1991, p. 37).

Analysis is a necessary component of community/problem oriented policing from conceptualization through evaluation. At its onset, there are several questions that can be answered through analysis:

1. What is the definition of community to be used? What boundaries does this community have?
2. What are the serious crime problems in this community?
3. What are the serious noncrime problems in this community?
4. Who lives (works in, or uses) this community? What is their racial, socioeconomic, religious, and educational background?
5. What police resources do we have available to work with this community? Are there other resources available to us (through grants, etc.)?
6. What nonpolice resources are available to work with this community? Are there other resources available to us (through grants, etc.)?
7. What resources are needed to effect community policing in this environment?
8. What other police agencies work in this community? Have we established liaison with them?
9. What other agencies work with issues that impact on the community? Have we established liaison with those agencies?
10. Are there community groups already organized? Have we established liaison with those groups?
11. What has the community's relationship with the police been in the past?

The answer to these questions should give police administrators an overview of the community, what needs are present, and what resources are available to meet those needs. To answer questions 2, 3, and 4, a community survey might be made to incorporate those questions into some questions similar to those found in the "fear reduction surveys" earlier. Survey development, compilation, and analysis can all be done by the agency's analytical staff.

Once the community/problem oriented policing effort has begun, analysis becomes part of the daily routine of those involved. The standard "model" of community policing provides the foot patrol officers with a "beat book" in which he can record the issues, crimes, and other problems which arise as the days and weeks go by. While some cities have provided rudimentary crime analysis training to their community police officers, others have not. Moreover, many issues cannot be solved by simple crime analysis and many officers do not have the time to go back over what they have recorded, looking for patterns and commonalities. An ongoing analytical capability should be written into each community policing program, to take these materials gathered by the officers, analyze them, and return the analyzed information to the officers for their action. A centralized analytical function would also allow multiple beats to be searched for patterns.

Herman Goldstein's book *Problem Oriented Policing* devotes a chapter to "Analyzing Problems." He comments that the type of analysis needed for problem solution goes "far beyond traditional crime analysis" (1990, p. 80). In one example cited, convenience store robberies were analyzed to determine commonalities. One finding was that in most cases, the store was robbed when only one clerk was on duty. Following the lead of other communities in solving the problem, the town council passed an ordinance requiring two clerks to be on duty in convenience stores at all times. Robberies dropped by 65 percent (Clifton, 1987, quoted in Goldstein, pp. 80–81).

Information to be analyzed is examined in the context of the problem. For example, when there are thefts from parked vehicles, particular questions are asked:

What is the incidence of the thefts?

What is the total magnitude of the problem? Do such thefts often go unreported? Are there factors that encourage reporting?

What is known, based on traditional crime analysis, about the reported offenses? . . . What is the correlation between incidence of reported thefts and specific circumstances (physical characteristics) in the parking facility? . . . What happens to the stolen items?

What are the characteristics of those who have been apprehended for theft from vehicles? . . .

What interest, if any, do nearby merchants, residents or employers have in the theft problem? . . .

How does the problem of theft from vehicles in this city compare with the problem elsewhere? . . . (Goldstein, 1990, pp. 82–83)

In Portland, Oregon, a seminar on community policing highlighted the Survey-Analysis-Response-Assessment (SARA) method of problem solving, developed by John Eck and William Spelman in Newport News, Virginia. The questions which this "workbook" presents strongly reflect the analytical process (see Figure 8.6).

Analytical skills can also support other aspects of community/problem oriented policing. Community newsletters, disseminated in conjunction with community groups, can be produced in the analytical shop. Community meetings can be enhanced by maps and charts produced by analysts. The analytical unit can serve as a conduit between the community policing efforts and the rest of the agency (and other law enforcement agencies) through information sharing. Information on emerging street-level crime groups, for example, can be forwarded to the appropriate investigative unit by analysts who can interpret the signs of gang development. The analysts can, on the basis of the data submitted by the patrol officers, identify problems and recommend strategies to solve those problems.

The evaluation of community policing programs is heavily reliant upon the types and quality of data collected and analyzed. Some agencies survey the residents every six months to record changes in actuality of victimizations or in

Figure 8.6
SARA Community Policing Problem-Solving

1. Survey
   a. Have you identified a problem?
   b. What is your perception of the problem?
   c. How do others outside law enforcement
      perceive the problem?
   d. How serious is the problem?

2. Analysis
   a. Who are the involved persons?
   b. Where is the problem occurring?
   c. Describe the sequence of events.
   d. What is the root cause?
   e. What is the current response to the
      problem?

3. Response
   a. What will be the goal of your action
      against this problem?
   b. What strategies will be used to meet
      the goal?
   c. Who can assist in developing these
      strategies?
   d. What obstacles exist?
   e. What is your plan of action?

4. Assessment
   a. What are the actual results of the plan
      of action?

Source: Adapted from John Eck and William Spelman, *Problem-Oriented Policing in Newport News,* Washington, DC: U.S. Department of Justice, National Institute of Justice, 1987.

perceptions of danger. The results of the program—not limited to arrests and seizures but extended to include community group progress, town watches, vacant lots cleaned up, and so on—must be analyzed and reported.

URBAN INITIATIVE APPLICATIONS

The development of the federal "Weed and Seed" program in cities starting with Trenton, New Jersey, and Kansas City, Missouri, brought out a positive example of the support to effective policing which analysis can provide. The purpose of Weed and Seed was to use a four-level program to reduce street crime in the cities. These four components included the Violent Offender Removal Program (VORP), community policing, the Safe Haven program, and community revitalization. The VORP program was an enforcement task force with federal, state, county, and local law enforcement working together to target recidivist offenders and perform initial "clean-up" operations in the areas chosen as Weed and Seed communities. The Safe Haven program was an after school and summer program for school-aged children in the schools. Programs for adults were also scheduled in the Safe Havens during the evenings. The summer program emphasized sports activities. The community revitalization program was a mixture of social and redevelopment programs including job counseling, high school equivalency diploma tutoring, abandoned building destruction, affordable housing construction, cleaning up of parks and trash in alleys, and replacement of street lights.

In New Jersey, the "street sweep" method of urban intervention had been previously tried in most of the state's major cities, including Trenton. While these enforcement actions (picking an area known for high crime, sending a large number of policemen in, and arresting everyone in the area on charges from drug sales, to prostitution, to loitering) generated arrest statistics, their effectiveness in removing significant drug dealers and violent criminals was minimal. The majority of those arrested in street sweeps were arrested on minor charges and received disorderly persons adjudications. These violators were often back on the street before the arresting officers had completed their paperwork.

To prevent this outcome, the Weed and Seed enforcement component, the Violent Offender Removal Project (VORP) Task Force, decided that strategic targeting of individuals or locations would be most effective. This strategic targeting took several forms. It was dependent upon records analysis, intelligence gathering from informants, and "tips" received from the community.

In the initial stages of the project, an analyst working with the Trenton Police Department reviewed fifteen thousand arrest records from the previous two years. The analyst culled from these records individuals and locations with multiple drug or violent crime arrests during that period which were within or contiguous to the designated Weed and Seed enforcement zones. The analyst then checked other sources of information (NCIC, MAGLOCLEN, state and county records) to determine whether there were other arrests involving the same people. Once a complete records check was done, the packages of data were handed to the VORP Task Force Coordinator for targeting by the investigators.

An intelligence/analysis function of the VORP Task Force was developed to allow for input from a variety of information sources. In addition to data from police records, informant data, "tip line" (an anonymous complaint line at the police department) information, intelligence data on gangs and organized criminal groups possibly operating in the area from local, state, and federal agencies, and community referrals were collected. Information from all these data sources was compiled, analyzed, and compared to create a comprehensive look at the people and locations being targeted.

One particularly effective source of data was the community. Their information was forwarded through the community policing component of Weed and Seed and through letters to the Attorney General. Once information was received on these individuals, background checks were done by the analyst and their files were passed on for targeting by the VORP Task Force.

By picking significant targets, the Task Force was assured of higher bail, guaranteed jail time, and stiffer sentences. Whenever possible, targets which would meet federal career offender of "Triggerlock" criteria were chosen. (Triggerlock cases involved persons carrying guns while involved in narcotics trafficking.) These meant federal prosecution, which affords less opportunity for short jail sentences. Such actions sent the message to the community that people will be caught and will go to jail.

High crime locations were also identified through arrest records analysis or through data provided by community residents. This aspect opened the door to possible seizure of property and its later forfeiture since it was being used, on an ongoing basis, to further criminal activity. Further checks by analysts into data bases uncovered the owners of the property and its value.

Depending upon the ownership and the level of knowledge of the owner of criminal activities, the property might be taken by the authorities. Within the Weed and Seed program, the property was then turned over to the city for rehabilitation into low-cost housing or into other uses which served the community. Thus, the enforcement component of the program supported the community revitalization component.

Building on this concept of strategic targeting within Weed and Seed initiatives, other sources of information to be analyzed could be brought into the overall data base. They could include information on calls for service to the police department (by location or name); graffiti indicating the presence of gangs or groups, by location; locations of abandoned houses or buildings in the area; locations of homicides or serious assaults.

CONCLUSIONS

The "new policing" calls for even more dependence on the analytical function in law enforcement. Problem oriented policing, which also forms the basis of community oriented policing, cannot be effective unless problems are identified and analyzed and solutions (strategies) are found to deal with them. As more communities move toward this philosophy of policing, the integration of analytical techniques and methods will become more a part of standard operating procedures in law enforcement agencies around the world.

CHAPTER IX

Specialists in Analysis

In the two decades since analysis began to carve a niche in law enforcement, certain organizations and individuals have emerged as significant figures in this process. They have become significant because of their work, their writing, their teaching, their furtherance of analytical goals, and their dedication. This chapter includes those organizations and individuals known to the author and, undoubtedly, does not reflect the actual number of people and individuals who deserve to be recognized. One of the drawbacks to the intelligence genesis of analytical work is that talent is often hidden and techniques closely guarded. There are those who would argue that the best analysts are those not known to the general community.

Those included here had to meet three criteria: they had to be known by (or brought to the attention of) the author, they had to have done something in the field by which they could be judged, and they had to respond to their nomination by submitting information to the author. Those who did not respond are listed separately. To encourage people to meet the first criterion, a blanket invitation for nominations was extended to the membership of the analysts' organization IALEIA and several dozen requests for nominations were sent to the top law enforcement agencies in the United States and several other countries. Personal letters were sent to all those nominated to request biographical data.

The people and organizations listed have contributed significantly to the art and science of criminal analysis, and for this they deserve the recognition and thanks of all of those in the field.

ORGANIZATIONS

The organizations which have made the most significant contribution to analysis fall into two categories: law enforcement agencies or departments which have used analysis to such an extent that they have expanded the techniques or understanding of the field and private organizations which are dedicated to furthering the profession of criminal analysis.

Law enforcement agencies or departments which initially used analysis were either state or federal agencies. Four state agencies known for encouraging analysis in the 1980s in America were the California Department of Justice, the Florida Department of Law Enforcement, the New Jersey State Police, and the New York State Organized Crime Task Force; in Canada, the Royal Canadian Mounted Police; and in Australia, the Criminal Justice Commission, Queensland, made analytical strides. During the 1980s, the emergence of the RISS projects brought analytical expertise to the county and local levels of law enforcement. Federal agencies including the Federal Bureau of Investigation were also strong proponents of analysis. The following are profiles of those agencies from this list which submitted material for publication.

California Department of Justice, Bureau of Investigation/ Intelligence Operations

The Bureau of Investigation/Intelligence Operations of the California Department of Justice (formerly Bureau of Organized Crime and Criminal Intelligence [BOCCI]) is dedicated to providing high-quality criminal intelligence information to law enforcement. Its primary focus is on traditional organized crime, gangs/criminal extremists, and Asian organized crime. It employs thirteen criminal intelligence specialists and two research analysts.

The Bureau of Investigation responds to thousands of inquiries each year and produces numerous strategic reports for both law enforcement agency and public consumption. Examples of publications include annual reports to the California Legislature on the status of organized crime, special reports on the emergence of gangs, the influence of eastern organized crime figures in the state, Forecast Bulletins, Criminal Information Bulletins, and threat assessments.

The Bureau of Investigation is the Central Coordinating Agency for the Law Enforcement Intelligence Unit (LEIU), an international association of over 250 law enforcement agencies in the United States, Canada, and Australia.

New York State Organized Crime Task Force

The New York State Organized Crime Task Force (OCTF) was established in 1970 by Executive Law. Its mandate is to investigate and prosecute multi-county organized crime activity and to assist local law enforcement agencies in their efforts against organized crime.

Its approach to the control of organized crime is based on developing strategies; employing a wide variety of remedies; using specialized skills, including legal, analytical, accounting, investigative, and research; addressing special state or regional interests; and holding its staff accountable for results consistent with team mission statements and strategy papers.

Analytic techniques, both tactical and strategic, are used, including financial analysis, economic analysis, and historical analysis. OCTF uses teams composed of an attorney, an analyst, an investigator, and an investigator/accountant who are assigned by industry, region, crime group, or criminal activity.

It is also part of OCTF's mission to provide training in the use of analytical and investigative techniques to other law enforcement agencies. OCTF annually presents a three and one half day seminar at Cornell University, a two-day seminar on Asset Forfeiture, and several four-day Analytical Techniques seminars. Technical Surveillance seminars are also given.

OCTF research projects have resulted in the publications *Corruption and Racketeering in the New York City Construction Industry* (1990) and *Racketeering in Legitimate Industries, A Study in the Economics of Intimidation* (with the Rand Corporation, 1987).

Royal Canadian Mounted Police (RCMP)

The Royal Canadian Mounted Police has been involved in intelligence, organized crime, and analysis for many years. For a time, its intelligence analysis function was distributed over different sections of its work; however, in 1991, it centralized the function into the Criminal Intelligence Directorate. Chief Superintendent J.W.M Thivierge stated, "The failure to develop a sophisticated strategic as well as tactical intelligence capability within the RCMP has seriously hindered the Force's ability to accurately measure and prevent crime having an organized, serious, or national security dimension in Canada." (Royal Canadian Mounted Police, 1991, p. i). Created along with this Directorate was a centralized automated data bank. Within the Directorate are a Criminal Intelligence Division and a Criminal Analysis Branch which includes thirteen analysts, two research analysts, one desktop publishing specialist, and six supervisors.

The RCMP is noted for producing analytical publications. It disseminates quarterly and annual crime trend publications (e.g., *RCMP Quarterly Drug Intelligence Trends*) as well as publications such as *Aerial Cocaine Smuggling into Canada* (1991). It received IALEIA Awards for Excellence in Law Enforcement Intelligence Publications in 1984 and 1985 as well as IALEIA Awards for Repeated Excellence in Law Enforcement Intelligence Publications in 1987, 1988, and 1989.

The RCMP also offers varied tactical and strategic analytical training courses to federal, state, and local police officers and analysts throughout Canada.

Criminal Justice Commission, Queensland

The mission of the Criminal Justice Commission is "to provide Queensland with an independent capacity to safeguard the integrity of public administration, facilitate reform within the criminal justice system, foster corruption prevention, and contribute to the elimination of organized crime'' (Criminal Justice Commission, 1992, p. i). It includes the following divisions: Official Misconduct, Research and Co-Ordination, Intelligence, Witness Protection, and Corporate Services.

Its Intelligence Division became operational in 1990 and provides both tactical and strategic intelligence support to Commission operations. It also oversees the intelligence function of the Queensland Police Service and the Service's liaison with other law enforcement agencies.

Prior to 1989, organized crime had received no systematic attention within Queensland. The advent of the Commission and its Intelligence Division has given the region a data base on organized crime and the capability to produce analytical work. During 1992, two strategic products on organized crime were produced by the Division.

The Intelligence Division also provides analysts to the Commission's Multi-Disciplinary Work Teams which investigate organized crime.

Regional Information Sharing Systems

In June 1981, the final link in the Regional Information Sharing System (RISS) was put into place, creating an organization of multistate agencies which span the United States. These projects were federally funded but provided support services, including analysis, to state, county, and local (and later even federal) agencies around the country. Their conceptual basis was "communication, coordination and cooperation."

There are six RISS projects—the Regional Organized Crime Information Center (ROCIC) in Nashville (covering Texas, Oklahoma, Alabama, Georgia, Florida, Arkansas, Kentucky, West Virginia, Tennessee, Virginia, North Carolina, South Carolina, and Mississippi); the Rocky Mountain Information Network (RMIN) in Tucson (covering New Mexico, Utah, Montana, Nevada, Colorado, Arizona, Wyoming, and Idaho); the Western States Information Network (WSIN) in Sacramento (covering California, Washington, Oregon, Alaska, and Hawaii); the Mid-States Organized Crime Information Center in Springfield, Missouri (covering North Dakota, South Dakota, Minnesota, Iowa, Nebraska, Illinois, Missouri, and Wisconsin); the New England State Police Information Network in Randolph, Massachusetts (covering Maine, New Hampshire, Vermont, Massachusetts, Rhode Island, and Connecticut); and the Middle Atlantic–Great Lakes Organized Crime Information Network in West Trenton, New Jersey (which covers New York, New Jersey, Delaware, Maryland, Washington, D.C., Pennsylvania, Ohio, Indiana, Michigan, and the contiguous Canadian provinces of Ontario and Quebec). Each RISS project may serve hundreds of member agencies. Over four thousand agencies are members of RISS projects.

One service offered by the RISS projects is analytical reports. This service is required by the grantor agency, United States Department of Justice, Office of

Justice Programs, Bureau of Justice Assistance, to be offered. The types of analytical products provided by RISS projects include network charts, telephone record analysis, event and commodity flow charts, financial analysis, crime scene charts, and analytical assessments.

The RISS projects have also been purveyors of analytical training. One rationale for this training is that it provides the local agencies they serve with knowledge about the use of analysis, which, in turn, encourages member agency use of RISS analytical services. Once some agencies have used these services for a period of time, they are ready to develop analytical abilities within their organizations, and thus their need for analytical training grows while their need for outside analytical assistance may diminish.

Specifically within the RISS projects, three projects have been recognized as the leaders in the analytical area: WSIN, MAGLOCLEN, and RMIN.

Western States Information Network

The Western States Information Network (WSIN) is a federally funded narcotics intelligence agency that collects and analyzes information from over 827 law enforcement agencies in five states. It employs eight criminal intelligence analysts and four research analysts.

WSIN has been instrumental in developing computerized analytical software that has been implemented throughout the RISS projects, called the Advanced Targeting, Analysis and Graphics System (AdTAGS). WSIN assists law enforcement in over 120 narcotics cases each year and prepares numerous strategic assessments for dissemination to member agencies.

WSIN received IALEIA awards for "excellence in law enforcement publications" in 1983, 1984, and 1990; for "repeated excellence in law enforcement publications" in 1988; and for being the organization that "has made the most significant progress in utilizing intelligence analytical techniques to support law enforcement objectives" in 1986, 1988, and 1990. Analysts from WSIN received the IALEIA "Analyst of the Year" award in 1984, 1985, 1988, and 1990.

MAGLOCLEN

The Middle Atlantic–Organized Crime Law Enforcement Network (MAGLOCLEN) was begun in 1981 as one of the six RISS projects. It provides both tactical and strategic analytical products, a monthly intelligence bulletin (*NETWORK*), and analytical training to over 350 agencies in eight states and two Canadian provinces.

On request, MAGLOCLEN provides member agencies tactical analytical products which are of assistance to critical investigations. Those products include case analyses, commodity flow charts, criminal association charts, event flow charts, evidential diagrams, financial analyses, and telephone record analyses.

MAGLOCLEN has provided strategic assessments on such topics as cocaine trafficking (1987), Jamaican organized crime (1988), Colombian organized crime (1988 and 1990), outlaw motorcycle gangs (1986 and 1991), Crips and Bloods (1989), organized sexual exploitation (1988), and Hispanic drug trafficking (1985). It has also distributed Special Reports including those on Nigerian organized crime (1991), Russian organized crime (1992), and Caribbean drug trafficking (1992).

MAGLOCLEN has won numerous IALEIA awards for its *NETWORK* publication and its strategic assessments.

Rocky Mountain Information Network

The Rocky Mountain Information Network (RMIN) is located in Phoenix and is another RISS project.

RMIN has been instrumental in raising both the level of awareness of intelligence analysis and the level of practice throughout its eight state region. It provides analytical support to over a hundred new investigations each year. It has trained several hundred law enforcement specialists in analytical techniques, and its staff members have made presentations at numerous conferences and training classes.

One example of RMIN's analytical work was accomplished through the Southwest Border Project. By analyzing information from cases along the United States/Mexico border, an RMIN analyst was able to uncover links among the cases which led to a six agency consortium of federal, state, and local agencies.

A RMIN analyst won an IALEIA Achievement Award in 1992.

Federal Bureau of Investigation

The Federal Bureau of Investigation (FBI) has a broad range of analytical capabilities and information sharing with agencies across the United States. The most basic of these, the Uniform Crime Reporting (UCR) Program, was implemented in 1930. On a monthly basis, statistical data concerning the incidence of criminal acts is collected from over sixteen thousand individual law enforcement agencies nationwide. This reporting supports the yearly publication of criminal activity as well as special publications on crime analysis and crime trends.

The National Crime Information Center (NCIC) is a nationwide computerized information system which provides a readily available computerized data base of accurate and timely criminal justice information. Although the FBI funds and operates NCIC, approximately 99 percent of NCIC use is by state, local, and other federal agencies. NCIC was founded in 1967; by October 1992 it had more than 24 million records maintained in its data base.

Also within the FBI is the National Center for the Analysis of Violent Crime (NCAVC). It has been operational since 1985 and brings a multidisciplinary approach to agencies confronted by unusual, high-risk, vicious, or repetitive crimes. Its services include consultation on major violent crimes, profiles of unknown offenders, personality assessments, investigative strategies, and other investigative aids. It includes the Violent Criminal Apprehension Program (VI-CAP), which was established to alert law enforcement agencies that might be seeking the same offender for crimes in their respective jurisdictions. The work of the FBI's Behavioral Sciences Unit is done in conjunction with the NCAVC.

The FBI uses computer systems including the Automated Information Systems (AIS) and the Computer Analysis and Response Team (CART). The AIS program's goal is the collection, analysis, maintenance, and dissemination of investigative data, while CART supports specific investigations and prosecutions. In addition, in 1985 the FBI began developing an artificial intelligence application with knowledge-based expert systems. The systems support labor racketeering, narcotics trafficking, and terrorism investigations.

In 1993, the FBI hosted a two-day conference for twenty-one analysts from around the country at the FBI Academy to discuss developing a curriculum for a three-week crime analyst training course to be held by the Bureau.

Private organizations were also instrumental in spreading the use of analysis through training, publications, standards, and networking.

Law Enforcement Intelligence Unit

The Law Enforcement Intelligence Unit (LEIU) was established in 1956 to coordinate the exchange of criminal information on traveling criminals between local law enforcement agencies. For nearly forty years, LEIU has performed a valuable coordinating function among law enforcement agencies in the United States, Canada, and Australia. Forty-five states are represented in the organization.

LEIU member agencies have formed the vanguard of analytical users over the decades of its experience. Also, it has provided training seminars on intelligence, organized crime, and analysis. It currently has over 250 member agencies. LEIU is governed by an Executive Board and facilitated by a Central Coordinating Agency, the California State Department of Justice.

ANACAPA Sciences

ANACAPA Sciences of Santa Barbara, California, began as a contractor to the California Department of Justice in the area of analytical training development and implementation. It pioneered the development of intelligence analysis and investigation methods and has been conducting training courses on these methods since 1971. The company has now conducted more than six hundred training courses for analysts, investigators, agents, attorneys, security officers, and others from over fifteen hundred agencies, institutions, intelligence networks, and companies throughout the world.

λ

It currently offers six courses: Criminal Intelligence Analysis, Analytical Investigation Methods, Financial Manipulation Analysis, Environmental Investigation Analysis, Advanced (Computer-Aided) Intelligence Analysis, and Management of Intelligence Analysis. It provides the seminars, on a request basis, throughout the United States and in other countries. It has been a sponsoring (corporate) member of the analysts' organization IALEIA since its inception.

ANACAPA instructors have included Douglas Harris, Walter Harper, Richard Fuller, Jack Kinney, James Howlett, Glen Ridgeway, and Robert Hamilton.

International Association of Law Enforcement Intelligence Analysts

The International Association of Law Enforcement Intelligence Analysts (IALEIA), of Washington, D.C., was formed in 1981 to promote the professionalism of analysis throughout law enforcement.

It publishes the semiannual *IALEIA JOURNAL* (formerly the *Law Enforcement Intelligence Analysis Digest*) and the newsletter *INTELSCOPE*. It holds an annual meeting in conjunction with the International Association of Chiefs of Police. A semiannual training conference is held in varied locations. There are nineteen regional chapters and active members in the United States, Canada, France, Great Britain, Hong Kong, Singapore, Russia, the Czech Republic, and Australia. Working committees of the association include membership, standards and accreditation, technology, private security, international relations, awards, bylaws, and training and education.

Past Presidents of IALEIA are the following:

Brian Boyd, U.S. Department of the Treasury, Bureau of Alcohol, Tobacco and Firearms (founder)

James B. Howlett, Federal Bureau of Investigation, Behavioral Science Unit

R. Glen Ridgeway, New York State Organized Crime Task Force

Jerry Walters, U.S. Department of the Treasury, Customs Service

Jack Morris, California Department of Justice

Emma E. Fern, Florida Department of Law Enforcement (current President)

Society of Certified Criminal Analysts

The Society of Certified Criminal Analysts (SCCA) in Purchase, New York, was begun in 1989 to develop standards and criteria for the certification of analysts. It is an offshoot of IALEIA and its relationship to IALEIA is expressed in several ways. First, the Board of Governors reserves one seat for an IALEIA representative. Second, the initiating Board of Governors comprises several IALEIA directors, officers, and past officers. Third, all analysts certified are required to maintain their membership in IALEIA.

In order to be certified as lifetime analysts, people must have at least ten years of analytical experience and a college degree and must have completed standardized analytical training. As of the time of publication, the following persons have met these strict criteria and are Lifetime Certified Criminal Analysts:

Robert Abramson, Kingsbrook Medical Center, New York

S. Woodruff Bentley, Security Consultant, formerly of the Department of Defense Office of Inspector General

Paula Carter, New Jersey State Commission of Investigation

Howard Clarke, Combined Law Enforcement Unit, Vancouver, British Columbia

Nigel Colyer, Rank Xerox (Australia), formerly of the Australian Bureau of Criminal Investigation

Robert Fahlman, Royal Canadian Mounted Police

Emma E. Fern, Florida Department of Law Enforcement

Charles Foley, New Jersey Division of Criminal Justice

Charles Frost, Northeast Missouri State University, formerly of the Drug Enforcement Administration

Barbara A. Haggerty, Drug Enforcement Administration

James B. Howlett, criminal justice consultant, formerly with the Federal Bureau of Investigation

Leo Jacques, Arizona Department of Public Safety

Richard Kedzior, Criminal Intelligence Services Ontario

Charles Lavine, New York State Department of Taxation and Finance

Sondra Lavine, New York State Department of Taxation and Finance

Francine Levert, Royal Canadian Mounted Police

Ritchie A. Martinez, Arizona Department of Public Safety

Joseph Mauz, New York Transit Authority (retired)

Terry Mercer, Rocky Mountain Information Network

Jan Nelson, Tempe, Arizona, Police Department

Marilyn B. Peterson, New Jersey Division of Criminal Justice

R. Glen Ridgeway, New York State Organized Crime Task Force

Paul Roger, Queensland, Australia, Crime Commission

Warren Sweeney, Canadian Police College

Serell I. Ulrich, Pennsylvania State Police

John Zondlo, Arizona Department of Public Safety

Analysts with less experience can be certified through an application and testing process. Regular certificants are required to have two years of college, IALEIA membership, completion of basic analytical training, and current employment or three years of experience as an analyst. Regularly certified analysts include Gloria Holloway, U.S. Customs Service; Robert Powers, Edmonton Police Force; Randy Martinak, Oregon Department of Justice; Gregory Thomas,

Pennsylvania Office of Inspector General; and David Barn, Pennsylvania Office of Inspector General.

Australian Institute of Professional Intelligence Officers (AIPIO)

The Australian Institute of Professional Intelligence Officers was begun in 1990 to further the professional standing of those in the intelligence, security, and analytical community, and of those who utilize intelligence techniques and products to improve the reliability of their decision making. Regular membership in AIPIO is limited to Australians with at least three years experience in the intelligence field. International Associate memberships are also available; several hundred persons are members.

The AIPIO holds an annual conference in Australia which attracts participants from law enforcement, regulatory agencies, the military, academia, and private security. It produces a semiannual journal, *The Journal of the Australian Institute of Professional Intelligence Officers,* which, in one issue, features the papers presented at its annual conference. Conference papers are also made available, on computer disk, to attendees.

Its current officers are Don McDowell, President; Jack L'Epagniol, Vice President (Administration), Australian Bureau of Criminal Intelligence; Bevin Wigan, Vice President (Program), Queensland University of Technology; Paul Roger, Registrar, Criminal Justice Commission, Queensland; Rod Kennett, Treasurer; and Glenn Jones, General Secretary, Australian Customs Service.

INDIVIDUALS

Jay S. Albanese

Jay Albanese is a Professor and Chair of the Department of Political Science and Criminal Justice, Niagara University, Niagara, New York. He has participated in various studies in New York and New Jersey.

He is the author of seven books, including *Organized Crime in America* (1985), *Crime in America: Some Existing and Emerging Problems* (1993; with Robert Pursley), and *Dealing with Delinquency: The Future of Juvenile Justice* (1993). He has also written twenty-two journal articles and book chapters on aspects of crime and justice and has made thirty-five presentations at universities, professional meetings, and police academies.

Dr. Albanese was the recipient of the Teaching Excellence Award from the Sears Foundation in 1990. He was a Visiting Professor at the School of Criminology at Simon Fraser University in British Columbia, Canada, and is a past president of the Northeastern Association of Criminal Justice Sciences.

Albanese received a B.A. in Sociology from Niagara University and an M.A. and a Ph.D. from the Rutgers University School of Criminal Justice.

Paul P. Andrews, Jr.

Paul Andrews is a Special Agent/Analyst with the New Jersey State Commission of Investigation in Trenton. He was employed by the New Jersey Division of State Police as Principal Intelligence Analyst from 1977 to 1985.

He is the coeditor of the book *Criminal Intelligence Analysis* (1990) and has also written the articles "Tactical Network Analysis" (1983) and "Zero-Sum Enforcement: Some Reflections on Drug Control" (coauthor; 1982). He was on the staff of the IALEIA *DIGEST* from 1985 through 1991; is the author of the column "The Analyst's Bookshelf" for the IALEIA newsletter the *INTEL-SCOPE;* and writes book reviews for the *IALEIA JOURNAL.*

He codeveloped and administered the New Jersey State Police Intelligence Analysis Seminars from 1977 through 1985. He codeveloped the first advanced intelligence analysis training course in 1985 and has lectured at John Jay College of Criminal Justice (CUNY) and at several police academies.

Andrews has an M.S. in Criminal Justice and a B.A. in Law Enforcement from Eastern Kentucky University. He attended the U.S. Army Command and General Staff College in 1986 and is presently a Lieutenant Colonel, U.S. Army Reserve, Military Intelligence.

David L. Carter

David Carter is an Associate Professor at the School of Criminal Justice, Michigan State University. In the past he has served on the staff of the Department of Criminal Justice, University of Texas, and of the College of Criminal Justice, Sam Houston State University. He was a training officer and police officer in Kansas City and at Central Missouri State University.

Carter has authored numerous articles, chapters, and books, including "The Application of Computer Simulation to Forecast Violent Crime" (1993) and "Organized Crime: Changes for the Future" (1993). He has authored a four hundred-page monograph on law enforcement analysis and teaches an academic course on the subject. He provides technical assistance to a wide range of federal and state agencies on intelligence issues and management and is currently conducting research on intelligence related issues as they apply to the future. He is the first academician to be chosen to participate in an exchange program with the FBI Behavioral Science Unit.

Carter has a B.S. in Criminal Justice from Central Missouri State University, an M.S. in Criminal Justice Administration from Missouri State University, and a Ph.D. in Criminal Justice Administration from Sam Houston State University in Texas.

Paula Carter

Paula Carter is an Investigative Analyst with the New Jersey State Commission of Investigation in Trenton. She was previously employed by the New

Jersey Division of State Police as Principal Organized Crime Intelligence Analyst for eight years.

She is the former managing editor of the IALEIA *DIGEST* (1986–88). She is a charter member of the International Association for the Study of Organized Crime and served on its Board of Directors in 1987–88. She presented a lecture on the State Commission of Investigation at the Fifth Round Table Conference in Virginia Beach in 1989. She has done extensive writing in her positions, including work on public reports on traditional and nontraditional organized crime, motor fuels tax evasion, municipal corruption, and private carrier company profit skimming.

She has received several honors and commendations for her work on various investigations. She is a Lifetime Certified Criminal Analyst of the Society of Certified Criminal Analysts.

She has a B.S. in Business Administration from Rider College, Lawrenceville, New Jersey.

Robert Clark

Robert Clark is a detective sergeant and the Project Manager of the Analytical Pool, Criminal Research Bureau, State Intelligence Group, New South Wales Police Service, in Australia. He has been a police officer for twenty-six years and has spent the last thirteen in intelligence and organized crime.

He personally or his unit has received three IALEIA awards: for "Repeated Excellence in Law Enforcement Publications," for "The Most Significant Contribution to the Literature of Law Enforcement Intelligence" (1992), and for "Criminal Analysis Techniques."

He has written several articles for professional journals and is currently involved in joint authorship of three books on intelligence, organized crime, and casinos.

Clark has a Bachelor of Arts degree in Social Science from Curtin University in Western Australia and a Master's Degree in Literature from Armidale University in Australia. He has received several research scholarships from the Australian and New Zealand Police College, the New South Wales Law Foundation, and the New South Wales Police Research Scholarship and a Visiting Scholarship at the Institute of Criminology, Canberra, Australia.

Robert Fahlman

Robert Fahlman is the Officer in Charge of the Criminal Analysis Branch of Criminal Intelligence Directorate, Royal Canadian Mounted Police, in Ottawa, Canada. He has served with the RCMP throughout his career, beginning as an intelligence analyst, and has also served as officer in charge of the strategic analysis section. He initiated and launched several RCMP publications, including the *RCMP National Drug Intelligence Estimate,* the *RCMP Monthly Digest of Drug Intelligence Trends,* and the *RCMP Drug Intelligence Bulletin.*

Fahlman served on the RCMP's Criminal Intelligence Task Force (1990–91), which resulted in the formation of the RCMP National Criminal Intelligence Program. He is the founding president of the first Canadian Chapter of IALEIA and serves on the IALEIA Board of Directors and on the Society of Certified Criminal Analysts' Board of Governors. He holds a certification as a Lifetime Certified Criminal Analyst. He received an award from IALEIA in 1992 for his significant contribution to law enforcement intelligence analysis.

He has written or edited numerous publications including "The Current Drug Situation in Canada" (195), "Illicit Traffic and Abuse of Cocaine" (1984), and "The RCMP's Criminal Intelligence Program" (1992). He has lectured on tactical and strategic intelligence in the United States, Thailand, Canada, France, and the Czech Republic. He served in 1993–94 on loan to INTERPOL in Lyon, France, for the purpose of establishing an analytical unit there.

Fahlman has a B.A. in Applied Arts from Ryerson Polytechnical Institute in Toronto, Canada.

Edward Feingold

Edward Feingold is an Intelligence Analyst working with the Rocky Mountain Information Network (RMIN) in Arizona for five years. He retired from the U.S. Army in 1986 after twenty-one years of military service. Eight years of his service was spent with the Defense Intelligence Agency in the attaché system holding posts in Poland, Mexico, and the Dominican Republic.

He has conducted several training classes on Toll Analysis and has developed a three-day Toll Analysis course. He is certified as an instructor by the Arizona Law Enforcement Officers Advisory Council. He has also spoken on topics including the use of computer-aided analysis, charting for courtroom presentations, and use of analysis in multijurisdictional task force cases.

Feingold attended the University of the State of New York and the Defense Intelligence College. He has been awarded Lifetime Certification by the Society of Certified Criminal Analysts.

Emma E. Fern

Emma Fern is an Intelligence Analyst with the Florida Department of Law Enforcement in Miami. She has been in law enforcement for twenty-three years.

She served as the President of the International Association of Law Enforcement Intelligence Analysts from 1990 to 1994 and as Interim President in 1986. She is a member of the Board of Governors of the Society of Certified Criminal Analysts and is a Lifetime Certified Criminal Analyst. She founded the Florida Chapter of the International Association of Law Enforcement Analysts and has been its President since 1981.

She has received numerous awards during her career, including a United States Department of Justice Award for Public Service in 1983 and the Florida Department of Law Enforcement Distinguished Contribution to Criminal Justice Award in 1984. The latter award was the result of her work on the "Outrigger Case" from 1978 to 1984. She received the IALEIA Award for Outstanding Contributions in 1984.

She has designed and administered numerous training seminars for IALEIA; her chapter has hosted the semiannual training conference for the organization a number of years.

She has an Associate of Arts degree in Criminal Justice from Metro Dade Community College.

Charles C. Frost

Charles Frost is a Professor of Justice Systems at Northeast Missouri State University in Kirksville. He has been an analyst, trainer, management adviser, and program analyst for agencies including the Drug Enforcement Administration, the White House Drug Prevention Office, and the Central Intelligence Agency.

He has written several publications on report writing including the chapter "Intelligence Report Writing," in *Criminal Intelligence Analysis* (1990). He is the author of *Police Intelligence Reports* (1983; with J. Morris) and wrote "Choosing Good Intelligence Analysts: What's Measurable?" for the IALEIA *DIGEST* (1985).

He is a member of the editorial review board of the *IALEIA JOURNAL,* has served for several years on the IALEIA Board of Directors, and is on the Board of Governors of the Society of Certified Criminal Analysts. He was the editor of the *IALEIA INTELSCOPE* for two years. He is a member of the International Association for the Study of Organized Crime and the Academy of Criminal Justice Sciences.

He received several awards and commendations while in the Central Intelligence Agency and the Drug Enforcement Administration.

Frost has a B.A. in History from Tufts University and an M.A. and a Ph.D. in International Finance from the Fletcher School of Law and Diplomacy.

Richard G. Fuller

Richard Fuller is a consultant for law enforcement programs to ANACAPA Sciences, Inc., where he was a Senior Scientist from 1978 to 1992. He was a criminal intelligence analyst for the Santa Barbara County, California, Sheriff's Office from 1974 to 1978.

While with ANACAPA, he presented numerous analytical training courses on beginning and advanced levels.

His publications for ANACAPA include *Sources of Information for Criminal*

Investigators (1986 and revisions), *Design for a Litigation Control Room* (1984), and *Advanced Criminal Analysis Training* (coauthor; 1980).

Fuller has a B.S. in Military Science from the University of Maryland and an M.A. in History from Arizona State University.

Ronald Goldstock

Ronald Goldstock is the Executive Director of the New York State Organized Crime Task Force in White Plains. He was Acting Inspector General, U.S. Department of Labor, from 1980 to 1981; Director and Executive Director of the Cornell Institute or Organized Crime, 1975 to 1979; and Assistant District Attorney, New York County, from 1969 to 1975.

He is on the faculty of Cornell Law School and New York University Law School. He has also made presentations at numerous professional conferences on organized crime topics. He has written numerous publications, including *Rackets Bureaus: The Investigation and Prosecution of Organized Crime* (with G. R. Blakey and C. H. Rogovin; 1978), *The Investigation and Prosecution of Complex Narcotics Cases: A Simulated Investigation* (with M. Goldsmith; 1989), and "The Prosecutor as Problem Solver" (1991). He has written, with G. R. Blakey, several Manuals of Law and Procedure, including *Techniques on the Investigation and Prosecution of Organized Crime* (1976), *The Investigation and Prosecution of Organized Crime and Official Corruption* (1977), and *The Investigation and Prosecution of Organized Crime and Labor Racketeering*.

Goldstock has an A.B. from Cornell University and a J.D. from Harvard University.

Steven L. Gottlieb

Steven Gottlieb is the Special Services Manager of the Chino, California, Police Department, supervising the department's crime analysis, crime prevention, and serious habitual offender programs. Before joining the Chino department in 1982, Gottlieb was a sworn police officer with the West Covina, California, Police Department and a Deputy Sheriff for Los Angeles County.

He is a consultant to the California Department of Justice and teaches statewide crime analysis courses. He recently developed a crime analysis curriculum for the California State University at Fullerton and San Bernadino. He is the coordinator for the Crime and Intelligence Analysis Certification program developed in conjunction with the California Department of Justice.

His publications include *Crime Analysis* (coauthored with Sheldon Arenberg and Raj Singh, 1992), *Crime Analysis: From Concept to Reality* (coauthored with Sheldon Arenberg, 1989), *Measuring and Evaluating Crime Analysis and Prevention Programs* (1984), and the recently released *Crime Analysis: From First Report to Final Arrest* (1994).

He is a member of the International Association of Crime Analysts, the California Crime Analysts, and the National Speakers Association. In 1993, he served as a consultant to the FBI Academy for the purpose of developing a curriculum for a three-week crime analysts' training program; the following year he was one of the principal instructors in the FBI's Crime Analysis Training. Gottlieb has a B.S. in police science and administration from California State University and a master's degree in Public Administration from the University of Southern California.

Walter Harper

Walter Harper is retired from—but continues to consult for—ANACAPA Sciences in Santa Barbara, California. While with ANACAPA, he participated in the initiation of the criminal intelligence analysis training course. Between 1971 and 1985, he conducted over a hundred of these courses in the United States, Canada, Germany, and the United Kingdom.

He has authored or coauthored about eighty publications, including "Intelligence Analysis Training Program" (with D. H. Harris, 1979), "The Application of Link Analysis to Police Intelligence" (with D. H. Harris; 1977), and "Intelligence Analysis Training Courses: Results and Evaluation" (with D. H. Harris; 1972).

Harper has a B.A. in psychology from George Washington University and an M.A. in educational psychology from the University of California.

Douglas Harris

Douglas Harris is the Chairman and Principal Scientist of ANACAPA Sciences, Inc., in Charlottesville, Virginia. Along with Walter Harper, Harris developed and conducted the first course in criminal intelligence analysis in the United States. He developed and conducted training courses in the United States, Canada, Singapore, the United Kingdom, and Venezuela. Courses included analytical investigation methods, criminal intelligence analysis, and computer-aided intelligence analysis.

He is the author of over one hundred publications, including journal articles, technical reports, and books. These include "Development of a Computer Based Program for Criminal Intelligence Analysis" (1978), "The Application of Link Analysis to Police Intelligence" (1975), and "Analytical Techniques and Computer Aiding" (1988). He is a Fellow of the Human Factors Society, American Psychological Association, and American Psychological Society.

Harris has a B.S. in industrial psychology from Iowa State University and an M.S. and a Ph.D. in industrial psychology from Purdue University.

James B. Howlett

James Howlett is an independent consultant specializing in criminal justice training, information management, microcomputer applications, and data management. He retired from the Federal Bureau of Investigation in 1993 after eight years as a Senior Crime Analyst for the Violent Criminal Apprehension Program (VICAP). Previously, he was employed by the Charlotte, North Carolina, Police Department, by ANACAPA Sciences, and by the Lakewood, Colorado, Department of Public Safety.

During his tenure with the FBI, Howlett received many commendations for his work on psychological profiling and serial crime. He taught for the FBI and for ANACAPA Sciences and spoke before numerous investigative and analytical conferences in the United States and Europe. He is a former President of IA-LEIA.

Howlett has a B.S. in accounting from Penn State University and a M.P.A. from Pepperdine University.

Richard Kedzior

Richard Kedzior is a consultant to the Criminal Intelligence Service Ontario supervising its intelligence analysis activity. A native of Quebec, Canada, he has worked as an intelligence analyst for the Quebec Police Force and the New York State Organized Crime Task Force and as a senior analyst with the Pennsylvania Crime Commission. He was a criminology consultant to the Quebec Police Commission's Division of Inquiry into Organized Crime, trained and supervised analysts for that inquiry, and wrote three of the nine volumes of the final report which dealt with the infiltration of the garment industry by organized crime; the legal, sociological, and criminological aspects of organized crime in Canada; and a statistical study of the ladies' wear industry.

He has taught organized crime and analysis while in Canada. He coauthored a chapter in *Organized Crime: A Global Perspective* (Robert J. Kelly, ed.; 1986). He has also presented papers before the American Society of Criminology ("The Evolution of Criminal Rackets in a Small City: A Case Study" in 1990) and the Quebec Police Academy's Third Annual Conference on White-Collar Criminality ("Organized Crime and White Collar Crime" in 1982).

Kedzior has a B.A. in psychology from McGill University in Montreal and an M.Sc. in criminology from the University of Montreal and has completed the course work for his Ph.D. in criminology from the University of Montreal. He is a Lifetime Certified Criminal Analyst.

Robert J. Kelly

Robert Kelly is Broeklundian Professor at Brooklyn College and Professor of Criminal Justice at the Graduate School of the City University of New York. He is President of the Board of Directors of the Edward Sagarin Institute for the Study of Deviance and Social Issues and is past President of the International Association for the Study of Organized Crime.

He has authored and edited numerous publications, including the *Handbook on Organized Crime in the United States* (edited with K. Chin and R. Schatz-berg), *Deviance: Domination, Denigration and Dehumanization* (coeditor and contributor), *Organized Crime: A Global Perspective* (editor and contributor), "The Evolution of Criminal Syndicates" (1987), "The Nature of Organized Crime and Its Operations" (1987), "Dirty Dollars: Organized Crime and Toxic Waste" (1988), and "The Development of Inferences in the Assessment of Intelligence Data" (1990).

He has received various research grants from the National Institute of Justice. He was a Faculty Honoree (for research) at the Graduate School of the City University of New York in 1987. He was nominated for the post of Distinguished Professor at Brooklyn College in 1992.

Kelly received his B.A. in Philosophy from Brooklyn College in 1963, his M.A. in Sociology from City College of New York in 1975, and his Ph.D. in Sociology from the Graduate School of the City University of New York in 1978.

Jack A. Kinney

Jack Kinney is a Consulting Scientist to ANACAPA Sciences, Santa Barbara, California. He has forty-three years of experience in the analysis of systems and organizations and in the development, conduct, and evaluation of training programs. He has eighteen years of experience with ANACAPA.

He has presented numerous papers on analytical techniques, including "Analytical Methods for Credit Card Fraud Investigation" (September 1991) for the International Association of Credit Card Investigators; "Analytical Investigation Methods: An Overview" (January 1985), for the Insurance Security Association; "Analytical Investigation Techniques as Tools in Bank Security" (March 1982), for the Bank Administration Institute; and "A Model for Urban Terrorism as a Function of Commitment" (November 1976), for the American Society of Criminology. He has participated in several studies of police organizations, such as the Bureau of Alcohol, Tobacco and Firearms (1980) and the Texas Department of Public Safety (1978). He is the author or coauthor of over fifty articles, pamphlets, and monographs.

He has won awards for "noteworthy service to the profession of law enforcement intelligence analysis" from IALEIA (1987), and for services to the organization from the Royal Hong Kong Police, Canada Customs, Metro-Dade (Florida) Police Department, Australian Bureau of Intelligence, Victoria Police Bureau of Crime Intelligence, and others.

Kinney has a M.A. in sociology and education from the University of Chicago and a Ph.D. in public administration from LaSalle University.

Peter A. Lupsha

Peter Lupsha is a Professor of Political Science at the University of New Mexico in Albuquerque. He has been with the University of New Mexico since

1972 and was previously an Assistant Professor of Political Science at Yale University. He is also an Academic Research Associate at Los Alamos National Laboratory in New Mexico, providing "domain expertise" to computer simulation and modeling systems analysis on organized crime and international drug trafficking.

Lupsha has received various grants, awards, and honors, including a Carnegie Mellon Travel Study Grant (1984–85), University of New Mexico Faculty Research Grant (1976–77), Yale Junior Faculty Social Science Research Fellowship (1971–72), and a Ford Foundation Travel Study Grant (1971), and was a National Science Foundation Research Fellow (1964–65).

His publications include "Organized Crime," in *Local Government Police Management,* 3rd ed. (1991); "Organized Crime: Rational Choice Not Ethnic Behavior," in *Law Enforcement Intelligence Analysis Digest* (1988); "Organized Crime in the United States," in *Organized Crime: A Global Perspective* (1986); "Networks Versus Networking: An Analysis of an Organized Crime Group," in *Career Criminals* (1983); and "Steps Toward the Strategic Analysis of Organized Crime," in *The Police Chief* (1980).

Lupsha has a B.A. from Oklahoma State University, an M.A. from the University of California (Berkeley), and a Ph.D. from Stanford University.

Frederick T. Martens

Frederick Martens is an independent consultant and investigator. He is the former Executive Director of the Pennsylvania Crime Commission in Conshohocken, Pennsylvania. Prior to his appointment to the Commission in 1987, Martens had achieved the rank of Lieutenant in the New Jersey State Police. While there, he was in charge of the Analytical Section of the Intelligence Bureau, and of the Narcotics Bureau/North. He had also served as Executive Assistant to the Deputy Superintendent and in other positions with the State Police.

Martens wrote *Police Intelligence Systems in Crime Control* with Justin J. Dintino (1983) and has authored or coauthored numerous articles in professional journals. He has served as a consultant to several documentaries on La Cosa Nostra and has lectured and appeared in the media across the United States, in Australia, Europe, and the Far East. He has taught intelligence and organized crime courses at police academies throughout the world.

Mr. Martens has received numerous commendations for his law enforcement work, including an IALEIA award (with Justin Dintino) for the "Most Significant Contribution to the Literature of Intelligence Analysis" in 1984. He has also received awards from the New Jersey State Police, New Scotland Yard, and Pennsylvania County and State Detectives.

He has a baccalaureate degree from Fairleigh Dickinson University, and two master's degrees, one from the City University of New York (criminology) and one from Fordham University (sociology). He has taught at Pennsylvania State University and at Upsala College.

Donald W. McDowell

Donald McDowell is a consultant who teaches tactical and strategic analytical methodologies to law enforcement agencies internationally. He is the former Director of the Strategic Crime Studies Unit of the Australian Attorney General's Department, Canberra. He has been involved in law enforcement intelligence work since the mid-1980s. His previous background was in military and governmental political and economic intelligence analysis in Indo-China, Pakistan, Afghanistan, and Bangladesh.

He is the founding President of the Australian Institute of Professional Intelligence Officers. His publications include "Comparative Analysis of Illicit Drug Strategy: Law Enforcement" (1992), "Australia's Illegal Drug Problem: A Strategic Intelligence Assessment," "The Environment and Crime: A New Challenge for Intelligence" (1992), and *Strategic Intelligence in the Law Enforcement Environment* (forthcoming). He has presented courses on intelligence in Australia, Malaysia, and Canada, on the topics Intelligence Practice and Management, Strategic Intelligence and Management, Basic Analysis, and Strategic Intelligence Analysis.

McDowell has a diploma in Vietnamese Studies and undertook postgraduate business management studies at the Australian Graduate School of Management in the University of New South Wales.

Jerry P. Marynik

Jerry Marynik is the Manager of the Gangs/Criminal Extremists Unit in the Bureau of Investigation/Intelligence Operations of the California Department of Justice. He was the former supervisor of the Organized Crime Unit in the Bureau of Organized Crime and Criminal Intelligence (BOCCI). Marynik was one of the first crime analysts in the country in 1972 to adapt telephone toll analysis from the national security environment to the law enforcement community. He has testified in court proceedings and has produced numerous analytical products. He has also been responsible for several special publications, such as *Gangs 2000* (1992), *Organized Crime Contract Killings* (1976), and *Migration of Eastern Organized Crime Figures* (1975).

He was a consultant to the Federal Law Enforcement Training Center in Glynco, Georgia, in its development of a criminal intelligence analyst training course. He also served as a consultant to the California Attorney General's Organized Crime Control Commission in 1978.

Bob R. Morehouse

Bob Morehouse is the Manager of the Organized Crime Unit in the Bureau of Investigation, Intelligence Operations, California Department of Justice. He has worked in the field of criminal intelligence for over twenty years. He has produced numerous analytical products, many of which have been used nationally. He has been responsible for several special publications, such as *Organized Crime Involvement in California Pornography* (1976), *Non-Traditional Organized Crime* (1982), *Issues of Interest to Law Enforcement—Information Sources* (1984), *Columbian Cocaine Cartels* (1991), and *Southern California Organized Crime* (1992).

Morehouse provides training at the California Department of Justice's Advanced Training Center on "Traditional Organized Crime," "Gambling in California," "Link Analysis," and "Public Information Sources." He coordinates the Bureau's Organized Crime and Criminal Intelligence Training Conference held each year.

In 1986, he received the California Attorney General's Sustained Superior Accomplishment Award. He presented the paper "Organized Crime Intelligence Collection and Analysis California Style" at the November 1991 conference of the American Society of Criminology; it was later reprinted in the IALEIA *Law Enforcement Intelligence Analysis Digest.*

Richard A. Nossen

Richard A. Nossen is a consultant and instructor at law enforcement academies throughout the United States and Canada. He spent twenty-four years with the U.S. Department of the Treasury, Internal Revenue Service, rising from special agent to Deputy Assistant Commissioner of the Criminal Investigation Division.

He has authored several publications, including *The Detection, Investigation and Prosecution of Financial Crimes, The Determination of Undisclosed Financial Interest, The Seventh Basic Investigative Technique,* and "The Dilemma of Prosecutors—One on One Uncorroborated Testimony" in the *Notre Dame Law Review.*

He teaches "Financial Crimes Investigative Techniques" and "Asset Seizure and Forfeiture Strategies" to federal, state, and local law enforcement agencies and associations. He has been a consultant to U.S. Attorney's offices in several cities for major criminal conspiracy prosecutions.

Marilyn B. Peterson

Marilyn B. Peterson is a Management Specialist with the Fraud Bureau of the New Jersey Department of Law and Public Safety, Division of Criminal Justice, in Trenton. She has previously been employed by the Pennsylvania Crime Commission and was Chief Writer of its *1980 Report: A Decade of Organized Crime* (1980). She was also senior analyst and later administrative and technical services manager for the Middle Atlantic–Great Lakes Organized Crime Law Enforcement Network (MAGLOCLEN). She worked for five years as an analyst and management specialist in the Narcotics Bureau of the Division of Criminal Justice.

Peterson has taught analysis across the United States and has developed basic, advanced, and strategic analysis courses. She has written extensively about analysis. Two of her writings have received awards from the International Association of Law Enforcement Intelligence Analysts for the most significant written contribution to law enforcement analysis for a given year. The first, "Law Enforcement Intelligence: A New Look," appeared in the *International Journal of Intelligence and Counterintelligence* (1986). The second, *Criminal Intelligence Analysis* (1990), was a volume she coedited and for which she wrote two chapters. Other written works to which she contributed, including the Pennsylvania Crime Commission *1990 Report: A Decade of Change* (1991), have also received awards for excellence.

She teaches for the Federal Law Enforcement Center in Glynco, Georgia, and at other training academies throughout the United States. She has spoken at the John F. Kennedy School of Government, Harvard University; before the Australian Institute of Professional Intelligence Officers; and at various colleges and universities. In 1993, she was a consultant to the FBI Academy for the purpose of developing a curriculum for a three-week crime analysts' training program.

She is the Managing Editor of the *IALEIA JOURNAL* and is the cofounder and Secretary/Treasurer of the Board of Governors of the Society of Certified Criminal Analysts, from which she holds the designation of Lifetime Certified Criminal Analyst. She is an International Associate of the Australian Institute of Professional Intelligence Officers.

Peterson has a B.S. in Criminal Justice from Thomas Edison State College in Trenton, New Jersey, and has completed an M.A. in Education from Seton Hall University, South Orange, New Jersey.

Michael Prodan

Michael Prodan is a Special Agent Supervisor for the California Department of Justice. His primary duties involve criminal investigative profiling.

Prodan has instructed students nationally and internationally on such subjects as "Criminal Investigative Analysis," "Serial Rapist Typologies," "Homosexual Homicide," "Adult and Juvenile Sex Offenders," and "Advanced Crime Scene Reconstruction."

He is one of thirty-four graduates worldwide of the Federal Bureau of Investigation's Police Fellowship in Criminal Investigative Profiling and Crime Scene Analysis at the National Center for the Analysis of Violent Crime. He is a nationally recognized expert in profiling serial sexual offenders, sexual homicide, and crime scene reconstruction.

Henry W. Prunckun, Jr.

Henry W. Prunckun is Chief Project Officer in charge of the police and research division of the State Courts Administration Authority, South Australia.

He has held the positions of police officer, research officer, principal research analyst, and manager of data operations and security.

Prunckun has lectured at the University of Adelaide and the Adelaide College of Technical and Further Education (Australia) on topics including computer crime and information security.

He is the recipient of an IALEIA award for the most significant contribution to the literature of law enforcement intelligence for *Special Access Required: A Practitioner's Guide to Law Enforcement Intelligence Literature* (1990) and the IALEIA professional service award in 1992 for his work with intelligence indexing software. He is also the author of *Information Security: A Practical Handbook on Business Counterintelligence* (1989) and *Shadow of Death: An Analytic Bibliography on Political Violence, Terrorism, and Low-Intensity Conflict* (forthcoming).

Prunckun holds a B.S. in criminal justice from Westfield State College. He has a postgraduate diploma in political science from Flinders University, South Australia, and is a candidate for a master of social science degree from the University of South Australia.

R. Glen Ridgeway

Glen Ridgeway is the Director of Training and Files for the New York State Organized Crime Task Force in White Plains. He was formerly responsible for the Strategic Analysis section of the State Organized Crime Task Force, has been an instructor for ANACAPA Sciences, Inc., and is a former New Jersey State Trooper.

Ridgeway is a past president of IALEIA and is Chancellor (and cofounder) of the Society of Certified Criminal Analysts. His publications include "Analytical Intelligence Training" and "Analytical Training in Today's Law Enforcement Environment" (both with M. Peterson).

He has a B.S. from Rider College and is completing his M.A. in Criminal Justice from Iona College.

Paul A. Roger

Paul Roger is the Director of Intelligence for the Criminal Justice Commission in Queensland, Australia. Previous to his 1991 appointment, he was principal intelligence analyst for the Commission and a sixteen-year veteran of the Royal Hong Kong Police. While there, he was primarily assigned to the Organised and Serious Crime Group.

He has lectured in Hong Kong, Canada, the United States, England, and Australia, primarily on Chinese organized crime. He has written several papers on organized crime, Chinese triads, and Chinese tongs. He has studied organized crime in the United States and Canada and presented a paper at the Third Annual Conference on Chinese Organised Crime in Manchester, England, "Triads in Hong Kong Past and Present." He lectures at the Queensland University of

Technology and the University of Queensland and has taught at the Australian Police College.

Roger is completing his bachelor justice studies at the Queensland University of Technology (Law Faculty). He is a Lifetime Certified Criminal Analyst and is a member of the Australian Institute of Professional Intelligence Officers.

Charles H. Rogovin

Charles Rogovin is a Professor of Law at Temple University Law School and has also served as vice-chairman of the Pennsylvania Crime Commission. Rogovin has been involved in law enforcement and intelligence since 1959, when he began his career as a public defender in Philadelphia. He was Assistant Director of the President's Commission on Law Enforcement and the Administration of Justice (Director, Organized Crime Task Force) 1966–67; the Administrator of the Law Enforcement Assistance Administration, 1969–70; President of the Police Foundation, 1970–72; and a member of the President's Commission on Organized Crime, 1983–86.

He has been a Fellow at the Institute of Politics, John F. Kennedy School of Government, Harvard University, and was a visiting professor at Brandeis University. He was Special Counsel to the Select Committee on Assassinations, U.S. House of Representatives (1978–79).

Rogovin has been a lifetime proponent of the analytical function in law enforcement and was one of the earliest lecturers in the ANACAPA program. He is an Honorary Member of IALEIA. He is a noted lecturer on a variety of intelligence, organized crime, and analytical topics. His writings include *A National Strategy for Containing White-Collar Crime* (co-author, 1980), *Rackets Bureaus: Investigation and Prosecution of Organized Crime* (coauthor, 1978), and *The Police-Prosecutor Relationship in the United States: An Uneasy Alliance* (forthcoming).

Rogovin has a B.A. in History from Wesleyan University and a L.L.B. from Columbia University Law School.

Karen L. Sanderson

Karen Sanderson is the Manager of the Research and Analysis Unit of the Western States Information Network (WSIN) in Sacramento, California. Over the past ten years she has produced over two hundred different analytical products, including link analysis, event flow analysis, telephone toll analysis, financial analysis, and visual investigative analysis. She has testified as an expert witness in federal court on telephone toll analysis.

Sanderson has provided training in the United States and Canada. She has instructed at the Federal Law Enforcement Training Center (FLETC), the California Department of Justice Advanced Training Center, and numerous training conferences. She is an Associate Editor of the *IALEIA JOURNAL,* a semiannual professional publication.

In 1985, she received the California Attorney General's Sustained Superior Accomplishment Award and the IALEIA Analyst of the Year award.

Sanderson has a B.S. in forensic science from the California State University at Sacramento.

Malcolm Sparrow

Malcolm Sparrow is a Lecturer in Public Policy at the John F. Kennedy School of Government, Harvard University. He is also the Faculty Chair of the M.P.P. and M.P.A. degree programs at the School. Prior to working at Harvard, he was a Deputy Chief Inspector in Kent County, England. He is currently doing research on the application of network analytic techniques to fraud control in the credit card and health care industries, with emphasis on early detection and prevention of organized multiparty collusive fraud schemes.

He is a coauthor of *Beyond 911: A New Era for Policing* (1990) and *Ethics in Government: The Moral Challenge of Public Leadership.* He has also written several publications on intelligence analysis, including "The Application of Network Analysis to Criminal Intelligence: An Assessment of the Prospects (1991), "Network Vulnerabilities and Strategic Intelligence" (1991), "Information Systems and the Development of Policing" (1993), and *Imposing Duties: Government's Changing Approach to Compliance* (1994).

Sparrow has a B.A. and an M.A. in mathematics from Trinity College, Cambridge; an M.P.A. from the John F. Kennedy School of Government, Harvard University; and a doctor of philosophy in applied mathematics, University of Kent, Canterbury, England.

OTHER PROMINENT ANALYSTS

The following organizations and individuals have established reputations of dedication and excellence in the field of intelligence and analysis.

Organizations

Financial Crimes Enforcement Network (FinCEN)

Florida Department of Law Enforcement

New Jersey Division of State Police

Royal Hong Kong Police

Individuals

Col. Justin J. Dintino, New Jersey Division of State Police

David Icove, Federal Bureau of Investigation

Mark H. Moore, Harvard University

Peter Reuter, The Rand Corporation

CHAPTER X

Intelligence, Analysis, Policy, and the Future

In October 1993, the author presented a keynote speech at Intel '93, the Annual Conference of the Australian Institute of Professional Intelligence Officers in Canberra, Australia. The topic was the link between analysis and policy setting in law enforcement. Following are excerpts from that speech.

I am pleased to be here participating in a discussion on policy, ethics, and technology. I believe that the future of law enforcement rests on our ability to use intelligence, analysis, and technology wisely and ethically in support of policy making.

During the years that I have been in analysis, I have seen policies created that bore no relation to analysis, no relation to intelligence, no relation to fact. Instead some policies reflected wishful thinking, personal opinions and knee-jerk crisis management. Strategic planning and strategic decision making have had only small footholds in many enforcement agencies.

McDowell commented that law enforcement planning has been viewed as a special prerogative of managers to the exclusion of the intelligence function (1992). But the planning process—defining the organization's mission; gathering information; analyzing the information; developing strategies, goals, and objectives; and developing measurements and evaluation data to look at the results of the strategy—has as its basis information collection, analysis, and conclusion-drawing, in short, the analytical/intelligence process.

Today, I see an emerging need for greater analytical support of policy making. I also see a need for the analysts of the future to be all-source, cross-trained, and full-service so they will be able to provide that support to policy making.

Analysis is the key which should link thinking and policy. Information gathering and analysis should play a central role in the planning process. Good planning is good decision making. It is the job of intelligence professionals to provide the information necessary to management to make those decisions.

Major corporations in the United States and Australia realize the importance of intelligence gathering and analysis to support decision-making. Many have built or are building intelligence systems to maintain information on their environment and their competitors that will allow them to gain or maintain a competitive edge. In the book *Liberation Management* Tom Peters says that by the year 2020, 80 percent of business profits and market value will come from the part of the organization that is built around what he calls info-business. That is, the information collection, analysis, and dissemination function will represent 80 percent of the value of the company. I believe this will be true for law enforcement and regulatory agencies even sooner.

Analysts and intelligence officers form an "expert network" which can change the face of law enforcement on this continent and on other continents. How well, and how real-time, we can connect to each other may make the difference between not finding the criminal, reinventing the technological wheel, or re-devising policies and strategies that have been tested elsewhere. Electronic hook-ups, teleconferencing, and telefaxing make us all only minutes away from each other, even when there is more than a half-day's time difference between us. There is no excuse for our refusing to share and benefit from the input of others in this expert network.

If good planning is informed decision-making, then being as informed as possible should be the desire of those responsible for management planning. But they need to be informed in a rational, workable way. The amount of data available in this "information age" far surpasses the assimilation ability of most people. The intelligence or information unit is designed and trained to act as a filter between the information and the manager—to accept all this data and turn it into something usable. To review countless facts and derive meaning from them. To provide the manager with factual bases for his or her decisions.

The connection between the intelligence unit and planning lies with strategic analysis. The IACP wrote, in 1985, that strategic analysis is "probably the single-most important activity" that police executives could use to support their strategic planning.

Meyer noted that "to achieve your objectives in a fast-paced, multi-national, information-driven world like ours, you need to know . . . as much as possible about what's going on—and what's likely to go on—throughout the total environment in which you and your adversaries are operating . . . intelligence is a tool of awesome power and flexibility" (1987, pp. 5–7). What did he mean by flexibility? I think he meant that all-source intelligence allows you to be familiar with all the sides to the problem and with the different ways you can look at it and solve it. All-source intelligence can provide a chief with several approaches to problem-solving, evaluated according to their probable impact, from which he can choose.

Intelligence provides us with the flexibility to look at the alternatives before or during the game, not after it is over. Why wait and be a Monday morning quarterback?

Why is intelligence maligned or ignored? Perhaps because of what has been called "failures in intelligence." This is used to refer to instances where an intelligence product has failed to support a decision-maker in coming to the "right" conclusion. This wrong conclusion can be the result of incorrect information being collected, wrong conclusions being drawn by the analyst, or wrong decisions being made by the manager in spite of having available data to the contrary.

A word of advice to managers: do not use the so-called failures of intelligence to hold you back from using intelligence in support of decision making and planning. More mistakes are made by managers who chose to ignore the data provided by their intelligence process than by those who use the intelligence function.

One difficulty we have faced in law enforcement is a lack of internal coordination and cooperation between units and bureaus. This holds true of analysis. There are crime analysts, intelligence analysts, strategic analysts, policy analysts, and operations analysts. They all receive different training, sometimes so specialized they must be re-trained when they move from one investigative unit to another. As a result, their value to the agency is more limited than it might be. Analytical cross-training is imperative. Analysts should know as much about the range of tools [e.g., as shown in Chapter 2 of this volume] available to them as possible.

Cross-training would breed full-service analysts who would be capable in their current roles and would be prepared for more advanced roles within law enforcement. Analysis is an evolving field. New techniques and new technology are moving its applications forward at a rapid pace. A full-service analyst is one who can take on any analytical assignment and complete it; one who has the confidence and creativity to adapt the basic tools to fill the need of the specific analytical task.

Analysts who possess a range of basic skills have more flexibility to work not just as analysts, but as planners, as public information officers, as speech writers, as special assistants to the chief. Analysts who possess a range of tools and techniques are confident enough to draw conclusions, to make recommendations, to take risks.

The future of analysis is what we, in the field, make it. Analysts must prepare to take their rightful place in the law enforcement community. We must use our organizations and our "expert network" to further the professionalism of the field and to serve law enforcement to the fullest.

Glossary

Definitions reflect the usage of these phrases in this book and may not necessarily reflect the most common use of the phrase.

ANALYSIS—the review of information and the comparison of it to other information to determine the meaning of the data in reference to a criminal investigation or assessment; also the fourth step in the intelligence process.

ARTIFICIAL INTELLIGENCE—computer software program which is able to "think" on the basis of preestablished criteria. This is used, for example, to identify potential tax evaders by reviewing the amounts they declare as deductions. Certain combinations "flag" officials to pull the return for a closer look.

ASSESSMENT—an overview of a crime group or crime problem.

ASSET—property a person owns that is readily convertible into cash. *See* NET WORTH ANALYSIS.

ASSOCIATION ANALYSIS—the compilation, review, and analysis of data to provide information about the strength and occurrence of relationships among persons, businesses, or groups.

ASSOCIATION CHART—also called a link or network chart. Depicts the associations and relations among individuals, businesses, and groups connected to an illegal enterprise.

ASSOCIATION MATRIX—the arrangement of data on relationships among people and entities into a column and row format. It is generally an intermediate step between raw data and creating an association chart.

AUSTRALIAN INSTITUTE OF PROFESSIONAL INTELLIGENCE OFFICERS (AIPIO)—the intelligence analyst organization in Australia.

BANK ACCOUNT ANALYSIS—the compilation, review, and analysis of records obtained from a bank to determine the flow of currency in and out of the account to determine its potential connection to criminal activity.

BANKER—a large-scale illegal betting operation which takes bets from smaller betting operations to ''cover'' the bets the smaller operation took from its customers.

BAR CHART—the depiction of data in comparison to each other in a measurable two-dimensional format.

BID RIGGING—where proposals to sell an item or service to another entity (often the government) are deliberately submitted in a way that ensures that a particular vendor receives the contract.

BIOGRAPHICAL SKETCHES—short biographical pieces on the primary participants in a criminal conspiracy which are developed in conjunction with other analytical products.

BODYCOUNT—the number of arrests made.

BOLO—Be On the Look Out. A form of Crime Bulletin.

BRIEFING—the oral presentation of data analyzed for the purpose of informing investigators or managers about the facts of the case, the analytical products completed, and the conclusions drawn.

BUST-OUT SCHEME—bankruptcy fraud; where a retailer orders merchandise and sells it cheaply while not paying the manufacturer for the items and then declares bankruptcy.

BUY-BUST—a narcotics transaction between an officer and a drug seller after which the drug seller is arrested.

CASE ANALYSIS—the overall analytical treatment of all materials gathered in a particular investigation. Can include several analytical techniques or products.

CHRONOLOGICAL TABLE—a table which lists activities which are to occur and the time frame in which the activities are to be completed. Is also called a TIMELINE.

COLLATION—the manual or computerized organization of data collected into a format from which it can be retrieved and analyzed; the third step in the intelligence process.

COLLECTION—the act of gathering data; the second step in the intelligence process.

COLLECTION PLAN—the determining of what materials should be gathered to complete the research necessary for a strategic analysis and the sources of the materials and the time frame in which the materials can be gathered.

COMMODITY FLOW ANALYSIS—the compilation, review, and analysis of data relating to goods, currency, or services which pass from one person or entity to another.

COMMODITY FLOW CHART—the graphic depiction of the flow of goods, currency, or services from one person or entity to another.

CONCLUSION—a decision based on the facts obtained through the analytical process.

CONTENT ANALYSIS—the review, analysis, and attribution of meaning to oral or written communications.

CONVERSATION ANALYSIS—the review of oral communication to uncover further information about the relationship of the conversants and their involvement in the subject being discussed.

CORPORATE RECORD ANALYSIS—the review of corporate documents to determine whether the corporation was involved in any illegal activity.

CRACK HOUSE—a place where "crack" cocaine is sold and used.

CRIME ANALYSIS—the compilation, review, and analysis of data generated by criminal activities which allow one to determine key factors in the activities.

CRIME BULLETIN—a short analytical compilation which generally includes a warning about a criminal or a criminal activity.

CRIME RATE—the number of crimes committed in a particular area divided by the population of the area; usually expressed in crimes per 1,000 or crimes per 100,000.

CRIMINAL HISTORY RECORDS CHECK—a check of police department records to determine the past criminal activities of a suspect. The record is sometimes called a "rap sheet."

CRIMINAL INTELLIGENCE—the body of information received on known or suspected persons involved in criminal activity or the data resulting from the analysis of criminal data collected on persons known or suspected of being involved in criminal activity.

CRIMINAL INVESTIGATIVE ANALYSIS—the analysis of crime scene and other data to determine a psychological or criminal profile of a suspect.

DATA BASE—usually a computerized set of files, called "records," broken down into columns, or "fields," which allows the analyst to retrieve and manipulate the data for analysis.

DEDUCTIVE REASONING—arriving at a conclusion which takes the known facts and restates them.

DEMOGRAPHIC ANALYSIS—the review and analysis of such factors as age, sex, race, socioeconomic status, geographic location, and education level.

DESCRIPTIVE ANALYSIS—the verbal (rather than mathematical) analysis of a situation, event, group, or entity.

DIRECTION—the first phase of the intelligence process in which direction for the collection of information is provided, usually by management.

DISSEMINATION—the release of information, usually under certain protocols; the final step in the intelligence process.

DOCUMENT SEARCHES—the review of public record documents (corporate records, deeds, marriage and divorce records, wills); performed by analysts (rather than investigators) in some agencies.

DNR—dialed number recorder. Records numbers dialed from particular phone, the time they were dialed, the time the telephone is deactivated, and the date. Informs enforcement personnel of numbers someone is in contacts without their hearing the actual conversations.

DRUG ENFORCEMENT ADMINISTRATION—United States agency with primary responsibility for investigating drug trafficking and related crime.

ELECTRONIC MONITORING—the recording of a conversation (in person or over a telephone) for the purpose of gathering information on a criminal activity.

EVALUATION—the process of reviewing data received for validity and reliability; also the review of the effectiveness of a program or the achievement of an objective.

EVENT FLOW ANALYSIS—the compilation, review, and analysis of data relating to events which have occurred over time. May result in the creation of event flow charts and drawing of conclusions about the events and their meaning.

EVENT FLOW CHART—a chart which depicts events in the order of their chronological occurrence.

EXPERT SYSTEMS—computer programs which are based on knowledge of particular crimes and allow input of data on current crime to determine whether there are any similarities between them and earlier crimes.

FACTORS—the components of a crime, including where it occurred, when it occurred, how it was done, to whom it was done, as well as use of weapons, means of escape, and so on.

FACT PATTERN—a brief summary of the facts of the case and its current status.

FEAR REDUCTION SURVEY—a survey of residents to determine their perception of the level of danger in their community.

FIELDS—the columns of data in a computerized data base. The field would include data of the same type about a number of incidents. For example, in a telephone record analysis data base, one field would be "time of the call."

FINANCIAL ANALYSIS—any one of several forms of analysis of financial records, including net worth analysis, bank record analysis, source and application of funds, and corporate record analysis.

FINANCIAL SUMMARY—a summary of account data, from either bank account records or corporate records, including deposits, withdrawals, and account opening and closing balances.

FORECAST—the prediction of what will occur in the future; the result of the forecasting process.

FORECASTING—a process which allows for the prediction of future activity. There are several forecasting methods, most of which rely upon past trends or current data.

FREQUENCY DISTRIBUTION—the determination of the number of times a particular element of an incident has occurred.

GEOGRAPHIC DISTRIBUTION ANALYSIS—the compilation of a series of locations into a geographic (map) format.

GEOGRAPHIC FLOW CHART—the depiction of the flow of commodities, persons, or other movable objects in a map format.

GEOGRAPHIC INFORMATION SYSTEMS—computer programs which are designed to hold data bases of information and output them onto maps.

GRAPH—a depiction, along x and y axes, of numeric data to show measurement in numbers or time.

HACKERS—computer users who gain illegal entry to private data bases, especially military and government systems.

HIERARCHY—the structure of a criminal organization; its leadership.

HYPOTHESIS—an educated guess about what happened; the result of a logical argument.

INDICATOR ANALYSIS—the compilation of information about criminal incidents to arrive at indicators of potential future criminal incidents.

INDUCTIVE REASONING—the arriving at a conclusion which goes beyond the facts on hand.

INFERENCE—a conclusion, hypothesis, or prediction.

INFERENCE DEVELOPMENT—the drawing of conclusions based on the facts as they are presented during the analytical process.

INFORMANT—an individual who provides information to the police about criminal activities. Includes anonymous callers on "tip" lines as well as confidential informants who regularly provide data.

INTELLIGENCE—the end product of the intelligence process; the data or conclusions drawn.

INTELLIGENCE ANALYSIS—the term applied to criminal analysis in law enforcement; so called because it produces intelligence.

INTELLIGENCE ANALYST—a person who has been formally or informally trained to derive meaning from raw data collected.

INTELLIGENCE PROCESS—the direction, collection, collation, evaluation, analysis, and dissemination of intelligence.

INTERNATIONAL ASSOCIATION OF CRIME ANALYSTS (IACA)—a group for crime analysts founded in 1990.

INTERNATIONAL ASSOCIATION OF LAW ENFORCEMENT INTELLIGENCE ANALYSTS (IALEIA)—a group for intelligence analysts founded in 1980.

INTERNATIONAL ASSOCIATION FOR THE STUDY OF ORGANIZED CRIME (IASOC)—a group for organized crime researchers, practitioners, and enthusiasts.

INTERPOL—an international police organization headquartered in Lyon, France, which collects, analyzes, and disseminates information on criminal subjects to police forces around the world.

INTERPRETIVE ANALYSIS—analysis which looks for the trends, meaning, and impact on the future of criminal activities and criminal groups. The term is used in California.

INVESTIGATIVE ANALYSIS—the analysis of data collected as part of an investigation of a criminal violation. Also called tactical analysis.

LIABILITY—a contractual obligation to repay; used in net worth analysis.

LINK ANALYSIS—see ASSOCIATION ANALYSIS.

LOGIC—the use of facts to draw inferences or conclusions.

MAP—a depiction of geographic boundaries used in a geographic distribution or flow analysis.

MARKET ANALYSIS—a business intelligence term also applicable to criminal intelligence. The study of the potential use of a criminal product (e.g., prostitution, gambling, extortion, narcotics) in a given area. Used to speculate on the probable success of criminal enterprises expanding into new areas.

MATRICES—arrangements of rows and columns with headings on one or two sides which allow the depiction of associations between the persons, places, numbers, or entities shown in the matrix.

MIDDLE ATLANTIC–GREAT LAKES ORGANIZED CRIME LAW ENFORCEMENT NETWORK (MAGLOCLEN)—a federally funded regional information sharing project headquartered in Pennsylvania.

MID-STATES ORGANIZED CRIME INFORMATION CENTER (MOCIC)—a federally funded regional information sharing project located in Missouri.

MODUS OPERANDI—the habitual way in which one commits a crime.

MONEY LAUNDERING—the movement of funds through several accounts or entities to hide its source and/or make it more available for use.

NARCOTERRORISM—the use of terroristic activities (bombings and assassinations) to dissuade authorities from enforcing narcotics laws.

NATIONAL CENTER FOR THE ANALYSIS OF VIOLENT CRIME—a unit at the Federal Bureau of Investigation Academy in Quantico, Virginia, which specializes in violent crime investigation and analysis.

NESPIN (New England State Police Information Network)—a federally funded regional information sharing project headquartered in Massachusetts.

NETWORK ANALYSIS—*see* ASSOCIATION ANALYSIS.

NET WORTH ANALYSIS—the compilation, review, and analysis of data relating to a person's assets and liabilities for the purpose of determining whether the individual was living within the confines of reported income or there are indications of income which was illegally derived. A standard format, developed by the Internal Revenue Service, is used. Conclusions based on the financial data are drawn about the person's potential for receiving and expending illegal profits.

ORAL INTERCEPT—an electronic intercept on a telephone line which allows the interceptor to hear and record telephone conversations.

PAPER CORPORATIONS—corporations which have been incorporated on paper but do not operate as businesses. They can be used to help launder money.

PEDOPHILES—persons (usually male) who find sexual gratification through activities with children.

PEN REGISTER—a machine which hooks up to a phone line and tells the interceptor when phone calls are made (or received), the number to which the calls were made, and the length of the call.

PIE CHART—a circular chart broken into wedges which represents the percentages of a whole or other statistical data.

POINTER INDEX—a computerized index of criminals which includes identifier data on individuals and reference numbers to agencies or files with further information on the criminals.

PONZI SCHEME—a form of investment fraud in which investor money is used by the perpetrator to pay personal expenses or to give earlier investors a token return. As the numbers of investors requiring return increases and the number of new investors decreases, the scheme collapses.

PREDICTION—*see* FORECAST.

PREMONITORY—a short-term strategic assessment which summarizes a particular crime situation and makes recommendations for undertaking a further investigation of the situation.

PRIMARY LISTING—a listing of the numbers called most often by a telephone subscriber whose records have been analyzed along with the date span of the calls to each number and the total length of time connected to each number.

PROBABILITY FACTOR—the degree to which an inference is believed to be accurate.

PROFILE—a psychological or criminal description of a suspect; the result of the criminal investigative analysis process.

RECOMMENDATIONS—suggestions for action to be taken by law enforcement management as a result of an analysis; they are usually investigative recommendations (e.g., subpoena bank records) or deterrence recommendations (e.g., four muggings have taken place in the 300 block of Mountain Avenue; recommend increasing police presence in that area in the evenings).

RELATIONAL DATA BASES—computer software which links files through a common field, thus allowing larger amounts of data on a subject to be connected.

RISS PROJECTS—six Regional Information Sharing Systems around the country, including MAGLOCLEN, MOCIC, NESPIN, RMIN, ROCIC, and WSIN.

RMIN—Rocky Mountain Information Network; a federally funded regional information sharing project headquartered in Arizona.

ROCIC—Regional Organized Crime Information Center; a federally funded regional information sharing project headquartered in Tennessee.

SELL-BUST—a transaction between a police officer and a drug user in which the police officer pretends to sell narcotics to the drug user and then arrests the user.

SHAREWARE—computer software that has been developed by an individual or company that wishes to share it with the general public at little to no cost.

SIGNATURE—an activity extraneous to a crime that is repeated by the criminal because of a need to express his or her personality.

SKIMMING—the removal of profits from a business for the purpose of avoiding paying taxes on the profits.

SOCIETY OF CERTIFIED CRIMINAL ANALYSTS (SCCA)—founded in 1990; provides standards for certifying analysts.

SOURCE AND APPLICATION OF FUNDS—a format which allows the investigator or analyst to determine whether the suspect has had the use of illegal income.

STATISTICAL ANALYSIS—the analysis of numeric data to determine its meaning, through averages, crime rates, percentages, norms, and other measurements.

STRATEGIC ANALYSIS—the analysis of a crime group, overall criminal activity, or situation which results in the production of a report on that group, activity, or situation and includes recommendations for future action.

SUBPOENAED RECORDS—records for which a court order is needed to allow investigators access to them.

SUBPROGRAMMING—development of computer routines within shelf software packages to allow the user to repeat certain manipulations or reports without reprogramming. Also called a "macro."

SUBSCRIBER INFORMATION—the name and address of the subscriber to telephone service; usually found in cross directories.

SUMMARY—a short statement of the facts of a case or a research project.

SURVEILLANCE—physical or electronic watching of someone suspected of participating in criminal activity. Physical surveillance can be done in person or through video cameras. Electronic surveillance is done through DNRs or pen registers, wire intercepts, or body wires.

SURVEY—a set of questions used to gather information.

SYNTHESIS—the reorganization of data into a cohesive whole which usually provides new information about the data.

TABLE—an arrangement of data, generally numeric, into rows and columns to organize the material for ease of accessibility and analysis. Most often used in frequency distributions or statistical analyses.

TACTICAL ANALYSIS—see INVESTIGATIVE ANALYSIS.

TELEPHONE TOLL ANALYSIS—see TELEPHONE RECORD ANALYSIS.

TELEPHONE RECORD ANALYSIS—the compilation, review, and analysis of records of telephone calls (from sources including dialed number recorders, telephone companies and long-distance services) to ascertain the contacts made by the subject of a criminal investigation to others who may be a part of the criminal conspiracy.

TELEPHONE RECORD CHART—a chart which depicts calls from one person to other persons suspected of being part of a conspiracy.

TELEPHONE RECORD MATRIX—an arrangement of rows and columns, shaped into a square, which depicts the calls to and from persons in a multiple-subscriber telephone analysis.

THIRD PARTY CALLS—calls that are made by one person to another, but billed to a third party.

THREAT ASSESSMENT—the analysis of a group and its potential to harm a particular target or target area. Used in examining the potential harm which might be encountered from terrorist groups, organized crime groups, or others.

TIMELINE—a listing of activities to occur and the dates by which they will occur. See also CHRONOLOGICAL TABLE.

TIME SERIES ANALYSIS—the analysis of information on a series of crimes and their occurrence over time.

TOLL BILLINGS—telephone bills showing long-distance calls made or mobile telephone bills listing all calls made and received.

TREND ANALYSIS—the review of historical and current data to determine patterns.

TREND—the product of a trend analysis; a conclusion drawn about the patterns found in the analysis.

TRIBUTE—money paid to an organized crime group for the "privilege" of running a criminal business in its territory. Also called "street tax."

VIA CHART—the graphic depiction of activities in chronological order; can be used to track progress in an investigation.

VICTIMOLOGY—the analysis of the attributes of victims to uncover similarities in the victims which may aid in the construction of a psychological profile of the perpetrator.

VISUAL INVESTIGATIVE ANALYSIS—the compilation, review, and analysis of data relating to investigative steps taken which may support the management of a major case or task force effort.

VULNERABILITY ASSESSMENT—a study to determine the potential for harm to a person, event, or location as a result of criminal activity.

WARNING—the product of a vulnerability assessment which warns of the potential threat and makes recommendations on how to deal with the threat.

WSIN—Western States Information Network; a federally funded regional information sharing systems located in California.

APPENDIX II

Analytical Software

A recurrent subtheme in the pages of this volume has been the use of computers to assist the analyst in accessing, compiling, and collating data. Expert systems, artificial intelligence, relational data bases, and geographic information systems are only a few of computer programs that are available.

The software that supports analysis generally falls into five categories: data base software, statistical software, graphics software, desktop publishing software, and financial software. Some programs combine attributes from more than one category; for example, Lotus 1,2,3 provides a financial spreadsheet, statistical analysis capabilities, and graphics.

There are two schools of thought about computers and analysis. Some believe that computers "do" analysis, while others think that computers are helpful in organizing and reorganizing data, but that analysis is best done by human analysts. Expert systems and artificial intelligence, both of which make use of the computer's decision-making abilities, are capable of simple "thinking." Systems now being developed are said to use "fuzzy logic," which is more similar to the processes of the human mind.

It should also be noted that computers have made the work of analysts different, but have not decreased the workload; rather they have increased it. For example, prior to the common use of computers, analysts were limited by practicality in the number of telephone records that could be reasonably analyzed. Now, with the computer to organize the data, tens of thousands (rather than five hundred or fewer) of records make up a routine assignment.

Computers have been and are certain to continue to be a great boon to analysts and to law enforcement. As new uses for them are found, wider varieties of hardware and software will be seen in departments of all sizes.

In keeping with the resource aspect of this text, a short listing of computer programs which are used in analytical shops follows. The programs listed are those on which information was known and the listing reflects neither a preference for the programs listed nor an endorsement of them.

ANALYST'S NOTEBOOKS

The Analyst's Notebooks are four related products: the Link Notebook, the Link Analyser, the Case Notebook, and the Case Analyser. The Link Notebook combines a graphics editor with a data base for storing the information which supports each chart. Link and commodity flow charts can be created through the Notebook. The Case Notebook is a chronologically ordered program which draws a time axis along the top of each chart and positions every event in relation to it. Case notebook charts can have either an event flow chart format or a visual investigative analysis chart format.

The Notebooks can be used to analyze data taken from other investigative software data bases. Analyst's Notebooks run on Microsoft Windows 3 or on conventional IBM compatible personal computers. A 386 machine with 4 megabytes of available memory, a color VGA screen, a hard disk, and a mouse are required.

Contact: MEGG Associates Inc., 2716 Enterprise Parkway, Richmond, VA 23294; 800/666-6344.

DBASE IV

DBase IV is a data base management system which allows the user to create data bases and make reports from the information stored in them. Earlier versions of DBase were among the first desktop computer data base programs. DBase allows files to be linked (relational data bases) and has a Chartmaster component with which the analyst can make rudimentary charts.

DBase runs on IBM compatible computers.

DRAWPERFECT

DrawPerfect is graphics software that is complementary to the WordPerfect word processing program.

Contact: WordPerfect Corporation, 1555 N. Technology Way, Orem, Utah 84057-9913; 801/225-5000; fax 801/222-5077.

EXCEL

Excel is a data base management/financial spreadsheet program that supports financial analysis. Excel 5.0 is compatible to Lotus 1,2,3 and can run Lotus macros in the Excel environment. Its Scenario Manager allows the analyst to name a set of input variables and have it run a report which shows the different inputs and their results. It also includes an Analysis ToolPak that provides statistical and financial analysis within Excel.

Drawing may also be done within Excel. With ChartWizard you can create nearly one hundred chart formats (including line, bar and column charts), or you can draw freehand. The TipWizard function keeps track of how you work and makes suggestions on how to get the same results faster.

Excel runs in an Apple or Windows environment.

Contact: Microsoft Corporation, One Microsoft Way, Redmond, WA 98052-6399.

FREELANCE GRAPHICS

Freelance Graphics 2.0 is a presentation software by the Lotus Corporation. It includes an animated on-line tutorial and 65 SmartMaster presentation types. Freelance Graphics has 108 ready-made chart styles and allows for animated transitions, sound effects and full-motion video. It accepts text from WordPerfect, Microsoft Word, and Ami Pro.

Contact: Lotus Development Corporation, 55 Cambridge Parkway, Cambridge, MA 02142; 800/343-5214.

HARVARD GRAPHICS

Harvard Graphics is a presentation graphics software that allows for thirty-one presentation styles in its 2.0 version. With it, the analyst can design pie charts, bar charts (vertical, horizontal and stacked), area charts, line charts, scatter diagrams, organization charts, and free-form charts. It also has symbol files including humans, animals, maps, common objects, flags, and computers. It has a "Five-Minute Coach" that tutors the user on specific application pieces and makes learning the software on an as-needed basis easy. It also has a help screen (the Advisor) which can be displayed or hidden, provides design tips, and tells what to do next.

Contact: Software Publishing Corp., 1901 Landings Drive, Mountain View, CA 94043; 800/234-2500.

INTELLIGENCE ANALYST WORKBENCH

The Intelligence Analyst Workbench is a combination of computer hardware and software. Using information in the owner's data base and/or through links to other information sources, the user can do network (association) analysis through the matrix to the chart.

The Intelligence Analyst Workbench runs on a SUNSPARC2, UNIX-based workstation.

Contact: ICL, 1 High Street, Putney, London SW15 1SW; 011-44-81/788-7272 (international); fax 011-44-81/785-3936.

LEADS (Law Enforcement Analysis Data System)

LEADS, by Orion, is a fully integrated management system that provides for the automated indexing of text, graphics, images, sound, and reports. It provides processing and review of government and commercial open-source electronic and hard-data copy. Retrieval can be customized by the user and then translated into link diagrams (association charts) or telephone link diagrams (telephone record charts). Pictures and graphics can be scanned into the system; data can also be displayed in a spatial format. Specialized data bases in LEADS created by Orion include the NARC data base and the Modus Operandi data base.

Orion also has a number of documents which can be accessed through its system, including "Criminal Acts Against Civil Aviation," "Guide to Analysis of Insurgency," "Global Terrorism: 1990," and "Terrorist Group Updates."

LEADS runs on a variety of UNIX platforms and can be used in portable and desktop workstations as well as in larger systems.

Contact: Orion Scientific, Inc., 4601 North Fairfax Drive, Suite 703, Arlington, VA 22203; 703/524-0504.

LINK

LINK software allows analysts to place information on associations among individuals or businesses as well as on dates, activities and reliability of the data into a data base, and then automatically creates a link chart. The entities on this chart are "filtered" through choices made by the analyst while searching the database.

LINK works on IBM PS/2 or 386/486 PCs with color monitor, DOS, OS/2, or Windows.

Contact: Scientific and Technical Analysis Corporation, Suite 300, 11250 Waples Mill Road, Fairfax, VA 22030; 703/278-9395; fax 703/591-7861.

LOTUS 1,2,3

Lotus 1,2,3 is a financial spreadsheet program which allows analysts to complete financial analyses including bank record analysis and corporate record analysis. It supports a number of accounting and auditing functions.

Lotus runs on IBM compatible systems.

Contact: Lotus Development Corporation, 55 Cambridge Parkway, Cambridge, MA 02142; 800/343-5214.

MAPADS (Micro-Computer Assisted Police Analysis and Deployment System)

MAPADS is not a commercially available software and hardware package; it was developed for the Chicago Police Department and includes various products. Although MAPADS uses an Apple Macintosh and Business Filevision (marketed by Marvelin), researchers have stated that MAC II, MapGrafix, and FoxBase+ provides the best combination for geographic analysis.

For more details on MAPADS, see *Mapping Crime in Its Community Setting Event Geography Analysis* (Maltz, Gordon, and Friedman, 1990).

MAPINFO

MapInfo combines a data base component with a map graphics component. It includes a relational database manager that allows the analyst to combine data from several sources onto a "layered" map. For example, calls for service can be shown along with crimes reported, vacant properties, and other related data, on the same map. The vendor supplies base maps and data from worldwide to street level. MapInfo also has demographic data bases including information on population, income, retail and business, airports, zip codes and railroads. A selection of data bases with Canadian information is available.

MapInfo is available on five platforms: Windows, DOS, Macintosh, Sun, and Hewlett-

Packard. It works with many data formats, including Oracle, Sybase, Excel, Paradox, and dBASE. Free demonstration disks are available in 5¼ and 3½ sizes.

Contact: Mapping Information Systems Corporation, One Global View, Troy, NY 12180; 800/327-8627; 518/274-8673; fax 518/274-0510.

NETMAP

NETMAP, distributed by Alta Analytics, is a program used to integrate and graphically display the contents of data bases in a circular spokelike format which has the connections between the spokes depicted by lines through the open center of the circle. It also uses color and groupings to differentiate between types of associations or other distinctions. Information from multiple data bases can be brought into NETMAP for visual examination and analysis; it integrates video and other sources with text retrieval for all-source information array.

NETMAP runs on UNIX-based platforms with NASIC, X-Windows, and OSF/Motif. It is currently supported on the Hewlett Packard 400/700 series, SUNSPARC, DEC, and Apollo.

Contact: Alta Analytics, 2111 Wilson Boulevard, Suite 700, Arlington, VA 22201; 703/875-8752.

PAGEMAKER

Aldus Pagemaker 5.0 is used to produce a number of analytical reports and publications. It handles color separation, font matching, and substitution. It allows multiple columns, varied font types and sizes, and graphic importation. This version also has import filters for Kodak Photo CDs.

Pagemaker works in a Windows environment.

Contact: Aldus Corporation; 800/627-8880.

PEN-LINK

Pen-Link is a PC data base management system designed for telephone record analysis applications. It contains two data bases: Call Data and Subscriber Data. It allows for automatic interfaces with all major DNR equipment and has optional interfaces with CD-ROM products such as NYNEX Fast Track. A custom report generator allows the user to design specialized reports.

Pen-Link has also developed City-Link as companion software to Pen-Link 4.0. This contains a third data base, which holds city, state, Zip, and country data which can be matched up with the subscriber and call data base files.

Asset/f is a separate program developed by Pen-Link for financial investigation management, analysis, and reporting. It includes net worth analysis summary reports and form letters for seized asset management.

Pen-Link runs on an IBM XT, AT, PS/2, or compatible that has 640K RAM, a floppy drive, and a hard drive.

Contact: Pen-Link Ltd., 6000 South 58th Street, Suite C, Lincoln, NE 68516; 402/421-8857; fax 402/421-9287.

POLICE RETRIEVER

The Police Retriever is a text search and retrieval system. It searches up to ten thousand pages in four seconds through word searches that use simple English commands.

The first step in the Police Retriever's functions is cataloguing every word and number in documents with a special Index File. The second step is the search function. On command, it searches the index for all references to the document required.

Police Retriever runs on IBM-PC compatible machines (386 or 486).

Contact: Binomial, Binomial International Corporate Center, 812 Proctor Avenue, Box 707, Ogdensburg, NY 13669; 613/692-4000; fax 613/692-2425.

Q & A

Q & A is a data base program which allows the user to create a file which contains as many fields and records as are required and to create reports and summaries based on the information that has been stored. It is integrated software and includes Q & A Write, a word processing program.

Q & A is user-friendly software which enables the analyst to add fields to the file at any time, as needed. Up to fifty fields of information can be included in a report. It also has a query and "intelligent assistant" function which allows the analyst to build summary reports and English language reports. It allows for the importation of data from other data base and spread sheet programs, including Lotus 1,2,3; Paradox; and dBase II, III, and IV.

Q & A runs on IBM compatible machines.

Contact: Symantec Corporation, 10201 Torre Avenue, Cupertino, CA 95014; 408/253-9600.

SIUSS (Special Investigative Unit Support System)

SIUSS is a combination criminal intelligence system, case manager, and analytical tool. SIUSS stores information on subjects, locations, telephone calls, surveillances, financial data, arret data, and group affiliations. It performs association, telephone record, and event flow analysis routines. It features the Major Crime System, which tracks incident/alibi information, subjects involved, property, vehicles, and more. Fragmentary information, such as partial license plates, can also be entered.

SIUSS runs on an IBM PC/AT, PS/2, or compatible using MS-DOS 3.3 and 640K of memory.

Contact: Criminal Investigative Technology Incorporated, U.S. Rt. 2, Jefferson, NH 03583; 603/586-7156.

TOPIC

TOPIC, by Verity, is an information retrieval system which allows you to search and retrieve information from your own data base as well as from links to other relational data bases. Graphics are also supported.

TOPIC REAL-TIME, a second form of TOPIC, reads, filters, and selectively disseminates information from real-time news and information sources such as financial and intelligence newswires. It is used in corporate intelligence as well as law enforcement. It operates on varied computer platforms (systems), including IBM, Apple, DEC, and SUN. Its minimum requirement is 8 megabytes of memory.

Contact: Verity, 1550 Plymouth Street, Mountain View, CA 94043; 425/960-7600; fax 415/960-7698.

WATSON

Watson combines data base tools, analytic functions, and automatic chart drawing to help organize, analyze, and present investigative information. Watson specializes in managing vast amounts of data. It can import telephone records from SQL data bases, Access, Paradox, dBASE, Excel, Lotus 1,2,3, Holmes, and ASCII text. It develops charts on associations, commodity flows, telephone calls, and activity flows.

Contact: Harlequin Incorporated, One Cambridge Center, Cambridge, MA 02142; 617/252-0052; fax 617/252-6505.

WORDPERFECT PRESENTATIONS

WordPerfect Presentations 2.0 can be used in a DOS environment without Windows and is supported by the WordPerfect wordprocessing software. It offers features including the import of spreadsheet data, and displays charts in a window for the user to see how they change as the spreadsheet is edited. It has a full-featured graphics editing module and a hand scanner.

Contact: WordPerfect, 1555 N. Technology Way, Orem, UT 84057; 800/451-5151.

Bibliography

Albanese, Jay S. (1991). "Organized crime and the oldest vice." Paper given at Annual Meeting of American Society of Criminology.

Alexander, Herbert E., and Gerald E. Caiden, eds. (1985). *The Politics and Economics of Organized Crime.* Lexington, MA: D. C. Heath.

Amherst Police Department. (Undated). "Death of a jogger: investigation of a serial rapist–murderer." Amherst, NY.

Anderson, Annelise G. (1979). *The Business of Organized Crime: A Cosa Nostra Family.* Stanford, CA: Hoover Institution Press.

Andrews, Paul P., Jr. (1983, January). "Principles of network analysis." *Issues of Interest to Law Enforcement, Intelligence: The Ultimate Managerial Tool."* Law Enforcement Intelligence Unit.

———. (1990). "Collection and analysis plans." *Criminal Intelligence Analysis,* Paul P. Andrews Jr. and Marilyn B. Peterson, eds. Loomis, CA: Palmer Enterprises.

Andrews, P. P., C. H. Longfellow, and F. T. Martens. (1981, March). "Zero-Sum Enforcement: Reflections on Drug Enforcement." *Federal Probation.*

Andrews, Paul P., Jr., and Marilyn B. Peterson. (1985). "The Bustamonte case." Training course. Trenton, NJ.

———, eds. (1990). *Criminal Intelligence Analysis.* Loomis, CA: Palmer.

Associated Press. (July 25, 1993). "Crazy Eddie trial: soap opera meets retailing." *Trenton Times.*

Blakey, G. Robert. (1985). "Asset forfeiture under the federal criminal law." *The Politics and Economics of Organized Crime,* Herbert E. Alexander and Gerald E. Caiden, eds. Lexington, MA: D. C. Heath.

Bloom, Lynda. (1993, May). "Wichita p.d. facing a gang problem head on." *Law and Order.*

Bouza, Anthony V. (1976). *Police Intelligence—The Operations of an Investigative Unit.* New York: AMS Press.

Buck, George A., Robert Austin, Gary Cooper, Don Gagnon, John Hodges, Kai Martensen, and Michael O'Neal. (1973). *Police Crime Analysis Unit Handbook.* Washington, DC: Law Enforcement Assistance Administration and National Institute of Justice.

Bureau of Justice Assistance. (1993, October). *A Police Guide to Surveying Citizens and Their Environment.* Washington, DC: U. S. Department of Justice.

Bureau of Justice Statistics. (1983, March). *Prisoners and Drugs.* Washington, DC: Bureau of Justice Statistics.

———. (1987). *BJS Annual Report Fiscal 1986.* Washington, DC: U.S. Government Printing Office.

———. (1988, July). *Drug Use and Crime.* Washington, DC: U.S. Government Printing Office.

———. (1992, December). *Drugs, Crime and the Justice System.* Washington, DC: U.S. Government Printing Office.

Bureau of National Affairs. (1990, May). Conversational analysis can turn tape cases around. *BNA Criminal Practice Manual, 4,* No. 10.

Burgess, A. W., C. R. Hartman, R. K. Ressler, J. E. Douglas, and A. McCormack. (1986, September). "Sexual homicide: A motivational model." *Journal of Interpersonal Violence, 1,* No. 3.

Burns, Edward, and Thomas J. Deakin. (1989, October). "A new investigative approach to youth gangs." *FBI Law Enforcement Bulletin, 58,* No. 10.

California Department of Justice, Bureau of Organized Crime and Criminal Intelligence. (1989). *Organized Crime in California, 1989.* Sacramento, CA.

———. (1993, March). *Gangs 2000: A Call to Action.* Sacramento, CA.

Clede, Bill. (1993, June). "Cellular phone fraud a growing problem." *Law and Order, 41,* No. 6.

———. (1993, July). "Investigating computer crimes." *Law and Order, 41,* No. 7.

Cole, Allen W., and David Kelley. (1992, October). "Fear and disorder index: measuring what really matters." *Law and Order, 40,* No. 10.

Cook, John, and Marilyn (Peterson) Sommers. (1987, January). "From gaming to tax evasion: going after the distributors." *Police Chief, LIV,* No. 1.

Cressey, Donald. (1969). *Theft of the Nation: The Structure of Organized Crime in America.* New York: Harper & Row.

Criminal Justice Commission. (1992, September). *Annual Report 1991/1992.* Toowong, Queensland, Australia: Criminal Justice Commission.

Davis, Roger W., and Charles H. Rogovin, "Indicators of the Impacts of Organized Crime." Report funded by grant 80-IJ-CX-006, National Institute of Justice, 1985.

Denver Police Department. (September 15, 1987). "Indicators of Suspected Drug Traffickers." Public memorandum.

Dintino, Justin J., and Frederick T. Martens. (1983). *Police Intelligence Systems in Crime Control.* Springfield, IL: Charles C. Thomas.

District of Columbia Government. (1991, January). *Drug Abuse Indicators Trend Report for the District of Columbia.* Washington, DC: Statistical Analysis Center, Office of Criminal Justice Plans and Analysis.

Douglas, John E., and Alan E., Burgess. (1986, December). "Criminal profiling a viable investigative tool against violent crime." *FBI Law Enforcement Bulletin, 55,* No. 12.

Douglas, John E., Robert K. Ressler, Ann W. Burgess, and Carol R. Hartman. (1986). "Criminal profiling from crime scene analysis." *Behavioral Sciences and the Law, 5,* No. 4, p. 407.

Douglas, John E., Ann W. Burgess, Allen G. Burgess, and Robert K. Ressler. (1992). *Crime Classification Manual* and *Pocket Guide to the Crime Classification Manual*. New York: Lexington Books.

Douglas, John E., and Corrine Munn. (1992, February). "Violent crime scene analysis: modus operandi, signature and staging." *FBI Law Enforcement Bulletin, 61,* 2.

Drug Enforcement Administration. (1985, August 15). *EPIC Reference Document RD-03-85 Commonly Encountered Concealment Methods—Revised*. El Paso, TX: Intelligence Center.

————. (1988). *Drugs of Abuse*. Washington, DC: U.S. Government Printing Office.

————. (1989, July). *Financial Source Debriefing Guide*. Washington, DC: Office of Intelligence.

————. (1989). *Intelligence Trends: Special Report from the Source to the Street*. Washington, DC: U.S. Department of Justice, *16,* No. 2.

————. (1990, December). *Argentina* (Country Profile). Washington, DC: Office of Intelligence.

————. (1990). *Intelligence Trends Special Report from the Source to the Street*. Washington, DC: Office of Intelligence, *17,* No. 1.

————. (1991, February). *Chile* (Country Profile). Washington, DC: Office of Intelligence.

————. (1991, February). *Cuba* (Country Profile). Washington, DC: Office of Intelligence.

————. (1991, January). *Worldwide Cocaine Situation 1990*. Washington, DC: Office of Intelligence.

————. (1991, May). *Worldwide Heroin Situation 1990*. Washington, DC: Office of Intelligence.

————. (undated). *Source Debriefing Guide*. Washington, DC: Office of Intelligence.

Eck, John E. (1983). *Solving Crime: The Investigation of Burglary and Robbery*. Washington, DC: Police Executive Research Forum.

————. (1984). *Using Research: A Primer for Law Enforcement Managers*. Washington, DC: Police Executive Research Forum.

Eck, John E., and William Spelman. (1987). *Problem-Oriented Policing in Newport News*. Washington, DC: U.S. Department of Justice, National Institute of Justice.

Edelhertz, Herbert. (1970). *The Nature, Impact and Prosecution of White Collar Crime*. Washington, DC: U.S. Government Printing Office.

Edelhertz, Herbert, and Charles Rogovin. (1980). *A National Strategy for Containing White Collar Crime*. Lexington, MA: Lexington Books.

Edelhertz, Herbert, and Thomas D. Overcast. (1992). *The Business of Organized Crime*. Loomis, CA: Palmer Enterprises.

Emergency Solid Waste Assessment Task Force. (1990, July 6). *Preliminary Report*. Trenton, NJ: New Jersey Department of Environmental Protection.

Federal Bureau of Investigation. (1990). *Criminal Investigative Analysis of Sexual Homicide*. Quantico, VA: National Center for the Analysis of Violent Crime.

————. (1992). *Uniform Crime Reports for the United States 1991*. Washington, DC: U.S. Government Printing Office.

————. (1993). *Uniform Crime Reports for the United States 1992*. Washington, DC: U.S. Government Printing Office.

————. (undated). *Ted Bundy Multiagency Investigative Team Report 1992*. Washington, DC: U.S. Department of Justice.

————. (undated). *Visual Investigative Analysis.* Washington, DC: Criminal Investigative Division.

"Financial Recordkeeping and Reporting of Currency and Foreign Transactions," *31 Code of Federal Regulations* 103.

Florida Department of Law Enforcement. (1987, April). *Crack Cocaine in Florida.* Tallahassee, FL.

Flowers, Ronald Barri. (1989). *Demographics and Criminality: The Characteristics of Crime in America.* Westport, CT: Greenwood Press.

Frost, Charles C. (1990) "Intelligence report writing." *Criminal Intelligence Analysis,* Paul P. Andrews Jr. and Marilyn B. Peterson, eds. Loomis, CA: Palmer Enterprises.

Frost, Charles C., and Jack Morris. (1983). *Police Intelligence Reports.* Orangevale, CA: Palmer.

Galanos, Diogenes. (1988, Summer). "Cocaine trafficking in Florida." *Law Enforcement Intelligence Analysis Digest, 3,* No. 1.

Garson, G. David, and Robert S. Biggs. (1992). "Analytic mapping and geographic databases." *Qualitative Applications in the Social Sciences, 87.*

Gates, Daryl. (1989, June). "The role of analysis in combating modern terrorism." *FBI Law Enforcement Bulletin, 58,* No. 6.

Gay, William G., and Robert A. Bowers. (1985, September). *Targeting Law Enforcement Resources: The Career Criminal Focus.* Washington, DC: National Institute of Justice.

General Accounting Office. (March 19, 1979). *Resources Devoted by the Department of Justice to Combat White-Collar Crime and Public Corruption.* Washington, DC.

————. (1991, March). *Money Laundering Treasury's Financial Crimes Enforcement Network.* Washington, DC.

————. *Defense Procurement Fraud.* (1992, September). Washington, DC.

Gerbeth, Vernon J. (1983). *Practical Homicide Investigation: Tactics, Procedures and Forensic Techniques.* New York: Elsevier Science.

Godfrey, E. Drexel, and Don R. Harris. (1971). *Basic Elements of Intelligence.* Washington, DC: U.S. Government Printing Office.

Gold, Jeffrey. (1993, July 21). Crazy Eddie found guilty. *Trenton Times.* pp. 1, 13.

Goldstein, Herman. (1990). *Problem-Oriented Policing.* Philadelphia: Temple University Press.

The Gotti Tapes. (1992). New York: Random House.

Grabo, Cynthia M. (1987). *Warning Intelligence.* McLean, VA. Association of Former Intelligence Officers.

Grau, Joseph J. (1981). *Criminal and Civil Investigation Handbook.* New York: McGraw-Hill.

Green, Terrence J., and Jane E. Whitmore. (1993, June). "VICAP's role in multiagency serial murder investigations." *Police Chief, LX,* No. 6.

Greene, Jack R., and Stephen D. Mastrofski. (1988). *Community Policing Rhetoric or Reality.* New York: Praeger.

Greenwood, Peter W., Jan M. Chaiken, and Joan Petersilia. (1977). *The Criminal Investigation Process.* Lexington, MA: D. C. Heath.

Hagaman, John C., Gary W. Wells, Theodore H. Blau, and Charles B. Wells. (1987, December). "Psychological profile of a family homicide." *Police Chief, LIV,* No. 12.

Haller, Mark H. (1991). *Life Under Bruno: The Economics of an Organized Crime Family*. Conshohocken, PA: Pennsylvania Crime Commission.

Harris, Don R. (1976, September). *Basic Elements of Intelligence*. Washington, DC: Law Enforcement Assistance Administration.

Hazelwood, Robert R., and Janet Warren. (1990, February). "The criminal behavior of the serial rapist." *FBI Law Enforcement Bulletin, 59,* No. 2.

Hazelwood, Robert R., and Ann Wolbert Burgess, eds. (1987). *Practical Aspects of Rape Investigation: A Multidisciplinary Approach*. New York: Elsevier.

Hill, Mark. (1992, November). "RCMP setting up serial killer tracking system." *Law and Order*.

Holmes, Ronald M. (1989). *Profiling Violent Crimes: An Investigative Tool*. Newbury Park, CA: Sage.

Howlett, James B., Kenneth A. Hanfland, and Robert K. Ressler. (1986, December). "The Violent Criminal Apprehension Program." *FBI Law Enforcement Bulletin, 55,* No. 12.

Ianni, Francis A. J. (1974). *Black Mafia*. New York: Simon & Schuster.

Ianni, Francis A. J., and Elizabeth-Reuss Ianni. (1972). *A Family Business: Kinship and Social Control in Organized Crime*. New York: Russell Sage Foundation.

Icove, David J., and Philip R. Horbert. (1986, December). Automated crime profiling. *FBI Law Enforcement Bulletin, 55,* No. 12.

———. (1990, December). "Serial arsonists: an introduction." *Police Chief, LVII,* No. 12.

International Association of Chiefs of Police. (1971). *Criminal Investigation*. Gaithersburg, MD.

———. (1975). *Criminal Investigation Specific Offenses*. Gaithersburg, MD.

———. (1985). *Criminal Intelligence*. Gaithersburg, MD.

International Association of Law Enforcement Intelligence Analysts. (1984). *Report of the Standards and Accreditation Committee*. Washington, DC.

Karchmer, Clifford L. (1986). "Money Laundering and the Organized Underworld." *The Politics and Economics of Organized Crime,* Herbert E. Alexander and Gerald E. Caiden, eds. Lexington, MA: D. C. Heath.

Kelly, Robert J., Ko-lin Chin and Jeffrey A. Fagan. (1993). "Notes on the vulnerabilities of the Chinese business community to extortionate crime in New York City." *IALEIA JOURNAL, 7,* 2.

Keppel, Robert D., and Joseph G. Weis. (1993, August). "Improving the investigation of violent crime: the homicide investigation and tracking system." *Research in Brief*. National Institute of Justice.

Knoke, David, and James H. Kuklinski. (1990). "Network analysis." *Quantitative Applications in the Social Sciences, 28.*

Kramer, Samuel. (1990, Summer). "An economic analysis of criminal attempt: marginal deterrence and the optimal structure of sanctions." *The Journal of Criminal Law and Criminology, 81,* No. 2.

Kwitney, Jonathan. (1979). *Vicious Circles: The Mafia in the Marketplace*. New York: W. W. Norton.

Lanning, Kenneth V. (1989, December). *Child Sex Rings: A Behavioral Analysis*. Washington, DC: Center for Missing and Exploited Children.

———. (1986). *Child Molesters: A Behavioral Analysis*. Washington, DC: National Center for Missing and Exploited Children.

Lapierre, Dennis, and William Hunt. (1985, Summer/Fall). "Use of electronic flow charting for intelligence probes and major criminal investigation." *Law Enforcement Intelligence Analysis Digest, 1*, No. 1.

Law Enforcement News. (April 30, 1993). "Seattle arson task force gets computer assist." *Law Enforcement News.*

Lesce, Tony. (1993, May). "Gang resistance education and training." *Law and Order, 41*, No. 5.

Lettich, Linda. (1988, Summer). "The social impact of casino gaming on Atlantic City." *Law Enforcement Intelligence Analysis Digest, 3*, No. 1.

Lewyn, Mark, and Evan I. Schwartz. (1991, April 15). "Why 'the legion of doom' has little fear of the feds." *Business Week.*

Libonati, Michael, and Herbert Edelhertz, "Study of Property Ownership and Devolution in the Organized Crime Environment." Report funded by grant 80-IJ-CX-006, National Institute of Justice, 1985.

Lippmann, Walter. (1930, November). "A theory about corruption." *Vanity Fair,* quoted by Jack D. Douglas and John M. Johnson in *Official Deviance,* 1977, p. 334.

Los Angeles Police Department. (1988, January). "Strategic plan to eradicate street narcotics sales and gang related narcotics activity in the city of Los Angeles." Internal memorandum.

Lupsha, Peter. (1980, May). "Steps toward a strategic analysis of organized crime." *Police Chief, XLVII*, No. 5.

Macartney, John. (1991). *Intelligence: What It Is And How to Use It.* McLean, VA: Association of Former Intelligence Officers.

Maltz, Michael D. (1985). "Toward Defining Organized Crime." *The Politics and Economics of Organized Crime,* Herbert E. Alexander and Gerald E. Caiden, eds. Lexington, MA: D. C. Heath.

———. (1990). *Measuring the Effectiveness of Organized Crime Control Efforts.* Chicago, IL: Office of International Criminal Justice.

Maltz, Michael D., Andrew C. Gordon, and Warren Friedman. (1990) *Mapping Crime in Its Community Setting: Event Geography Analysis.* New York: Springer-Verlag.

"Managing an information overload." (1993, April 30). *Law Enforcement News,*

Martens, Frederick T., and Michele Cunningham-Niederer. (1985). "Media magic, mafia mania." *Federal Probation, 49*, No. 2.

McBride, Wesley D., and Robert K. Jackson. (1989, June). "In L.A. County, a high-tech assist in the war on gangs." *Police Chief, LVI*, No. 6.

McDowell, Don. (1992, December). "Strategic intelligence and law enforcement." *The Journal of the Australian Institute of Professional Intelligence Officers, 1*, No. 1.

Messick, Hank, and Burt Goldblatt. (1972). *The Mobs and the Mafia.* New York: Ballantine.

Meyer, Herbert E. (1987). *Real World Intelligence.* New York: Weidenfeld & Nicholson.

Middle Atlantic–Great Lakes Organized Crime Law Enforcement Network (MAGLO-CLEN). (1984). *Report.* Malvern, PA. MAGLOCLEN.

———. *Bunco Assessment.* (1986b). Malvern, PA.

———. *MAGLOCLEN '85.* (1986). Malvern, PA.

———. *MAGLOCLEN '86.* (1987). Malvern, PA.

———. *MAGLOCLEN Annual Report.* (1990). West Trenton, NJ.

Moore, Mark, and Darrel W. Stephens. (1991). *Beyond Command and Control: The Strategic Management of Police Departments.* Washington, DC: Police Executive Research Forum.

Morris, Jack. (1983). *Police Intelligence Files.* Orangevale, CA: Palmer Enterprises.

———. (1982). *Crime Analysis Charting.* Orangevale, CA: Palmer Enterprises.

National Advisory Committee on Criminal Justice Standards and Goals. (1976). *Criminal Justice Research and Development.* Washington, DC: Law Enforcement Assistance Administration.

National Institute of Justice. (1988, March). *Report to the Nation on Crime and Justice.* Washington, DC: U.S. Government Printing Office.

———. (1993). *Report to the Nation on Crime and Justice.* Washington, DC: U.S. Government Printing Office.

National Narcotics Intelligence Consumer's Committee. (1990, June). *The NNICC Report 1989.* Washington, DC.

New Jersey State Commission of Investigation. 1988. *Public Hearing Report and Recommendations on the Subversion of Organized Crime and Other Unscrupulous Elements of the Check Cashing Industry.*

New Jersey State Police. (1990). *ALERT.* West Trenton, NJ.

———. (1990). *Uniform Crime Report.* West Trenton, NJ.

———. (1992). *Uniform Crime Report.* West Trenton, NJ.

New Mexico Governor's Organized Crime Prevention Commission. (1990, July). *New Mexico Prison Gangs.* Albuquerque, NM: Governor's Organized Crime Prevention Commission.

———. (1991). *New Mexico Street Gangs.* Albuquerque, NM: Governor's Organized Crime Prevention Commission.

New York State Organized Crime Task Force. (1989, December). *Corruption and Racketeering in the New York City Construction Industry.* White Plains, NY.

Nossen, Richard A. (1982). *The Detection, Investigation and Prosecution of Financial Crimes.* Richmond, VA: Richard A. Nossen & Associates.

Nossen, Richard A., and Joan W. Norvelle. (1993). *The Detection, Investigation, and Prosecution of Financial Crimes.* Richmond, VA: Thoth Books.

O'Hara, Charles E., and Gregory L. O'Hara. (1980). *Fundamentals of Criminal Investigation,* 5th ed. Springfield, IL: Charles C. Thomas.

"Organized crime the white collar way: Litton indicted for adding fat to the chicken." (1986, July). *Organized Crime Digest, 7,* No. 7.

Osterburg, James W., and Richard Ward. (1992). *Criminal Investigation.* Cincinnati, OH: Anderson.

Ostrom, Charles W., Jr. (1990). "Time Series Analysis Regression Techniques." *Quantitative Applications in the Social Sciences, 9.*

Pagano, Clinton L., and Frederick T. Martens. (1986). "An enforcement paradox: the intelligence dilemma in narcotic enforcement." *Law Enforcement Intelligence Analysis Digest, 1,* No. 2.

Pate, Anthony M., and Wesley G. Skogan. (1985, January 31). *Reducing the Signs of Crime: The Newark Experience Technical Report.* Washington, DC: The Police Foundation.

Pavlock, Ron. (1993, May). "Suburban agencies fight gang activity." *Law and Order.*

Pennsylvania Crime Commission. (1974). *Report on Police Corruption and the Quality of Law Enforcement in Philadelphia.* St. Davids, PA: Pennsylvania Crime Commission.

——— (1980). *A Decade of Organized Crime: 1980 Report.* St. Davids, PA: Pennsylvania Crime Commission.

———. (1981, April). *Annual Report.* St. Davids, PA: Pennsylvania Crime Commission.

————. (1981, December). *Health Care Fraud: A Rising Threat.* St. Davids, PA: Pennsylvania Crime Commission.

————. (1984). *1984 Report,* St. Davids, PA: Pennsylvania Crime Commission.

————. (1985, February). *Coal Fraud: Undermining a Vital Resource.* St. Davids, PA: Pennsylvania Crime Commission.

————. (1986). *The Changing Face of Organized Crime.* Conshohocken, PA: Pennsylvania Crime Commission.

————. (1988). *1988 Report.* Conshohocken, PA: Pennsylvania Crime Commission.

————. (1989). *1989 Report.* Conshohocken, PA: Pennsylvania Crime Commission.

————. (1991). *Organized Crime in Pennsylvania: A Decade of Change: 1990 Report.* Conshohocken, PA: Pennsylvania Crime Commission.

————. (1993, April). *1992 Report.* Conshohocken, PA: Pennsylvania Crime Commission.

————. (1994, April). *An Investigation Into the Conduct of Lackawanna County District Attorney/Attorney General Ernest D. Preate, Jr.* Conshohocken, PA: Pennsylvania Crime Commission.

Peterson, Marilyn B. (1985, Summer/Fall). "Financial/corporate analysis with computerized applications." *Law Enforcement Intelligence Analysis Digest, 1,* No. 1.

————. (1986, July). "Reuben Sturman's pornography empire: an analytical look at white collar crime in the pornography industry." *Law Enforcement Intelligence Analysis Digest, 1,* No. 2.

————. (1989). "Strategic analysis for law enforcement." Training course. Trenton, NJ: New Jersey Department of Law and Public Safety.

————. (1990). "The context of analysis—from analysis to synthesis: exploring the context of law enforcement analysis." *Criminal Intelligence Analysis,* Paul P. Andrews Jr. and Marilyn B. Peterson, eds. Loomis, CA: Palmer Enterprises.

————. (1990). "Telephone record analysis." *Criminal Intelligence Analysis,* Paul P. Andrews Jr. and Marilyn B. Peterson, eds. Loomis, CA: Palmer Enterprises.

————. (1990, Summer). "Economic analysis and organized crime: a later perspective." *Law Enforcement Intelligence Analysis Digest, 5,* No. 1.

————. (1991–92, Winter). "Strategic intelligence for law enforcement." *Law Enforcement Intelligence Analysis Digest 6,* No. 2.

————. (1992, Winter). "The changes of a decade." *Criminal Organizations, 6,* Nos. 3, 4.

————. (1993, Summer). "Analysts in the 1990s: An IALEIA Survey." *IALEIA JOURNAL, 8,* No. 1.

————. (1993). "Strategic analysis for law enforcement, 2nd edition." Training course. Trenton, NJ: New Jersey Department of Law and Public Safety.

————. (1993). "Advanced investigative analysis." Training course. Trenton, NJ: New Jersey Department of Law and Public Safety.

————. (1993). "Bridging the analytical gap: from facts to visions." Training course. Trenton, NJ: New Jersey Department of Law and Public Safety.

————. (1994). "Intelligence and analysis within the organized crime function." *Handbook of Organized Crime in the United States,* Robert Kelly, Ko-lin Chin, and Rufus Schatzberg, eds. Westport, CT: Greenwood Press.

Peterson, Marilyn B., and R. Glen Ridgeway. (1990, May). "Analytical intelligence training." *FBI Law Enforcement Bulletin, 59,* No. 5.

———. (1990–91, Winter). "Analytical training in today's law enforcement environment." *Law Enforcement Intelligence Analysis Digest, 5,* No. 2.

President's Commission on Law Enforcement and Administration of Justice. (1967). *Task Force Report: Organized Crime.* Washington, DC: U.S. Government Printing Office.

President's Commission on Organized Crime. (1984, March). *Organized Crime and Money Laundering.* Washington, DC.

———. (1986, April). *The Impact: Organized Crime Today.* Washington, DC.

Prunckun, Henry W., Jr. (1987, Fall). "Would you buy a used car from this man: utilizing the intelligence process in combating consumer fraud in the second-hand motor vehicle industry." *Law Enforcement Intelligence Analysis Digest, 2,* No. 2.

Rackmill, Steven. (1992, Summer). "The impact of the Arab Israeli conflict on the 1972 Olympics and its aftermath." *IALEIA JOURNAL, 7,* No. 1.

RAND Corporation. (1988, March) *The Prevalence, Predictability and Police Implications of Recidivist,* as quoted in *Report to the Nation on Crime and Justice,* Second Edition. Washington, DC: U.S. Government Printing Office.

Ratledge, Edward C., and Joan E. Jacoby. (1989). *Handbook on Artificial Intelligence and Expert Systems in Law Enforcement.* Westport, CT: Greenwood Press.

Reboussin, Roland, and Jerry Cameron. (1989, August). "Expert systems for law enforcement." *FBI Law Enforcement Bulletin, 58,* No. 8.

Rebovich, Donald J. (1987, February). "Exploring hazardous waste crime characteristics: an examination of four northeast states." *Law Enforcement Intelligence Analysis Digest, 2,* No. 1.

Ressler, Robert K., Ann W. Burgess, and John E. Douglas. (1983, January). "Rape and rape-murder: one offender and twelve victims." *American Journal of Psychiatry. 140,* No. 1, pp. 36–40.

Ressler, Robert K., Allen W. Burgess, and John E. Douglas. (1986, September). "Sexual homicide patterns and motives." *Journal of Interpersonal Violence.*

Ressler, Robert K., and Tom Schachtman. (1992). *Whoever Fights Monsters.* New York: St. Martin's Press.

Reuter, Peter, Jonathan Rubinstein, and Simon Wynn. (1983, January). *Racketeering in Legitimate Industries* (Executive Summary). Washington, DC: National Institute of Justice.

Riechers, Lisa M., and Roy R. Roberg. (1990, June). "Community policing: a critical review of underlying assumptions." *Journal of Police Science and Administration, 17,* No. 2.

Ruxlow, Thomas R., and Stephen Henson. (1988, January). "New intelligence concept curbs crime." *FBI Law Enforcement Bulletin, 57,* No. 1.

Royal Canadian Mounted Police. (1988). *National Drug Intelligence Estimate 1987/88.* Ottawa, Ontario: Drug Enforcement Directorate.

———. (1990). *National Drug Intelligence Estimate 1988/89.* Ottawa, Ontario: Drug Enforcement Directorate.

———. (1990, November/December). *Monthly Digest of Drug Intelligence Trends.* Ottawa, Ontario: Drug Enforcement Directorate, *10,* No. 11/12.

———. (1991, Winter). *Drug Intelligence Trends.* Ottawa, Ontario: Drug Enforcement Directorate, *1,* No. 1.

Sanderson, Karen L. (1987, February). "An analytical response to the clandestine drug laboratory problem." *Law Enforcement Intelligence Analysis Digest, 2,* No. 1.

Sauls, John Gales. (1985, October). "Computerized business records as evidence." *FBI Law Enforcement Bulletin.*

Sears, Donald J. (1991). *To Kill Again.* Wilmington, DE: Scholarly Resources.

Serial Killers and Murderers. (1991). Lincolnwood, IL: Publications International, Ltd.

Shanahan, Donald T., and Paul M. Whisenand. (1980). *The Dimensions of Criminal Justice Planning.* Boston, MA: Allyn and Bacon.

Shapiro, Susan P. (1980, December). *Thinking About White Collar Crime.* Washington, DC: National Institute of Justice.

Shilling, A. Gary. (1991, July 22). "Plastic bombs." *Forbes, 148,* p. 326.

Shuy, Roger W. (1990). "Tape recorded conversations." Andrews, Paul P., Jr., and Marilyn B. Peterson, eds. *Criminal Intelligence Analysis.* Loomis, CA: Palmer Enterprises.

Slahor, Stephanie. (1993, May). "Nipping in the bud: the task force approach the gangs." *Law and Order.*

Sommers (Peterson), Marilyn B. (1986). "Law enforcement intelligence: a new look." *International Journal of Intelligence and Counterintelligence, 1,* No. 3.

Sparrow, Malcolm K. (1990). *Beyond 911: A New Era for Policing,* Mark H. Moore and David M. Kennedy, eds. New York: Basic Books.

―――. (1991, September). "The application of network analysis to criminal intelligence: an assessment of the prospects." *Social Networks, 13,* No. 3.

―――. (1994). *Imposing Duties: Government's Changing Approach to Compliance.* Westport, CT: Praeger Books.

―――. (1993, March). Information systems and the development of policing. *Perspectives on Policing.* Washington, DC: Department of Justice.

State of New Jersey Commission of Investigation. (1985, December 16). *Organized Crime in Boxing.* Trenton, NJ: State Commission of Investigation.

―――. (1987, October). *Report and Recommendations on Impaired and Incompetent Physicians.* Trenton, NJ: State Commission of Investigation.

―――. (1988, August). *Public Hearing Report and Recommendations on the Subversion by Organized Crime and Other Unscrupulous Elements of the Check Cashing Industry.* Trenton, NJ: State Commission of Investigation.

―――. (1989, April). *Solid Waste Regulation.* Trenton, NJ: State Commission of Investigation.

―――. (1989). *21st Annual Report.* Trenton, NJ: State Commission of Investigation.

―――. (1993, November). *Criminal Street Gangs.* Trenton, NJ: State Commission of Investigation.

―――. (1992, September). *Local Government Corruption.* Trenton, NJ: State Commission of Investigation.

―――. (undated). *18th Annual Report and Report and Recommendations on Organized Crime–Affiliated Subcontractors at Casino and Public Construction Sites.* Trenton, NJ: State Commission of Investigation.

State of New Jersey Department of Law and Public Safety. (1992, December). *The New Jersey Statewide Strategy for the FY93 Drug Control and System Improvement Formula Grant Program.* Trenton, NJ: State of New Jersey.

State of New Jersey Department of Law and Public Safety. (1993, March). *Attorney General's 1993 Statewide Narcotics Action Plan.* Trenton, NJ: State of New Jersey.

Sterling, Claire. (1991). *Octopus.* New York: Simon and Schuster.

Stern, Richard L., and Reed Abelson. (1991, June 24). "The second-oldest industry?" *Forbes, 147,* p. 239.

Stern, Richard L., and Amy Feldman. (1992, October 26). "But where are the cops?" *Forbes, 150,* pp. 160–164.

Stier, Edwin H., and Peter R. Richards. (1987). "Strategic decision making in organized crime control: the need for a broadened perspective." *Major Issues in Organized Crime Control,* Herbert Edelhertz, ed. Washington, DC: National Institute of Justice.

Stipp, David. (September 10, 1990). "Environmental crime can land executives in prison these days." *Wall Street Journal.*

Sutherland, Edwin H. (1983). *White Collar Crime: The Uncut Version.* New Haven, CT: Yale University Press.

Terry, Gary, and Michael P. Malone. (1987, November). "The Bobby Joe Long serial murder case: a study in cooperation (part 1)." *FBI Law Enforcement Bulletin, 56,* No. 11.

———. (1987, December). "The Bobby Joe Long serial murder case: A study in cooperation (conclusion)." *FBI Law Enforcement Bulletin, 56,* No. 12.

Trojanowicz, Robert C. (1992, May). "Building support for community policing." *FBI Law Enforcement Bulletin, 61,* No. 5.

Tucson Police Department. *Safe by Design: Enhanced Crime Prevention Grant Phases I–III Final Report, December, 1991.* Tucson Police Department undergrant numbers 87-SD-CX-K068, 89-DD-CX-K015 by the Bureau of Justice Assistance.

Tufte, Edward. (1990). *Envisioning Information.* Cheshire, CT: Graphics Press.

U. S. Attorney. (1989, August 23). *Attorney General's Report on Narcotics Trafficking for the Western District of Pennsylvania.* Pittsburgh: Acting United States Attorney.

U.S. Attorney General. (1980, August). *National Priorities for the Investigation and Prosecution of White Collar Crime.* Washington, DC: U.S. Department of Justice.

"U.S. Parole Commission proposed regulations." *Federal Register, 55,* No. 7 (January 10, 1990), p. 862.

Vaughn, Jerald R. (1991, June). "Community oriented policing . . . you can make it happen." *Law and Order.*

Wardlaw, Grant, Don McDowell, and John Schmidt. (1991, April). *Australia's Illegal Drug Problem: A Strategic Intelligence Assessment.* Canberra, Australia: Attorney-General's Department.

Weber, Robert Philip. (1990). "Basic Content Analysis. Second Edition." *Quantitative Applications in the Social Sciences, 49.*

Weiner, Neil Alan. (1989). "Violent Criminal Careers and 'Violent Career Criminals': An Overview of the Research Literature." *Violent Crime, Violent Criminals,* Weiner, Neil Alan, and Marvin E. Wolfgang, eds. Newbury Park, CA: Sage.

Wells, Joseph T. (1993, Spring/Summer). "Conquering Fraud Investigation Fears." *National FOP Journal.*

White, Alexander S., Lester M. Joseph, Deborah Watson, and Joseph Yenouskas. (1985, August). *Racketeer Influenced and Corrupt Organizations (RICO): A Manual for Federal Prosecutors.* Washington, DC: U.S. Department of Justice.

The White House. (1991, February). *National Drug Control Strategy.* Washington, D.C.

———. (1992, January). *National Drug Control Strategy: A Nation Responds to Drug Use.* Washington, DC: U.S. Government Printing Office.

Whitworth, Anthony W. (1993, May). "Computer program helps predict gang activity." *Law and Order.*
Wilson, Stephen V., and A. Howard Matz. (1979). "Obtaining evidence for federal economic prosecutions: an overview and analysis of investigative methods." *New York Law Journal, 1.*

Index

About the Author

MARILYN B. PETERSON is a management specialist for an agency having statewide responsibility for the investigation of criminal justice matters. She has worked in criminal analysis since 1980 for agencies in Pennsylvania and New Jersey. She is a Certified Criminal Analyst and has taught intelligence subjects internationally. She is co-editor (with P. Andrews Jr.) of *Criminal Intelligence Analysis* (1990); a contributor to *A Handbook of Organized Crime in the United States*, edited by Robert Kelly, Rufus Schatzberg, and Ko-lin Chin (Greenwood Press, 1994); and has written at length on analytical techniques for, and developed basic and advanced seminars on, criminal analysis.

CPSIA information can be obtained
at www.ICGtesting.com
Printed in the USA
BVHW040544140122
626195BV00016B/135

9 780275 964689